# A Will to Win
## The Manager's Diary

# A Will to Win
## The Manager's Diary
# Alex Ferguson
### with David Meek

ANDRE
DEUTSCH

First published in Great Britain in 1997
by **Manchester United Books**
an imprint of **André Deutsch Ltd** (a subsidiary of VCI plc)
106 Great Russell Street, London WC1B 3LJ
(www.vci.co.uk)
in association with
**Manchester United Football Club plc**
Old Trafford, Manchester M16 ORA

CIP data for this title is available from the British Library.

**ISBN 0 233 99106 9**

1 2 3 4 5 6 7 8 9 10

A **Zone** production

Designed by **offspring**
Photos by **Action Images, Rob Wilson, John Peters, Empics, Allsport**

Printed by **Butler & Tanner**, Frome, Somerset

# Contents

# List of illustrations

# Acknowledgements

Olivia Blair
*for her scrupulous editing*
Justyn Barnes
Hannah MacDonald
Faith Mowbray
Lou Pepper
Tim Forrester
James Freedman
and Ruby Blair

**To the team...
my staff, the players
and the supporters**

# 1
# Pre-season:
# chasing Shearer

Another season, another challenge.

The cheers have hardly died down and I'm already looking ahead, but that's how it goes in football. The last thing you can do is rest on your laurels – you are only really as good as your last match. Now is the time for me to weigh up the last 12 months and consider the future.

We've finished the 1995/96 season on a high, of course. Not many people thought we would complete a second League and FA Cup double so soon after the previous one. Fans and rivals alike watched me sell Paul Ince, Mark Hughes and Andrei Kanchelskis. Not everyone understood the reasons but of course it is a manager's job to see beyond the obvious and make decisions for the future.

Although we have had our ups and downs, like those early exits from the Coca-Cola Cup and Europe, I was always confident we would eventually achieve something. I knew our youngsters could and would deliver and they had to be given their chance. I didn't know exactly how they would cope with the big games but in fact they revealed they had that crucial, winning, key factor: temperament.

So it was a good year. Still, everyone needs to recharge their batteries and take a break so now I'm talking holidays with Cathy and making up my mind where she wants to go! We didn't have a holiday last year because of a family bereavement. It was essential we got away this time. I finally booked for us to leave the Saturday after we had won the FA Cup.

*Sunday 19 May*

I'm lying by the pool relaxing and letting the world, including football, go by. We're at a small hotel on the Riviera at Cap Ferat, in the south of France. It is near Nice, and expensive, but I've been before and it's a great area. The hotel is small and nobody knows me in these parts. A friend told me about it and it suits us fine because nothing much is happening.

*Monday 20 May*

You can only lie by the pool and think about nothing for so long. Now my thoughts are back on the game and I'm starting to structure the coming season. Uppermost in my mind is not so much savouring our recent success, but wondering how to handle its effect. Will it change me or the players? It's all very well people saying keep your feet on the ground, but it's more complicated than that. You need to have the character to heed the advice. You have to have been brought up the right way or have been in touch with the common side of life. Success undoubtedly changes people. I've seen one good game change players overnight and I've seen some managers change with just a little bit of success.

So it's not a glib saying that is meant for everyone. It's only meant for people who have the ability to stay true to themselves all their life. At 54 years of age I don't think I'm going to get carried away now. Whatever happens, the Double and all that, and people saying it is Manchester United's best-ever year, and an even more notable achievement with such a young squad, I think my greatest achievement is staying at the club for 10 years.

Probably everyone would like to manage this club, but how many could survive more than a few years? Nowadays the beast is so huge. Only Sir Matt Busby managed it before me and that was in a totally different era. Possibly my grounding – at East Stirling 22 years ago – has helped. I remember asking the chairman, Willie Muirhead, if I could have a look at the players' contracts. He took a nervous puff on his cigarette and I knew straightaway something wasn't quite right. It was only when I counted the contracts though that I realised he had whittled the playing staff down to eight. He'd given all the others free transfers to save on wages. We were bottom of the Second Division, which is about as low as you can get in Scotland, and I asked him if he realised it was normal to field 11 in a team!

Surviving that, then going on to St Mirren where the chairman was a megalomaniac, made me vulnerable. But it also taught me how to handle the vulnerability of football. I tasted some success as a manager at Aberdeen but still had to endure a rough spell early on at Old Trafford. Coming through it to complete 10 years is really my big achievement. You have to produce winning teams to stay at a club that long – doing that has been my biggest satisfaction.

When I first came to Old Trafford I couldn't understand how a club of such stature had gone 20 years without winning the Championship. For months I analysed the possible reasons, looking at former managers' records, their players, what period of a season they had fallen away, the training – until at the end I realised that it mattered not a jot. I had wasted valuable time instead of focusing on my own job. I'd been looking at yesterday, instead of working out what the club needed today and tomorrow. Once I'd sorted that out I was able to set my sights correctly and get to grips with the job.

*Tuesday 21 May*

So where are we going this coming season? Certainly the double was a good feeling, and I had the satisfaction of proving that my faith in the young players was justified. They'll improve still more, but even now I believe they are ready for the next challenge, ready to be judged on the European stage. I shall make it clear to everyone when I get back home that we are determined and ready to make our mark in Europe.

In 1991, the day after winning the European Cup Winners' Cup, I said at the press conference in Rotterdam that we were now going on to win the League. A close follower of the club asked me afterwards if I didn't feel I had put my head on the chopping block by making my ambition so public. But it's like everything else: you have to issue the challenge and create the demand. After winning the European trophy I felt entitled to expect my players to make a real effort in the League. The time was right and the team was right. Although we threw it away in the last few weeks of the season I believe I was right to set the expectation for myself, the players and the fans.

It's the same now. The time is right, and I have the right players to make a strong challenge in the European Cup. When I get into the build-up for the new season I shall spell out that we're not going to bask in the glory of another Double but move on to the next major challenge. It's a fair one to lay on both myself and the players. I don't accept that the recent lack of success by British clubs in Europe reflects a huge gap in tactics and technique. The record of late is not a fair reflection of what we can achieve. This season I am determined to prove it.

*Wednesday 22 May*

Had a phone call from the chairman today to say that Steve Bruce intended to exercise a clause in his contract which allows him to leave. He'd decided to accept an offer from Birmingham City. When I heard the extraordinary terms they were offering, I realised there was no way he could turn the opportunity down. You have to be fair. Steve is 35 and has started to get a few niggling injuries, and I'm looking to shore up that position anyway. I rang him to wish him all the best. It was a bitter pill to learn that the captain would be leaving but he has been a fantastic player and I can't begin to do justice to what he has done for Manchester United. It's not just been his obvious contribution on the field but his attitude in the dressing room and his personality away from the club. Time after time he bailed me out at the last minute, when I wanted a player to do something and others made an excuse. Nothing was ever too much bother. His sense of humour was tremendous; he had that likable daft Geordie streak. I think he was disappointed that I left him out of the Cup final team, not even putting him on the bench, but I had already gambled once by having him as a substitute for the final League match at Middlesbrough. He wasn't fully fit but I wanted him in his kit, so that he was there to receive the Championship if all went well. After we had won the match and the title, even though Steve hadn't come on, Eric Cantona turned to him immediately, to indicate that he should be the one to go up for the trophy. It said a lot for the team spirit, though it didn't surprise me. Steve was always a very popular skipper, as well as a much respected player.

*Thursday 23 May*

It's easy to dream of course, especially when you're soaking up the sun, but I'm thinking more and more about the harsh realities. I've been preparing for the European challenge for some time, as I know that if you are to tackle a major project you need the right tools for the job. It became evident last season, despite our domestic success, that we needed more quality in depth. We were fortunate in one or two areas, especially in midfield, to escape serious injury, but this season we must be prepared to handle anything up to 60 games. We might not be as lucky as last year, so I decided a while ago that we needed to bring in a few quality players.

With the departure of Steve Bruce in mind, we'd been looking at Norwegian international Ronny Johnsen for a whole year. In January, we'd been close to getting him from his club, Besiktas in Turkey, but at the last moment a legal problem developed with his contract. So we had to leave it until the end of the season, when we finally completed the deal for £1.4

million. That's what I call good value. He's mobile, really quick, can play as a third centre back or as a centre half or full back, as well as in midfield. He's a modern player: intelligent and a good passer of the ball.

I was delighted to sign Ole Gunnar Solskjaer, too. We had also been watching him for some time at Molde in Norway, and monitored all his international matches when he was suddenly thrust into the Norwegian national team. Les Kershaw, our chief scout, watched him, and the last report was from Jim Ryan. Jimmy saw him score twice and came home with the message – just sign him, you can't miss with this one. So we got him for £1.5 million.

The fees paid for these two players were modest, especially when compared to the huge sums other players look like moving for this summer. People will say we have plenty of money, so why should we skimp in the transfer market? Well, we certainly have cash available but there's no point in spending a lot of money just for the sake of it. If you do your homework right there are some prudent economical buys abroad at the moment. In fact Les Kershaw, Brian Kidd and Jimmy Ryan have spent as much time travelling this year as they've spent at home. When it comes to transfers, it's not what you pay, it's what you get! In any case, I haven't ruled out the possibility of getting Alan Shearer to Old Trafford and that would be a transfer which would certainly need our millions. I'm working on that one.

*Friday 24 May*

Now I have Steve Bruce's wife to sort out. Apparently one of the papers ran a story saying that Janet was having a go at me for the way I had treated Steve. The piece revolved round the fact that I left him out of the Cup final team. I did, of course, because I couldn't risk his hamstring breaking down as it had done at Wembley the previous season. Incidentally, I think Steve accepted the situation. Janet was very upset because she said she hadn't been critical of the decision. I phoned her and persuaded her there was no way we would believe a Daily Mirror story, which calmed her down. It's bad enough losing a great player without having to deal with an upset wife as well!

Of course, when he was younger, Steve could play on despite injuries. I recall a match at Anfield when he had done his hamstring the day before but played the full match. Any physio would tell you it was impossible, but it's true. He was one of those players, like Bryan Robson or Roy Keane, with a tough mental attitude who could overcome physical handicaps.

*Saturday 25 May*

Am I never going to get my holiday? The chairman phoned again today, this time with the news that Tony Coton had been in to say that he had enjoyed his season at Old Trafford but now wanted first-team football again. He had the chance of joining his old manager, Peter Reid, at Sunderland. I agreed he should be allowed to leave, but that leaves us still needing experienced cover for Peter Schmeichel. This evening I telephoned an old friend, Ton Van Dalen, a Dutchman. We've known each other for 16 years, since he brought a team to play a friendly at Aberdeen. He's a former goalkeeper himself, and a good contact in Holland. Ton recommended a goalkeeper to me years ago and I knew he might be able to help again. You can always get a decent keeper out of Holland. The standard at clubs like Ajax has been consistently high and the keepers are of a good standard down through the divisions. I told Ton I wanted a capable guy, but not someone who would always be knocking on my door if he wasn't in the team.

Ton said he had the very man for me, a player who would appreciate the experience of joining Manchester United – even if it did mean playing second fiddle to Peter Schmeichel. When he told me about Raimond van der Gouw from Vitesse Arnhem, I remembered I'd seen him a couple of years before. He had stuck in my mind not just for his goalkeeping, but because he played with his hair in a ponytail. I immediately set the wheels in motion to get him over to Old Trafford and the chairman completed the deal. It was more good business because he cost £200,000, replacing Tony Coton who we'd just sold for £600,000.

*Monday 3 June*

Finished my holiday in peace, eventually. Now it's down to business at Old Trafford, to tackle the mountain of mail and inquiries. Make a silent vow that I will not allow the many calls on my time to distract me from the main business of strengthening my squad and preparing for the new season. Spoke to Les Kershaw to say that we must make sure we watch Jordi Cruyff in all his games for Holland. I've had my eye on him for some time, and now that his father is leaving as manager of Barcelona, the boy might feel inclined to move too. In fact I want all the Euro 96 matches covered, because it's an ideal opportunity to look at the cream of European football. The big competitions nearly always reveal a player who's comfortable on the big stage and who can handle life at the top; not so much the big names who are already secure with their clubs, but an ambitious newcomer who's looking for a chance at a major club – like Manchester United.

*Saturday 8 June*

The curtain goes up today on the European Championship. Peter Schmeichel's boy is taking part in the opening ceremony; as the son of one of the reigning European champions he'll help hand over the trophy from Denmark back to UEFA.

It's a big family day for the Schmeichels. Likewise for the

Ferguson clan, when my mobile phone rings and Cathy screams down the line that we have two new twin granddaughters. They were nine weeks premature and weighed in at two pounds ten ounces and three pounds ten ounces, delicate but apparently doing well. The phone call was one of those lovely moments you get in life and the sparkle stayed with me all day.

After the opening game between England and Switzerland, I went to see them all in hospital and stayed overnight in Aylesbury, where my son Jason and his wife Tania live. Jason works for Sky television. They already have a son, Jake, who at two-and-a-half is master of the house.

Before I could go to see the twins I had my television work to do at Wembley, where I was also invited to a birthday party being thrown for Mick Hucknall, who was singing in the opening ceremony. I told him my news and he immediately insisted on a double celebration.

I also have another encounter and I'm not at all sure how this one will go. ITV have teamed me up with Kevin Keegan – we haven't met since he had a go at me on television after we had played Leeds. I'd ventured the opinion that it would be interesting to see if Leeds played as hard against Newcastle as they had done against us. Kevin came out with some amazing stuff linking my comments with the fact that he was taking a team to Leeds to play in a testimonial. I guess he thought I was suggesting that one good turn deserved another, and that it would be three easy points. Actually, the only thought in my mind was how teams raise their game to play us and that I thought Howard Wilkinson deserved better from his players, by seeing them at full throttle in every match.

Kevin had been in a right stew though, and I wondered what he would say. But it was as if nothing had happened. He offered me a drink and simply didn't mention it. So I let it go. I have always got on well with him and I put his outburst down to the pressure of the title run-in. Amazing really, because he had the whole country willing his team to win. They were the new challengers and every Geordie in the land had surfaced to rally round to the north-east cause. Every week the papers dug out another ex-pat Geordie to root for Newcastle. I wonder how Kevin would have reacted in my place, facing that kind of anti-Manchester barrage. As far away as Southampton, Dave Merrington remembered his roots and came out in support of St James' Park.

It seemed as if everyone was against us, but I wasn't trying to wind Kevin up because I didn't think it was necessary. I just felt that we were going to get back at them. They were losing a few games away from home and I knew after we had beaten them up there in March that they would be glancing over their shoulders. I don't say that disparagingly, because it is simply a matter of experience. In any case I have the greatest respect for Kevin Keegan, Newcastle and their supporters; for one thing they don't sing abusive songs about rival teams, none of this mocking Munich stuff. Their chants and songs focus entirely on their own team, and that's how it should be. I have done nothing but praise Newcastle – perhaps once the heat of battle was over, Kevin remembered that, and decided to let the issue drop.

*Sunday 9 June*

Watched Germany play the Czech Republic at Old Trafford today, as part of my plan to study emerging players in Europe. Before the game an agent came up and told me to watch Karel Poborsky, because he is going to be a star. The long-haired Karel was certainly one of their best players, along with Patrik Berger who came on as a substitute. The Germans were strong, both physically and technically. I've backed them to win the tournament and I think they're going to give me a good run for my money. But the Czechs were brilliant. Poborsky interests me because one of the items on my agenda is a wide right player to replace Andrei Kanchelskis. David Beckham has been brilliant but his future is in a more central role. In any case, this summer is all about developing and building up a squad of quality and depth. I have already spoken to Eric Cantona about Zinedine Zidane, the French international, and asked him if he thought he could play wide right. Eric said he would speak to him but thought Zidane now saw himself as a central midfield player. Les and I watched him play for Bordeaux several times and came to the conclusion that we should wait for the European Championship. But Poborsky interests me.

I felt sorry for the referee, David Elleray, who finished up booking 10 players, six of them Germans. It was a physical game and there was a lot of rolling about when players went down. I think David found it difficult to tell who had really been hurt, but he did the right thing with his cards. It could easily have got out of hand. I wonder, though, how it will go down in the press.

*Monday 10 June*

Went to watch Holland against Scotland, with a particular eye on Jordi Cruyff. Met Johann, and asked if his son would be interested in joining us. He said Jordi was talking to one or two clubs but that Manchester United would indeed be the kind of place to advance his career. Later I phoned Johann and made arranged to meet Jordi after the Holland–France match at Anfield. The boy can play in a variety of positions – centre forward, midfield or as a wide player. Aged only 22, he is a developing player who I see as a natural performer for Manchester United. Perhaps he now needs to develop his football away from his father's control.

*Wednesday 12 June*

Went to dinner at Mottram Hall, at the invitation of the German Federation. It gave me the opportunity for a long natter with Bertie Vogts. Mottram Hall was the German's base for Euro 96 and their players also attended the function. You couldn't help but be aware of their team spirit and their tremendous organisation and preparation. I sat next to Bertie for the meal and he outlined his injury problems, but that was only half the story. They were working hard on belief. You know the kind of thing: "We are Germany and nothing will be allowed to stand in our way."

The Germans have a reputation for being thorough, and it certainly shows in their Euro 96 campaign. They had even brought over a popular singing group from Germany for the night's function, to help create "the Germany thing". They went out of their way to make the right impact locally as well, with the team training at nearby Macclesfield so their supporters and local schools could see them in action. They also made a £10,000 donation to charity. I received the cheque on behalf of Destination Florida, the airport-based organisation which takes seriously-ill children to Disney World for what may be a last memorable holiday. I'm impressed. Administratively, they have everything under control and I can see where they get all their drive from. It made me even more convinced they will go all the way.

*Friday 14 June*

At Liverpool, to see the Czechs play Italy. What a turn up for the books ... Italy were beaten 2–1. The roof has fallen in for Arrigo Sacchi. He's getting hammered because he dropped five or six players, but I can understand why he decided to rest some of them. He has clearly come here with the intention of winning the European Championship and wants everyone nice and fresh for the big one, his final group fixture, against Germany. I think his strategy was to go for broke and put Italy in the position of being able to eliminate the Germans from the tournament, but it backfired on him. Probably Italy were the better team but you've got to give the Czech Republic credit. They are flying now and I certainly like the look of Poborsky. His hair may well get on my nerves if I sign him, but he can definitely play. He's a tenacious little blighter, with great ball control, and maybe he could give us something different playing wide right.

*Sunday 16 June*

Another big family day, with wedding bells for Darren, Jason's twin brother. He's rather left behind in the baby stakes – three down now – but never mind, Paula is a lovely girl. She comes from Prestwich and they met when he was playing for Manchester United. Not that it was planned this way, but the reception is at Mottram Hall, where the Germans are staying. I mentioned it to Bertie Vogts at their official dinner and true to style they sent a huge bouquet of flowers. A few of the German players came to the party following their match that day against Russia. They had won 3–0 so they were in good spirits.

*Monday 17 June*

The *Times* ran a story today that the German players had gatecrashed the reception. Not so, they were invited. It was the least I could do. Bertie Vogts had invited me to watch their private training, one professional to another; he knew I wouldn't rush around telling opponents his tactical plans.

As for Darren, I hope his career takes a turn for the better. He's a good footballer. It's all he's ever wanted to be and he's been unlucky. He was doing well under Graham Turner, the manager who bought him, then Graham Taylor took over and had different ideas. Now Mark McGhee is in charge, I'm surprised he hasn't used him more. Mark has brought some of his old players in from Leicester. One of my old managers, Alan McLeod, warned me against that kind of policy if you move to a bigger club. Moving players up a grade doesn't necessarily mean they can recreate their previous success. We'll see. Of course I wonder now whether I should ever have let Darren leave Manchester United, but we had reached the point where he needed to be away from his father. It worked fine when he was a youngster playing for Eric Harrison and Jimmy Ryan but once he started in the first team it became difficult for both of us. Our relationship complicated decisions on whether he should be in or out of the side. I think he needed to be away. Obviously he is not entirely happy at the moment, but I have counselled him to be patient. I'm sure his turn will come.

*Wednesday 26 June*

I thought England did well in the Euro semi final against Germany today. It's always tough to go out on penalties. Though I suppose England shouldn't complain too much, after needing a penalty shoot-out to get through their quarter-final against Spain. Overall I thought Terry Venables prepared his team brilliantly. He went on the offensive and took risks to win matches, playing Steve McManaman and Darren Anderton as wing backs. He showed great flexibility in his tactics and deserves all the credit that is coming his way. His departure is England's loss.

Overall, though, it hasn't been a great tournament; some good games, but some poor ones too.

*Saturday 29 June*

Old Trafford was packed with even more people than we get for our top matches. Mick Hucknall and Simply Red were the stars, backed by three other bands. It was fantastic to see the ground with 60,000 people in it. You always worry about the pitch, though they seemed so well organised that I'm sure there will be no problems. I was asked to introduce Mick at the start.

He is a great United fan and I said it would be a pleasure. I think he appreciated it. We've always got on well. I've been to his flat in Milan and he's smashing company.

*Sunday 30 June*

So to the final. The Czech tactics were fantastic – they played with just one-up. The Germans were left with the ball when they were in their own half, but once they crossed the halfway line they ran into a massed midfield. Then the Czechs got about them, snapping and winning the ball to set up counter attacks. Karel Poborsky played his part, although the fact that he had not missed a game started to show at Wembley. He looked tired but he still won them a penalty. I thought a shock was on the cards until I remembered they were playing Germany! After going a goal down, Bertie Vogts made a great substitution. He left on his experienced players, Hassler and Moller, and changed the younger ones. Within 10 minutes the Germans had equalised.

For me, the Czechs were the better side. They played tremendously well, but the Germans' mental strength saw them through. It was a triumph for their general organisation, which didn't fail them right to the end, on or off the pitch. They thought of everything. Even when they left their hotel they gave a hugely generous tip for the staff, as well as 100 autographed jerseys. Nice touch. I chatted to Terry Venables before the final. He fancied the Czechs and we had a bet, with me going for Germany. I wonder if he will remember!

*Monday 1 July*

I've decided to go for Poborsky. I'm flying out to Malta, to open a new headquarters for our supporters' branch there, but the chairman has stayed down in London. Today he's talking to Poborsky and his agent, at the Czech team hotel in St Albans.

I check with the chairman from Gatwick Airport and he tells me that a deal is now in place. The player wants to join us and will come to England in two or three weeks time.

*Tuesday 2 July*

Four of our young players are coming with me for the Malta opening: Gary and Phil Neville, David Beckham and Ben Thornley. We receive an incredibly enthusiastic welcome and I am proud of the way the boys handle themselves in the spotlight. Along with their parents, they can take great credit for the way they behave and conduct themselves.

We try to help our young players prepare for this kind of situation. Every now and again we run a media course. We ask an experienced journalist from the Press, television or broadcasting to come into the club, to teach them how to handle interviews and that kind of thing.

I don't think Ben Thornley needed any help. He's the star of the show. The others are comparatively shy, but when Ben gets up on the stage it's like the Gettysberg Address. He has a lovely, bubbly personality and he wins over all the fans. By the time I get up to say a few words he has already said them all, and it's time to go home.

*Wednesday 3 July*

Get up very early to fly home. The long flight gives me plenty of time to ponder the Alan Shearer position. I spoke to his agent at the end of the season and asked about Shearer's intentions. Since then there has been almost a public debate about his future. His performances for England in the European Championship have highlighted his value. I'm interested in trying to get him to Old Trafford, although I'm cautious because I have only spoken to Tony Stephens, the agent, and not the player himself. It's always a grey area when you deal with the agent. He assures me Shearer is ready to leave Blackburn and would like to play for United. My response is that if Blackburn are prepared to let him go, then we would be keen to talk. This follows on from conversations Shearer's had with some of our players when away on England duty, when he's told them of his desire to join us. I am still unsure, simply because he has turned us down before. Time is a great healer but I don't want to get my fingers burned twice. Certainly, he's a fine player. His scoring record alone makes you sit up and take notice. His Euro '96 form has elevated him through dark clouds of criticism concerning his scoring drought. I'll discuss the situation with the board tomorrow.

*Thursday 4 July*

Our chairman has approached Blackburn about Shearer and has been given a very definite refusal. Apparently he met with an emotional response from Robert Coar, the Blackburn chairman, who said he would only sell Shearer over his dead body. I can see that this transfer saga is likely to run and run. But there seems to be no question that the player has made up his mind to move on.

It's always very difficult when a star player decides to leave, especially if he has a good relationship with his club and the fans idolise him. It's difficult for both the club and the player himself. But things change. Perhaps Shearer's taken the view that Blackburn's best days are behind them. Sometimes a club needs more than a winning blend to hold on to a player; sometimes it takes a tradition built up over decades. Blackburn were prominent in the 1960s, when teams like Ipswich and Burnley won championships, but they've never been a dominant force.

I imagine these are the kind of thoughts that have run through Shearer's mind, and that he's come to the conclusion he wants a bigger stage. I'm sure the fact that Blackburn have not bought any new players has also influenced him.

*Friday 5 July*

I'm in America for a few days, mainly to attend a wedding. Mark, my eldest boy, is best man for a pal. It's a super occasion, though I am constantly on the phone to the chairman to see if there is any movement with Shearer. The chairman tells me he has had a letter from Blackburn containing just one word ... 'No!' Jack Walker seems to be like the original dog with a bone who won't let go. I enjoy the break, as does Cathy, who loves weddings. But I'm still anxious about the Shearer situation.

*Saturday 13 July*

Back from the States. Top of my agenda is to get an update from Tony Stephens on the Shearer position. Apparently nothing much has changed.

*Sunday 21 July*

At last, things are moving. I took a call from Tony Stephens to say that he and Shearer had had a meeting with Blackburn. They've reached an agreement allowing them to talk to clubs. He said Shearer would like to meet me. I quickly fixed an appointment for the next day at a secret rendezvous – secret because there is no point advertising our plans. This is the most important meeting of his career and it is vital for us, too.

*Monday 22 July*

I'm due to meet Shearer and Stephens at 2 pm. Before that, I have a board meeting to attend at Old Trafford. Shearer isn't on the agenda, but naturally I tell the directors where I am going. They are as excited as me. Nobody brings up the matter of money at this point, which is perhaps just as well because this boy is going to cost plenty. I leave the board meeting in good time to make sure I'm not late.

# Pre-Season: chasing Shearer

When I arrive I'm greeted by Tony Stephens, who tells me that they will be talking to Newcastle the following day and then Arsenal. I find this disturbing. It reminds me of the breakdown the previous time we tried for Shearer. Stephens says today's meeting is important for the player and I reply it is a big one for me, too.

I'm soon convinced that Shearer is interested in joining us. The meeting is going well and I do my best to stress the advantages of joining us. I tell him that he can improve and develop in areas such as handling tight markers. I point out that he will be able to tap into the experience and enormous talent of Eric Cantona. I explain that I'm bringing in new, exciting players, like Jordi Cruyff and Karel Poborsky. We mean business, with a very young team that can only improve. I ask him to consider how young many of our players are, and the way we play our football: patient when we need to be patient, quick when we need to apply pressure. I outline our big challenge in Europe. When I'm finished, I feel sure he won't be able to resist coming to Old Trafford.

Shearer had two main questions for me. He wanted to know if he would be able to take the penalty kicks and if he could wear the number nine shirt. I tell him that Eric Cantona hasn't missed a penalty for us since he arrived but that if he ever did, then, possibly. As for the number nine shirt, no problem. I thought that if they were the only things worrying him, we would get our man.

All the feedback suggested that if he left Blackburn there was only one club which interested him, and if it didn't work out with us he would be staying at Blackburn. As far as I'm concerned, you either want to play for Manchester United or you don't. It's as simple as that, especially with Alan Shearer. He'd changed his mind about coming to us once before.

Incidentally, I pick up the vibes that the reason he didn't sign last time was to some extent due to Southampton's influence. If that's the case, I'm very disappointed. Anyway, Tony

Stephens' last words were that he would phone me on Thursday, after meeting the other clubs. We must wait and see.

*Tuesday 23 July*

No time to brood about Alan Shearer. Along with the chairman and Maurice Watkins, our director and club solicitor, I went to negotiate a deal with Barcelona for Jordi Cruyff. The boy's father met us at the airport. We have all come a long way when someone like the great Johann is picking us up.

Johann took us back to his house for a cup of coffee. It's beautiful, packed with paintings by Dutch and Spanish artists. He was, of course, the manager of Barcelona before Bobby Robson, so obviously he knows the people at the club extremely well. He did his best to prepare us, warning us who we could trust and who we couldn't, and that we would probably be messed about.

Johann then took us to the Barcelona offices, where we found a stack of television and press people waiting. We went into session with Gaspart, the general manager. It was soon clear that they were going to be difficult over the fee. We are talking here about a boy of 22, who was brought to the club by his father for nothing, and who they no longer wanted. He had just one more year to go on his contract and they were talking about a £1.2 million fee. That's not what we had in mind and I told the chairman that I wasn't comfortable with Gaspart. There was a stumbling block, but we left to go and sort out Jordi's terms. Then back to Gaspart's office, once more with all the press there. It's their way of trying to put pressure on you to give way, in order to get a solution.

Johann told them in no uncertain terms how he felt, but the arguing and haggling went on for hours. The terms of the deal changed several times without us reaching an agreement. At 6.30 pm we adjourned. The Barcelona people said they would call us to arrange dinner and further discussions. Johann told us

Nunez, the president, would be there this time – nothing really happens at Nou Camp without his blessing.

We hung about the hotel until after 9 pm, ravenously hungry because we hadn't eaten properly all day. In the end we went off on our own, to a restaurant someone recommended to us, leaving a contact number at the hotel. We'd just started eating when the chairman got a phone call from Gaspart, asking us to join them at their restaurant. We said we were in the middle of a meal, but agreed to go over at 11.30 pm.

Again, the media were waiting as we went in to meet the Barcelona people. Johann was right, Nunez and his son were there, along with Bobby Robson. Once again they were trying to box us in and wear us down. It's an amazing difference in culture when you try to buy a player from a club like Barcelona. I thought Gaspart was a powerful man, but with Nunez there he didn't open his mouth except to remark about the weather. I detected that Nunez's son is preparing to take over control of the club, which was half the problem. He certainly tried to make his presence felt and we argued the toss until 1 am.

Barcelona said they didn't have to sell Jordi, but Bobby doesn't particularly want the son of the former manager staying on. I can relate to Bobby, an experienced manager of passion and commitment. He was getting as vexed as us. At one stage he said Manchester United were a big club who shouldn't object to paying the asking price. But when Johann claimed that Barcelona hadn't even paid his son's hospital bill following an injury and knee operation, Bobby was quite knocked back. He didn't say another word.

We still couldn't agree so said we'd had enough. The waiting press wanted to know what was happening, but we said pre-cisely nothing. I don't particularly enjoy this part of the job. We had flown out in good faith, thinking it was virtually all settled. It had been a long day with nothing to show for it, not even the opportunity to discuss other aspects, like football!

I'm bemused at the difference in culture regarding transfers in Spain and England. Transfers at home can be tricky. You get managers who sometimes use the press in an effort to unsettle a player they fancy, but when it comes down to the nitty-gritty the negotiating is much more business-like.You may argue about the size of the fee but usually you can reach agreement without the hassle we experienced in Spain.

*Wednesday 24 July*

Up early, for what I call the 'red-eyed shuttle'. I hadn't been back at the training ground very long when the chairman phoned. Gaspart had called and they had agreed a deal for £500,000. They'd realised that we weren't going to be bullied. Back in Spain, Johann was going to do some work on it.

*Thursday 25 July*

Barcelona confirmed that Jordi would be coming over. I've arranged for him to have a medical tomorrow. Everything seems to be falling into place now. Tony Stephens also phoned to say that he and Alan Shearer had seen the other clubs, and that Manchester United are still the club the player wants to join. They are going to see Jack Walker at his tax retreat in Jersey tomorrow, the next step to getting away.

*Friday 26 July*

Leaving today for our pre-season tour in Ireland. Just before departure, I take a call from Tony Stephens. Immediately, I detect a difference in attitude. They have seen Jack Walker, the man who's put all the money into Blackburn, and apparently he is not in favour of a transfer to Manchester United.

I'm not sure what to do. Jack's attitude is a problem, but if the player really wants to come to us, then he is in the driving seat. Ultimately, it's up to Shearer which club he joins. I tell

Stephens I'd like to speak to Shearer. We're just about to fly to Belfast but my mobile will be switched on as soon as we land. I have a deep suspicion the transfer has turned against us.

That night I am at the Milk Cup in Coleraine, a competition for Under-14s and Under-16s. I'm making the presentation. It's always a great occasion and has progressed from its early days. As I'm driving to the ground with Bertie Peacock my mobile still hasn't rung. Halfway there I can't wait any longer, so I phone Tony Stephens. No reply, and that's the moment I regret the whole thing. I can't get hold of our chairman either. Instead I switch on to auto pilot and enjoy the tournament. Manchester United always get a good reception and tonight is no different.

Back at our hotel in Belfast, I have a couple of beers and a sandwich with Bertie. Brian Kidd comes up and asks if I have heard anything. He knows how I am feeling.

*Saturday 27 July*

I keep trying Stephens on my mobile but no joy. So I just concentrate on our match against Portadown. We win 4–0, which is comfortable enough. Then we leave for Dublin, for our next match tomorrow.

*Sunday 28 July*

The goals keep coming against Shelbourne, in a 4–1 win. At least the tour is going OK, although I wish I could say the same for the Shearer saga. I keep trying to make contact but without success. Can't even discuss it with the chairman, he's out for the day in Derbyshire.

The mobile phone seems the most important part of my life at the moment, an instrument which sooner or later is going to be the bearer of very good or extremely bad news. I'm desperate for it to ring but it doesn't, so in disgust I switch the damn thing off.

*Monday 29 July*

I start phoning at 8 am, early enough to get hold of Tony Stephens. When I finally make contact he simply says: "I'm sorry, Alan has agreed to join Newcastle."

I'm pretty sure I know how Jack Walker would feel if Shearer were to join us. Perhaps the player feels such loyalty to someone who bought him from Southampton and made him a wealthy young man that he doesn't wish to upset him by joining us. At any rate, there was clearly an undisclosed agenda, and one day I'll find out what really happened.

My reply to Tony Stephens was simply that I was very unhappy about the whole business but that I accepted the boy had the right to choose. Initially, I feel sick and then angry. However, I've always made it a rule never to get too disappointed when a transfer attempt doesn't work out. Over the years I have missed John Barnes, Paul Gascoigne, Peter Beardsley and, now, Shearer. But because we didn't sign Gascoigne, we got Paul Ince, and when the first effort for Shearer failed, I signed Eric Cantona – so I can't complain. Sometimes what appears to be a setback turns out for the good.

I must admit that because we had been so sure of getting our man in this particular case we don't have any other striker irons in the fire. I really thought Shearer was stitched up for Old Trafford. But, in any case, I now have a group of players who will be a dominant force in England for some years. As long as they remain ambitious, these players can progress. It's not as if I am still looking for the final piece in the jigsaw. Those days have gone. I can relax really, because I'm more than happy with the players I have got. It's not going to be an easy day with the press – but let's get on with it.

*Tuesday 30 July*

The team are flying out to Milan for a friendly, agreed as part of the Paul Ince transfer, but I am staying on for two engagements in London. The first is a surprise 60th birthday party for Richard Greenbury, the Marks and Spencer's chairman, which I am invited to this evening at the company's offices. It's a funny night for a football man because I hardly know anyone. It's a totally different world but Richard is easy going. He's quite a Manchester United fan and I enjoy it.

*Wednesday 31 July*

My second appointment is football business, an appeal at the Home Office against the decision refusing Jovan Kirovski, our young striker, a work permit. Jovan, an American of great promise, has been with us for three years as a student. While he's been at college there has been no problem about him staying in this country. However, now his studies are complete he needs permission to join us on a professional basis. At the Home Office I'm met by Stan Orme, one of our local MPs, who will be representing us along with our solicitor, Maurice Watkins. Gillian Shephard, who's dealing with the case, is friendly. She tells me her husband is an avid Manchester United fan, who had faxed her from Belgium that day to tell her to do the right thing. I thought at least the outcome would be better than Barcelona or the Shearer saga.

Kirovski is going to be a very good player. I am keen to have him but amazingly, the Home Office are demanding that he should be offered the same terms as our top players. We explain that that would be ridiculous. The pay on offer is as good as anywhere in Britain for someone of his age, but he isn't Eric Cantona. I get the impression a decision has already been made by the civil servants and Gillian Shephard isn't prepared to go against them. I have to leave to make it in time to Heathrow, to catch up with the team who play in Milan tonight. My worst fears are confirmed later, so it's another long hard night.

I needn't have rushed from the Home Office. My flight is delayed for an hour-and-a-half because of a furious row between a man and his girl. She ends up running through an emergency door, triggering a full alert with police and security officers all over the place. Their baggage had to be identified and taken off our plane because they weren't travelling with us – hence the long delay.

We eventually landed in Milan, where I was met by the Reebok representative, David Williams. He's an avid Welshman who reckons the real reason United are successful is because they play in the Welsh red!

I was late. I hate missing any kick-off, and have done ever since Rangers played Montrose in the Summer Cup years ago. It was a two-leg affair and Rangers seemed to be cantering to a 2–1 aggregate win. When the whistle blew I was on the way out when I suddenly spotted the teams lining up again. Montrose had scored an early goal before I'd arrived; it's embarrassing when it turns out a football man doesn't even know the score. Anyway we had a hair-raising ride to the San Siro Stadium, did it in about 20 minutes, but were still six or seven minutes late.

We were playing quite well but the balance in midfield – David Beckham wide on the left with Nicky Butt and Brian McClair – was not right. We kept the ball OK and I told them at half time not to relax their concentration and start charging forward. I was wasting my breath. I wonder if they'll ever change. It was like the Charge of the Light Brigade, with the result that we lost two goals in five minutes to finish with an embarrassing, undeserved 3–0 defeat.

My post-match thoughts were interrupted by Paul Ince coming into the dressing room to chat for half an hour. When he left our club, I didn't enjoy the circumstances – although he denied it at the time, I felt that privately he had made up his mind that he wanted to play in Italy. I was also worried about his dressing room attitude. But all that is water under the bridge now. I have great affection for him. He is still very much a Manchester United man and has retained a friendship in particular with Ryan Giggs and Andy Cole.

# Pre-Season: chasing Shearer

*Thursday 1 August*

Trained at the San Siro Stadium today. Wondered why the players were laughing at me until I looked down to see I was covered in mosquito bites, about 45 of them, and was in a right state. Flew back to Manchester in the afternoon.

*Friday 2 August*

A big shock this morning – Andy Cole has developed pneumonia and will be out for maybe a month. How on earth do you get pneumonia in sunny August? That one is a puzzle. I didn't have much time to dwell on it, though. We were travelling in the afternoon to Nottingham, for the Umbro Trophy, to be played over the weekend.

*Saturday 3 August*

Our first match is against Ajax. We lose a goal early on, so at half-time I reorganise to play three-up, with Brian McClair joining Eric Cantona and Paul Scholes. We get back to 1–1 through McClair. Then it's the old thing, a lapse of concentration, and Ajax score a second goal. It was an interesting press conference afterwards. I thought I might get some difficult questions but all the Dutch journalists wanted to ask about was a story in that day's papers. Supposedly, we were going to sign Patrick Kluivert, the young Ajax international striker. The Dutch people simply said that United hadn't even phoned them and it killed the conference. I had taken Brian McClair along with me but he wasn't asked a single question so that was a waste of time.

*Sunday 4 August*

Today we played Nottingham Forest and looked more the part, with a 3–1 win. Our scorers were McClair (again) along with David Beckham and Phil Neville – his first senior goal. Now we have  a free week, which will give us the chance of some decent practice for the FA Charity Shield against Newcastle next weekend.

*Wednesday 7 August*

Jordi Cruyff is settling in well. Maurice Watkins has been to Prague to complete a deal with Slavia Prague for Poborsky, who is due any day now. Our two Norwegian signings are also settling in well. Along with Van Der Gouw, they have got themselves places to live. After our experience of 1989, when we had five players living in hotels for six months, I don't want the newcomers living in hotels any longer than necessary. It's not a good way of life for a sportsman.

*Friday 9 August*

The hype for the Charity Shield on Sunday is incredible. Normally this fixture is simply a nice day out for the fans, but this one is different. The intensity is building up all the time, played up by the press and television of course. I shall use it in my own build-up; I sense the players are ready for it. We'll travel down on the Saturday and stay at our usual place in Berkshire. The bookmakers have made Newcastle favourites. They're usually right, so who am I to argue!

*Sunday 11 August*

Surprised, when we arrived at Wembley, at the number of Newcastle supporters. Manchester United have a massive following, but the black and white favours were everywhere. I felt like General Gordon, arriving for the relief of Khartoum, only to find the Madhi waiting and taunting him. This Charity Shield is definitely different, there's a distinctly intimidating atmosphere which I haven't seen in the past. Perhaps the Newcastle fans have become more frenzied after watching Kevin crack up at the end of last season. Of course, this is a clash between the champions, and the team who thought they should be champions plus Shearer. I tried to swing the hype our way and told our players that they would love the atmosphere. Just make sure you express yourselves, I stressed to them.

A big game can do that for us and the team duly gave an excellent performance to win 4–0. Newcastle bombarded us for the first 20 minutes of the second half but the boys made it clear they were not going to be intimidated. Our defenders dealt comfortably with Shearer, so missing out on his transfer was not too agonising. History will prove whether he was right to pick Newcastle ahead of us. And I do feel that there's often a sting in the tail when you sign someone for that kind of money. Afterwards my players tell me that there is already muttering in the Newcastle team about some of them looking for new contracts. It's very difficult keeping some kind of pay parity in a club, especially in these days of agents.

*Charity Shield / Wembley / Att: 73,214*

**Manchester United 4**
Schmeichel, Irwin (G Neville), May, Pallister, P Neville, Butt (Poborsky), Keane, Cantona, Beckham, Scholes (Cruyff), Giggs
*Scorers: Cantona, Butt, Beckham, Keane*

**Newcastle 0**
Srnicek, Beresford, Batty, Peacock, Lee, Beardsley (Asprilla), Shearer, Ferdinand, Ginola (Gillespie), Watson, Albert

*Tuesday 13 August*

Milan are here for the second leg of our pre-season friendly. I have to leave Gary Pallister out to rest an injury, because I definitely need him on Saturday against Wimbledon. Nicky Butt has double vision – we must get him to the specialist and have the problem sorted out – but it gives me the opportunity to play the newcomers, Poborsky, Cruyff and Solskjaer.

We lose 1–0, a bad goal from our point of view, but the performance is reasonable. It's been good experience for some of our younger players. The new lads did well enough but, as foreigners, they need time to learn about English football.

*Thursday 15 August*

The players loosen off and I start thinking about the opening of the Premiership season. I'm struck by the wide variety of opposition ... Milan and Wimbledon, chalk and cheese. I don't mean any disrespect to Wimbledon, because I love going there. It's always a great test of your team's character. They ask searching questions and you have to admire their approach. I like Sam Hammam, who is the managing director these days. He's always very hospitable. On one occasion, when we played Wimbledon in the semi final of the FA Youth Cup, he invited the parents of the Youth team for a meal.

# 2
# Into battle

*Saturday 17 August*

Never mind the Charity Shield and all its hype, Wimbledon at Selhurst Park is the real challenge, with three League points at stake. I couldn't have hoped for a better start in defence of our Championship. We score three splendid goals, the final one by David Beckham which he hit from just inside his own half. Jordi Cruyff had tried something similar just a few minutes before, which hadn't come off. When Brian Kidd saw Becks shaping up he shouted out: 'Not you now!' Then when it sailed into goal I turned with a big grin on my face to tell Kiddo: 'Aye, him.' I am moved to say it is already the Goal of the Season. Early days I suppose, but it will take some beating. After the match, the Wimbledon trainer seemed a trifle miffed when he told us: 'It could have ended up in Brighton!'

*Premiership / Selhurst Park / Att: 25,786*
**Wimbledon 0**
Sullivan, Cunningham, Jones (Ekoku), Thatcher, Leonhardsen, Earle, Holdsworth, Gayle, Perry, McAllister, Clarke
**Manchester United 3**
Schmeichel, Irwin, May, Pallister, P Neville, Butt (Johnsen), Keane, Cantona (McClair), Beckham, Cruyff, Scholes
*Scorers: Cantona, Irwin, Beckham*

*Tuesday 20 August*

I'm thrilled to bits today with the news that Roy Keane is going to sign the new contract we have offered him. It will secure the heart of Manchester United for the next four years. The agreement consolidates the centre of our midfield for what should be the peak years of his career. His best seasons are ahead of him – and the ones just gone haven't been bad! I feel much happier about our involvement as a major football force now that the deal has been concluded. I have always seen Roy as a Manchester United man, the kind of player who belongs to a club like this, and I think he has always wanted to be here. At the same time, you never feel safe in these post-Bosman times, when a player is drawing close to the end of his contract and can move without a fee. So it's welcome news indeed. The plan is to announce it to our fans at the match against Everton tomorrow night.

Roy got into a bit of an argument during the close season with his Republic of Ireland manager, Mick McCarthy, when he pulled out of their summer tour. I can see both points of view, but I have to sympathise with Roy after a very hard season. No one drove himself harder and certainly Manchester United could not have expected more of him.

*Wednesday 21 August*

Joe Royle is not a happy man, and it turns out it's me who has upset him. He is here at Old Trafford with his Everton team but is studiously ignoring me. I have always got on well with Joe and I like him. It was disappointing when he didn't pop into my office for his usual cup of tea before the game, and failed to come for a drink afterwards.

I can only guess it has something to do with my quotes in this evening's paper, saying that in some respects Everton play like Wimbledon. What I had in mind is the long, high ball forward to Duncan Ferguson, so that the big man can knock it down for someone like Gary Speed to come on to. For instance, it's how they made the second goal against Newcastle. I was making the point that it is a danger we must be aware of, but Joe doesn't seem to like the comparison and has taken umbrage. So there's a bit of an atmosphere.

# Into battle

The game itself is OK. We were playing quite well when we got suckered by a marvellous goal from Ferguson, a sharp turn and explosive hit. I said to Gary Pallister at half time, "He's caught you by surprise there. You know about his ability in the air but you forget he has other qualities, that he's dangerous all round. He's a handful."

Anyway, we recover and our performance in the second half is magnificent. We get to grips with the game and overrun them, coming back from 2–0 down for a 2–2 draw. It's a reasonable result against an experienced team. It shows the character of Manchester United, our ability to get busy when the chips are down.

There's a good atmosphere and it's an entertaining game, though I lose my rag at the end. In my opinion the referee fails to allow for all the time the Everton players wasted in their longing for the final whistle. I'm bent on having a few words with the referee and march across the pitch towards him. Fortunately Brian Kidd senses I'm not in my most relaxed mood and heads me off. Instead, a BBC reporter catches the flak later at the press conference when he presses me just a little bit too hard on the incident. The media have the right to ask questions, but sometimes they don't show much sense. They fail to make allowances for the fact that during and immediately after a match you are in a highly emotional state. For those of us directly involved, it's a game of extreme passion and it takes time to come back down to earth.

One thing that would help with time-keeping is a third party, complete with klaxon, whose sole job would be to make sure a match runs its full course of ninety minutes' actual play. They have a time-keeper in rugby league and it's something our game should consider seriously. Then I wouldn't have to go looking for the referee at the end to discuss the matter! I don't see Joe Royle afterwards, of course, but I learn from the press that it is indeed my Wimbledon comments that have annoyed him. I'll phone him tomorrow.

*Premiership / Old Trafford / Att: 54,943*

**Manchester United 2**
Schmeichel, Irwin, May, Pallister, P Neville, Cantona, Butt, Beckham, Giggs, Cruyff, Poborsky (McClair)
*Scorers: Cruyff, Unsworth (own goal)*

**Everton 2**
Southall, Barrett, Hinchcliffe, Unsworth, Stuart, Ferguson, Speed, Ebbrell, Kanchelskis (Grant), Parkinson, Short
*Scorer: Ferguson 2*

### Thursday 22 August

I get through to Joe and he confirms he wasn't happy with my reference to Wimbledon. I just remind him of one or two things he has said in the past about Manchester United and point out that I hadn't gone sulking or making a big deal. It cuts both ways, and my mention of Wimbledon was not a criticism of him. In my opinion, there are parts of Everton's game involving Ferguson which do bear comparison. Anyway, we finish the conversation on good terms again. He's promised to buy me a drink. I'll wait now to see who gets their hand in their pocket first: Terry Venables, who still owes me that bet after the Germans won Euro '96, or Joe!

Roy Keane missed last night's match, because we've decided to go ahead with an operation on his knee, which has been bothering him since pre-season. Originally the plan was to have it done straight away, so he'd be ready for our big match against Juventus in the European Champions' League. Then the tournament format was changed, so that suddenly Juventus away is our first game. It was going to be impossible to have Roy ready in time, so he carried on and played in the Charity Shield and at Wimbledon. But the problem will keep surfacing if we don't have something done about it. He'll miss Juventus and be out for a month or so. It's a blow, and not my only injury worry. Sooner or later Phil Neville will need an ankle operation – but we are keeping that quiet for the time being.

Without Roy available last night I tried a new midfield, of Nicky Butt, David Beckham and Karel Poborsky. It was the

Czech's first match at Old Trafford and the helter skelter of it was something quite new to him; after a while I needed some experience on the pitch. So I put Brian McClair on, and he did really well to turn the game round for us. He is in my thinking for the next match against Blackburn, especially now that Nicky Butt is injured.

*Sunday 25 August*

Nicky Butt has taken another bang on the head so we'll have to be careful. It means I have to form yet another midfield for tonight's game against Blackburn. I go for David Beckham, Brian McClair and Jordi Cruyff, and bring in Ronny Johnsen for his first appearance. I'll play Ryan Giggs up front. It's hard on the wing, tracking up and down, and he is only just back from injury. It will be easier for him and his pace is always a factor through the middle.

That's the plan anyway, but it turns out we allow Blackburn to play so much that they begin to enjoy it. They have never played so well against us and we go one down. We get back to 1–1 when Jordi Cruyff does well to make an interception, but then Blackburn go ahead again with a terrific goal from Lars Bohinen. I change it to play three up, with Ole Gunnar Solskjaer on for his first appearance, with Cruyff and Eric Cantona just behind him. Then we get right on top and could have scored 10 goals. The final few minutes are amazing and we deserve our equaliser from substitute Solskjaer after a fine move by Cantona and Cruyff. The Norwegian's first goal sounds the bell that there is another player coming along at Old Trafford who is going to be a real star.

He amazes me. My intention this season, as I explained to him when he joined us, was that he should spend this season learning about how we play. Perhaps, I said, he would get a few games in the Coca-Cola Cup, or the odd appearance here and there. Lets see how you go, I said, but from the first training session he made everyone sit up and take notice. The improvement he makes each week is startling. As they say in football, a player's goals will pick him. This has been an excellent start on top of all the scoring he has been doing in training.

*Premiership / Old Trafford / Att: 54,178*

**Manchester United 2**

Schmeichel, Irwin, P Neville (G Neville), May (Solskjaer), Pallister, Cantona, Beckham, McClair, Cruyff, Johnsen, Giggs
*Scorers: Cruyff, Solskjaer*

**Blackburn Rovers 2**

Flowers, Coleman, Kenna, Sherwood, Hendry, Ripley, Gallacher (Fenton), Bohinen, Berg, Donis, Warhurst (Pearce)
*Scorers: Warhurst, Bohinen*

## *Tuesday 27 August*

I call a meeting of players and explain that, because we have to start thinking about how to handle Juventus, I am going to play three at the back in central defence at Derby in our next match. We toss the idea around. I leave it with them to think about while I set off with Brian Kidd on a scouting mission to check out Juventus in a Cup tie. We stay overnight in Rome.

## *Wednesday 28 August*

There's a six-hour delay at Rome Airport during a horrendous thunder storm and I panic that we won't reach Bari in time for the match. However, we are recognised by a group of Italian sports journalists and fill in time by quizzing them about the latest news on Juventus. Eventually get to the ground just outside Bari with an hour to spare and watch Juventus win comfortably enough, 2–0.

Kiddo knows quite a lot about Italian football as a result of going to watch them train whenever he gets a free spell during the season. He has been all over Europe in fact, and certainly knows the scene in places like Turin and Milan. Kiddo is sure that the system we're watching will be the one they'll play against us. "What you see, you will get," he says.

What strikes me in particular is the attitude of the Juventus players. Every one of them works his tail off. It gives you an idea of how the power base has changed in European football over the last 10 or 15 years. While our clubs were banned from playing in the European competitions, the Italians analysed our game and added our strengths to their own technical ability, thoroughness of preparation and organisation.

The result is that the two most powerful sides in Europe are AC Milan and Juventus. In addition to a high level of skill, they have a formidable work ethic and power. I've watched a tape of a pre-season Cup tie between the two and the commitment was unbelievable. Juventus lost 1–0, but clearly our match is going to be a tough, tough game.


*Thursday 29 August*

Back at the training ground.

There are World Cup qualifying fixtures at the weekend, which gives me a free week to plan how we will approach Juventus. I work at it mentally and tactically, thinking how best to handle three coming at us through the middle. Should we play three centre backs and let them handle one each, with one of the full backs the extra man?

Not having Phil Neville and Roy Keane isn't ideal. As we approach international weekend, I keep my fingers crossed that we don't have any more injuries.

We don't actually have many players left at Old Trafford but it does give Kiddo and me a chance to do individual exercises, technical stuff, one on one. The players enjoy that kind of thing.

On Sunday, England are in Moldova and Wales are handy at Cardiff, but with our match against Juventus in mind I'm keen to see Ronny Johnsen and Ole Solskjaer play at international level. So I am going to see Norway play Georgia.

*Saturday 31 August*

I fly to Norway and have dinner with an interesting football crowd. I meet up again with Archie Knox, who was my old sparring partner at Aberdeen, then Old Trafford, until he left to join Glasgow Rangers. He's still as keen as ever. Glenn Roeder, who is working for Glenn Hoddle now, is there too, with Tony Parkes, who's scouting for Blackburn Rovers, and Guido Mallents, coach of the Belgian club Mechelen. It's always good to get some football chat from a varied bunch of people like that.

*Sunday 1 September*

At the match, I sit next to Arrigo Sacchi, who congratulates me on our Double last season. I thank him, but say the real stuff starts now. "Juventus very strong," he says to me. In his polite way, I know he's telling me that we are in for a hard time. He says he is coming to the game and I tell him he will be very welcome.

As for the match itself, I see certain things in Solskjaer which confirm that he is an exceptional player. I like his style. Johnsen has an easy time in the game because his pace is good and he is comfortable on the ball. Georgi Kinkladze, the Manchester City player, is quiet for Georgia.

Norway win with a last-minute penalty.

*Monday 2 September*

Up very early after a late night, in order to get back to the Cliff. We take a roll call of the United players who have been away on international duty. Gary Neville, David Beckham and Gary Pallister have all come through OK. I know the Norwegian pair are all right, so it's just a matter of waiting for Denis Irwin, Peter Schmeichel and Jordi Cruyff. We've been lucky.

# Into battle

*Tuesday 3 September*

We are at Derby tomorrow night. I gather the players together to confirm that we're going to use three centre backs, because that's how we're going to play against Juventus. The way the Italians play, and the speed of their strikers, dictates that we need an extra man in the middle. I want to give our players the opportunity to practise the system.

I'm serious about it now, so I outline our formation: Cruyff forward in the inside-left position, Cantona similar on the right, three in the middle with Beckham, Butt and Giggs and then three centre backs – May, Johnsen and Pallister. Irwin and Gary Neville are pushed up as wing backs.

No matter what, I'm going to play Juventus with three in midfield. I'm absolutely sure that is the right thing to do. David, Nicky and Ryan are young and lack experience, but I'm confident they can pose problems so long as they relax and play to their true potential.

We have a practice match at the Cliff and I ask the Reserves to play like Derby. Sometimes that kind of match is a waste of time, because the Reserve team has its own way of playing and you really want to concentrate on working with the first team. I stop the game from time to time to discuss how it is working out. They look comfortable enough, but my players are flexible, adaptable and athletic.

I'm loaded with flu, so I go off to my bed early.

*Wednesday 4 September*

Match day. I don't travel with the team coach to the Baseball Ground because of the flu. I quarantine myself and follow in my car.

In the first half we do well, show great penetration The attacking players should have scored three or four goals. Then we have a terrible lapse and have just two men in a defensive wall against a free kick, which I just can't credit. Their Danish boy, Laursen, thunders his kick into the roof of the net and I spend five minutes of the interval on an inquest into why only two players were in the wall. Someone said that's what Schmeichel asked for, but Peter wasn't having any of that.

I cut through all the argument to discuss more important issues, such as why we're letting them get to the edge of our box too easily. We need to defend much earlier. They changed their system quite cleverly and, in fairness, produced a really good performance, full of grit and determination as well as attacking adventure.

David Beckham got us an equaliser but in the second half, Darryl Powell made more runs from midfield than I can remember for a long time. Derby deserved their draw.

Driving back on my own gives me plenty of opportunity to think. My conclusion is that playing three central defenders against Juventus would be too big a risk. It's a system that could do well but perhaps not just now. It needs practice would be too much of a gamble. We need to concentrate on it more in training, and then in the Premiership, before trying it in Europe.

It's the Continental style, and we must use it in the long run, at least in European competition. That's one of the reasons I have been investigating the possibility of getting Miguel Nadal from Barcelona. With him, I'd have the option. I could play Pallister with May or Johnsen but I need another player with great European experience alongside them. Maybe I'll give it another try at Leeds on Saturday. I'll talk to the players, but I must also take into account how Leeds are going to play against us.

*Premiership / County Ground / Att: 18,026*

**Derby County 1**
Hoult, Rowett, C Powell, D Powell, Stimac, Sturridge (Gabbiadini), Asanovic (Flynn), Willems (Simpson), Laursen, Carbon, Dailly
*Scorer: Laursen*

**Manchester United 1**
Schmeichel, G Neville, Irwin, May (Scholes), Pallister, Butt, Cantona, Beckham, Cruyff (Solskjaer), Johnsen, Gigg
*Scorer: Beckham*

# Into battle

*Thursday 5 September*

Cathy gives me a cutting from a paper in Scotland that had been sent down to her. The headline alleges that an old 'pal' of mine has been jailed for sex offences. Charming. I did know him. We were in the same class in Govan High in Glasgow. Little did I know how Robert Coglan was going to turn out. I phoned my old teacher, Elizabeth Thomson. I've kept in touch with her all my life; she must have turned 70 now. I told her to watch the television news and she'd see one of her old pupils. She called back later to say: "I've bred monsters." I wonder afterwards, does she include me in that?

*Friday 6 September*

Planning now for the trip to Leeds. First I talk with Kiddo, to say that Howard Wilkinson is sure to have watched us at Derby and will pick a team to make it difficult for us. I think they will play one up to upset our three at the back; Kiddo thinks they'll play with two strikers. He may be right. The matter is taken out of our hands when news comes in that Pallister has a knee injury. I must assume that he will be doubtful for Juventus next week as well, so we can definitely forget all about three at the back with a sweeper for the Leeds game.

*Saturday 7 September*

Pally has a final fitness test this morning before we set off for Leeds and is definitely out. I change the team, abandon three at the back and bring Karel Poborsky back into the side. Thinking ahead to Juventus, I have to consider how I can best make up the team with the experience, ability and penetration needed for a top European game. Poborsky, Cruyff and Cantona have quality and the experience of playing in Europe, so I must decide on the best way of utilising them against Juventus. I know I must play three in the middle of the park, so that means two wide with Eric through the middle. My main tactic will be to make sure that we are always left with two in the centre of midfield.

We arrive at Leeds and I go into Howard Wilkinson's office for a cup of tea, as usual. His wife Sam is there along with his son who, believe me, is a walking encyclopaedia of football knowledge. So I hit young Ben with a question: "Who was the only centre back in the European Championship Alan Shearer didn't score against?" Three seconds later comes the reply: "Nadal" – and he is dead right. Sam laughs and Howard gives a proud chuckle before asking me why I came up with that kind of question. From the searching way he looked at me, I know he's worked out why Nadal was on my mind. Negotiations for the Spanish defender are going well. I'm almost certain that he will join us after the Juventus match.

Into the match, and our performance is brilliant. They say that Leeds are a bad side, but they're not that bad. Their crowd, at their intimidating, pose a test of character for our young ones, who do us proud. They sprout wings, get the bit between their teeth and, with the benefit of an early goal, dominate the game. Poborsky is sensational, albeit against a young full back still learning the trade. It was a very good performance. This is the way to go against Juventus.

Then comes the sad part. It is difficult to appreciate how one game can change the fortunes of a man's life. The last thing the Leeds fans want was a 4–0 home defeat by Manchester United, and they vent their feelings on Howard. Their venom tells you he's really under pressure. I start to worry about him.

The last thing he needs at that moment is a television interview, but on he goes. I'm only six or seven yards away, doing a radio interview and I really feel for him. John Motson keeps pressing Howard with questions, asking how he thinks he can turn it round. The interview is long and tedious and only Howard's experience and strength of character gets him through. I'm disappointed in John Motson. He could have been

# Into battle

a bit more understanding. He is not normally the type to turn the screw but he does today. Perhaps he's getting his orders from his boss, down the line from the studio.

How the media has changed. They always want to get a result, so they go after a struggling manager. It's sad and it's wrong. I tell you one thing: if ever I am in that situation, I won't be doing a TV interview. Why should Howard subject himself to that ordeal and inquisition? There's not one benefit for him in it, except perhaps the satisfaction of knowing he hasn't lost his professional pride, and how many people watching and listening would give him credit for that? People say he is the manager and it's his job to do it. I say that that is bollocks. I'm surprised that, as a body of managers, we go along with the trend. The priority for a manager is to retain control, keep the players on track and get the team back to what they are good at. Frankly, doing a searching television interview immediately after a horrendous result shouldn't be on the agenda. He couldn't possibly be at his best. So why do it? Having watched Howard I have nothing but admiration for his mental toughness. Not every manager could have handled it.

I go into Howard's room for a drink. His staff are there, good guys like Paul Hart and David Williams, and you can sense the gloom. It's not a day for the usual joviality so I ask how the youth team are doing and things like that, trying to give some encouragement and support. It's difficult for me to handle as well, because I'm on a high after our good performance, particularly since it came at a vital time before a big European tie. However, at the same time I feel so badly for Howard.

*Premiership / Elland Road / Att: 39,694*
**Leeds United 0**
Martyn, Kelly, Palmer, Wetherall, Sharpe, Wallace (Hateley), Rush, Bowyer (Gray), Jobson, Harte, Ford (Radebe)
**Manchester United 4**
Schmeichel, G Neville, Irwin, May, Butt, Cantona, Beckham (McClair), Cruyff (Cole), Johnsen, Poborsky (Solskjaer), Giggs
*Scorers: Martyn (own goal), Butt, Poborsky, Cantona*

49

*Sunday 8 September*

It's Sunday but the lads are in to loosen off. It's the best time to get the stiffness and soreness out of their legs, while I think about how we are going to play against Juventus on Wednesday. There are areas in which we have to do well. I'm planning to arrange some sessions so that I can instil into them the discipline of always having two in the middle of the park when we attack.

Experience has taught us that it's not so much what happens when you have got the ball, or even necessarily when the opposition have the ball; the crucial moment is when you lose it. That's when you face the test, and it's where I miss Roy Keane. This is where a player of his experience and great awareness is so important. But I'm optimistic we will give a good account of ourselves and at least come away with a draw. I'm certain of it, so long as our players express themselves and don't get intimidated by the power of the Italians.

We have no new injuries. Hopefully we will have Pallister back, but it's going to be a last-minute decision.

*Tuesday 10 September*

This is it. We're in Turin, staying in a huge hotel which used to be the Fiat car headquarters. Each of the massive rooms has a picture showing the blueprints of the first and most recent Fiats ever built. It's an interesting place and I have no worries about our stay. You worry in some countries, but the Italians are very professional and everything is done to our liking.

We train tonight at the San Siro – you are allowed an hour at the actual ground. Pallister has to do well in training; I tell him I can't wait until tomorrow, the day of the match, to finalise the team. We must settle it this evening. He comes through the session OK, so I take the midfield and front players to give them an understanding of their part of the game. Strange as it may sound, the way Juventus play is like Wimbledon, only with more technical ability and power. They play the ball quickly to the front players. Don't get me wrong, they put in the long diagonal ball, but it's not in the air all the time. They work very hard at these things, close in behind you and don't let you out of your own half. We have to make sure we are always in close contact with each other. Our two wide players have to respond to where the ball is. In other words, if the ball goes out to Poborsky on the right, then Jordi Cruyff must move in from the left, to become a striker in support of Eric Cantona. Vice versa if the ball comes left, with Karel moving inside.

We try some shadow play to get the picture. The midfield players must judge their runs sparingly so that we have a grip on midfield and keep numbers in order to retain possession. That's my game plan, but the most important thing is that they must not come in at half time regretting the first half. I tell them: "You have got to express yourselves. You have the ability and this is the platform we have all been waiting for."

The build-up is right and I'm feeling more optimistic. You are always a little apprehensive, of course, and come the big game situation you start to question the European scene. Is it really an ogre? Is it such a big bad wolf that we can't handle it?

*Wednesday 11 September*

The first half is just what I didn't want and exactly the way I knew Juventus would play. It wasn't so much that we failed to handle it, more that we failed to express ourselves. The young players suffered.

At half time, I knew I needed Brian McClair's experience on to bring some order into our play. I stressed that Jordi must come in off the wide position to support Eric when Karel had the ball on the right; and the same thing for Karel if the ball was with Jordi. The second half was a transformation and I was pleased with them. Juventus are the hardest team in Europe to play against on their own ground at the moment, but we got near to them in the second half. It was a good performance, lacking only in strikes at goal. One thing you know is that when the Italians go one up, they're not going to give one away. The last 15 minutes were wasted with Juventus going down with injuries, making substitutions, and all the tricks they could get up to.

I was disappointed. The young players know what is expected of them now and I they won't let us down again. I'm sure of that. But though I'm disappointed by the result, I can understand it. And funnily enough, I enjoyed the occasion.

Through an interpreter I managed a few words with their coach, Marcello Lippi, who said what we had achieved at Old Trafford was incredible. I thanked him, but pointed out that what we wanted now was the big thing he won last season. He took a big puff on his cigar. He knew what I was talking about. Europe is our big challenge now. Hopefully, the reminder from Juventus of the difficulties will help us in the long term to achieve our goal.

*European Champions League / Stadio Delle Alpi / Att: 54000*

**Juventus 1**
Peruzzi, Ferrara, Montero (Juliano), Porrini, Pessotto, Conte, Deschamps, Zidane (Di Livio), Boksic, Vieri (Amoruso), Del Piero
*Scorer: Boksic*

**Manchester United 0**
Schmeichel, G Neville, Irwin, Johnsen, Pallister, Cantona, Butt, Beckham, Giggs (McClair), Cruyff (Cole), Poborsky (Solskjaer)

*Thursday 12 September*

Flying home in the early hours It feels like the morning after the night before, except of course I'm stone cold sober and wondering what the guys sitting behind us have written about our defeat.

One of the interesting things about European football is taking the press with you. In fact the media outnumber us, what with all the reporters, columnists, photographers, radio commentators, analysts and a few television representatives as well. They are sitting at the rear of the plane and I keep saying to the chairman that it's all wrong. The press should be in front of us rather than behind, where they keep us under the spotlight, assessing which player is taking a drink, and then perhaps hanging a story on it. There's no mileage in that direction for them with Manchester United. The players know I'm obsessively strict on how they behave when travelling and they never let me down.

I insist on blazer, flannels, shirt and tie when we travel, because a popular football team is a sort of icon for young people. It gives me enormous satisfaction and pride to see how our players conduct themselves abroad.

Another pressure that comes with taking the press on the club charter aircraft is the frustrating delays if they are held up getting reports back to England. It can be very frustrating if we are ready to go but have to wait for one chap who has had problems with his telephone link. Happily, this trip has gone like clockwork. I'm glad about that, because if the press can't get their stories and pictures back on time from a sophisticated country like Italy, then we're going to be in trouble on trips to less civilised parts of the world.

We get away on scheduled time, but even so it's 4 am when we land – or, by our body clocks of the last three days, 6 am. I'm wondering if the players will be fully recovered for the weekend.

Most clubs take the press with them on foreign trips. We did it at Aberdeen. Rangers don't because they use a lot of scheduled flights rather than hire charter planes, so there isn't the same opportunity. A little while ago we were approached by an executive airline offering us a first-class aircraft with seats reduced from around 140 to a roomy 50. It appealed to me because it would have meant just our own party travelling, with the media left to fend for themselves. But after discussion, the board stuck with tradition, in favour of presenting a united front of club and media abroad. It must be an enormous help when we go to places in Eastern Europe, where scheduled flights are minimal and subject to all kinds of delays with passports and visas.

I wish the media would remember the way we smooth out the wrinkles when they complain about the price of their trips – which always includes coaches to and from the airport, to training and to the match itself. Contrary to popular belief, Manchester United don't profit out of the situation. Hiring charter planes is a costly business and we don't make money out of the media. Admittedly, we always have the best for our players, and that comes at a price, but we are a big club. Every player is treated superbly, spoiled even. They are lucky lads. Everyone, from their immediate coaches and support staff to the girls in the office, really works hard to please them... but then again, they are the best.

Even the best have to go short of sleep. I ask them to come into the training ground for a team meeting about the Juventus match. It's not a question of hanging blame on people, or saying so-and-so let us down or failed. I want to sum up the game in the context of European football. The players need to be aware of the tactical implications and trust their ability, something which eluded them in the first half. Until they believe in and can express themselves, they will always allow a team like Juventus to dominate them.

It wasn't until I came into the changing room at half time to go bananas that they woke up. I asked them if they remembered my specific warning against coming in at the break regretting their performance, or lack of one. Everything I had warned them against was spot on, but nobody gets accused individually. That policy isn't productive. Everything said is to increase their determination and ambition. I tell them that I don't expect them to lose another game in this Champions' League.

It was a good meeting. They understood the points I was making exactly, and it's good if players accept the truth without making excuses. The real problems start when a team refuses to accept a lesson. It means the players are not prepared to advance on a bigger stage and develop their own personalities. Down the years, players like Bryan Robson and Steve Bruce, Brian McClair and Roy Keane have been prepared to hold up their hands and do something about it. They are the players you know you can depend on and I believe the others will show they are made of equally stern stuff.

## Saturday 14 September

You always worry about the aftermath of a big European tie. Initially, against Nottingham Forest at Old Trafford, our boys bore that out. They were slack and Forest took the lead, a habit of visiting teams so far this season. Then we got to grips with the game and for the next 20 minutes played some magnificent football to win 4–1.

Our display prompted Frank Clark, the Forest manager, to say after the game that he feels we are a better side than last year. It's nice to hear that because I feel the same way. There is a developing maturity about the side. The younger players look more experienced. They react with more maturity – witness their response to going two goals down against Everton. They are not so dependent on the older players to help them out. Youngsters like David Beckham, Nicky Butt and Gary Neville have done fantastically well in this respect. Yes, I was mightily pleased with this performance, a real pick-me-up after Juventus.

*Premiership / Old Trafford / Att: 54,984*

**Manchester United 4**
Schmeichel, G Neville, Irwin, Pallister, Johnsen, Butt (McClair), Beckham, Poborsky, Cantona, Giggs, Solskjaer (Cole)
*Scorers: Solskjaer, Giggs, Cantona 2 (1 pen)*

**Nottingham Forest 1**
Crossley, Lyttle, Pearce, Cooper, Chettle, Bart-Williams, Phillips, Saunders (Roy), Lee, Woan (Allen), Haaland
*Scorer: Haaland*

*Monday 16 September*

Time to do key work in training. A free week before next Saturday's match at Villa Park, and very welcome it is too. We can concentrate on the basics – getting our passing going and building up morale after the shattering experience of playing in Turin. There is always a price to pay when you play game after game at the tempo and intensity demanded of Manchester United. All our games are major, all full houses, and there can be no easing up. But I'm happy with the situation at the moment. Roy Keane is on the mend after his knee operation, Phil Neville's ankle operation looks to have gone well and Gary Pallister's knee injury seems to have cleared up. It has been niggling away and he hasn't been able to train. There is no doubt that when players don't train they lose their fitness, especially a big lad like Pally. Hopefully he can now get his fitness level back up.

I'm keeping tabs on the Nadal situation, but there is still no sign from Barcelona that they are ready to take our interest any further.

*Tuesday 17 September*

I go to see Preston against Spurs in a first-leg, 1–1 Coca-Cola Cup tie. We are excused this second round because of our European commitments – a welcome arrangement, and not before time!

I arrive early, park, and am escorted to the front door by a lovely police lady. I ask her if everyone at Deepdale gets a personal usher and she says, "I have to look after my manager!" We have fans everywhere!

I enjoy my celebrity welcome and then in the boardroom I run into a real celebrity figure. Every time I meet Alan Sugar I wonder why Terry Venables chose to take him on in court. You look into his eyes and you know he doesn't mess about. He is a substantial, formidable figure.

I always have a good banter with him, and tonight is no exception. He asks if I am here to buy any of his players. I say I have no money, he scoffs. Then he tells me I've missed a gem of a player – Rory Allen, a youngster from London. I say I've never heard of him. In fact we knew all about Rory when he was still at school, but we hadn't a facility in London where he could train, so we couldn't do anything about it. What Alan probably doesn't know is that the boy's mother is a dyed-in-the-wool United fan, and you never know what might happen in football. When Rory is older perhaps he will change his mind about which team he wants to play for. Certainly there aren't many promising youngsters we don't know about. But I let Alan have his moment of satisfaction, thinking we had slipped up!

Then I bump into Tom Finney, and I'm reminded of watching my first international at Hampden Park in 1954. I was just a kid at the time, hanging around outside. My parents would have slaughtered me if they'd known I was there. When I was spotted by a friend of my dad's, George McGonnal, I thought my number was up. Please don't tell them, I pleaded. George was great. "In you go," he said, and lifted me over the turnstile.

It was the greatest moment of my life, watching Scotland at home to England ... up until the moment when I saw Tom Finney inspire a 4–2 win for England and destroy my boyhood hero. Sammy Cox was probably coming to the end of his career at Ibrox, and Tom made sure of it. As sprightly as ever, the Preston Plumber is a lovely man, but I still wonder whether to forgive him for the pain he put me through as a 13-year-old. I decide to let bygones be bygones, and we have a good chat.

*Wednesday 18 September*
Fly to Vienna to watch Rapid play FC Lask, in preparation for our Champions' League tie at Old Trafford against the Austrians. I have reservations. Time and again you go abroad

to see games which turn out to be so low key that they bear little resemblance to a European match; you know the tempo will shoot up.

So I'm cautious about what I see. I look to see who their influential players are, who's bossing the game, who the team focuses on in the build-up and who's taking all the free kicks. I try to assess stamina and whether they will all go the distance. I watch out for defensive problems, but I don't look much beyond because, as I say, a low-key league game can mislead you. In any case Les Kershaw, our chief scout, will have done his homework. We will have covered four of their games in total, which paints an adequate picture of what we will be facing.

*Thursday 19 September*

Take the first flight out of Vienna and arrive in Manchester at 10.30 am via Amsterdam. I go straight to the training ground and chat to Kiddo. I tell him I think we can win the game and I'm a bit more set in my mind about how to approach it.

*Saturday 21 September*

It's Aston Villa away. My theme to the players is that Villa are a Championship threat to us this season. They are sound defensively and don't give goals away. Southgate, Staunton and Ehiogu do well for them; with Townsend in midfield and Yorke up front, they will make a challenge.

We start quite well and I'm disappointed that we go in at half time without a goal, because we had dominated. I'm pleased with our football but regret the missed chances. Before the match I explained to Solskjaer that I would take him off at the break, to give Andy Cole 45 minutes to assess his fitness for the Vienna game. Andy was unlucky not to score and Ryan hit the post, but at the end of the day we still hadn't scored. If you don't take your chances, you can't expect to win.

# Into battle

*Premiership / Villa Park / Att: 39,339*

**Aston Villa 0**
Oakes, Curcic (Taylor), Staunton, Southgate, Wright, Ehiogu, Townsend, Nelson, Draper, Yorke, Milosevic
**Manchester United 0**
Van Der Gouw, G Neville, Irwin, Johnsen, Keane, Pallister, Cantona, Solskjaer (Cole), Cruyff (Poborsky), Beckham, Giggs

## *Sunday 22 September*

Drive up to Glasgow first thing to pick up my mother-in-law. She is 86 and we have persuaded her to come and live with us. I'm back in the house by 3 pm. Well, Spurs were playing Leicester and I couldn't miss that, could I?

David Sadler and Alan Wardle would have been glad to know I was safely back in Manchester, as they waited for my arrival at their old boys' charity dinner. Unbeknown to me, they intended to make a special presentation to me, to mark the team's League and Cup Double, on behalf of their Association of Former Manchester United Players. Brian Kidd had told them I'd gone to Glasgow and naturally they wondered if I had forgotten and they would be left with an embarrassing situation.

There were two mightily relieved organisers when I strolled in for what was a great night! There is a wonderful camaraderie among the ex-players and I was very honoured to receive their award, one of the most appreciated honours I have had. My thanks to the old boys for the beautiful crystal and, more particularly, the thought behind it. The guest speaker was Jim Watt; a few funny stories and very clearly no sign of brain damage to this one-time boxing champion.

## *Monday 23 September*

I call in the players for a tactical discussion on how we are going to play against Rapid Vienna. I explain to Roy Keane that Kühbauer is their main player; knowing Roy, he'll attend to it. David Beckham's role will be to drop deeper in order to draw Zingler, who sits in front of their defence. This way I hope we'll find more space to play the ball forward to Cantona. I am satisfied that we have the players to be successful, but I stress that they mustn't wait until half time to get started. They must take the game by the scruff of the neck right from the start. There will be 50,000 fans at Old Trafford ... I want them lifted off their seats. The players musn't let the fans down.

### Wednesday 25 September

I couldn't have asked for a better response. The team's movement and determination were first class, as we carved out a highly satisfying 2–0 win. A lot of people say to me that Eric Cantona doesn't play well in Europe: I don't understand what they're talking about. He was unfairly criticised against Juventus, because he simply had no support in that game. Much of Eric's effectiveness is geared to people moving around him. In Turin it just didn't happen, so of course he was quiet. In this match I knew he would be man-marked so I asked him to play further upfield – which he did perfectly. Both he and Solskjaer did extremely well.

After just 15 minutes, we lost Ronny Johnsen with injury and replaced him with David May, a man who never lets you down. You  know you will always get an excellent performance. The Austrians did better in the second half but we kept our discipline and if anyone had asked me before the game if I would have settled for a 2–0 win I would have snapped their hand off. We mustn't be greedy ... we'll save that for another day.

*European Champions' League / Old Trafford / Att: 51,831*

**Manchester United 2**
Schmeichel, G Neville, Irwin, Johnsen (May), Pallister, Cantona, Beckham, Keane, Giggs, Poborsky (Butt), Solskjaer (Cole)
*Scorers: Solskjaer, Beckham*

**Rapid Vienna 0**
Konsel, Ivanov, Schöttel, Stöger (Barisic), Kühbauer, Prosenik, Lesiak, Ratajczyk, Wagner (Stumpf), Zingler (Jovanovic), Heraf

# Into battle

*Thursday 26 September*

On my way to Aberdeen to play golf. Yes, I know it's a long way for a round, but I accepted this invitation by mistake. I thought it was the run-up to an international and a free fortnight, so I agreed to take part in a charity event for old friends. And did I regret it! Normally I like going back to Aberdeen. Compared with Manchester, the air is so fresh and you can't help feeling revitalised. But on this occasion it was the wettest day imaginable and blowing a gale. I couldn't even get round in par ... and there's wishful thinking for you!

What really disturbed me, though, is that just before I went out I got a call from David Fevre, our physio, to say there was a problem with Roy Keane and that he was sending him straight to hospital. What had appeared to be a simple 'dead leg' last night had bled internally and Roy was now in a bad way. Apparently he had a hot bath after the match, which is the worst possible thing for that kind of muscle injury. He had also had a few friends over from Ireland and I'm afraid Roy thinks Guinness is medicine, which probably hasn't helped. I'm anxious to get back and see exactly what is happening.

*Friday 27 September*

The first thing I do after catching the early flight back to Manchester is get the players in to explain the situation with Roy and use him as an example of how important it is to avoid taking a bath if they have a damaged muscle. Jonathan Noble, the orthopaedic surgeon, says Roy can come out of hospital tomorrow if he promises to rest when he gets home. Roy gives me his word that he will literally put his feet up and be sensible. We are going to be without him for a few weeks, but the situation would have been a lot more serious if David Fevre hadn't taken such prompt action. The swelling was more than an inch round his thigh and, but for David's spot-on diagnosis, Roy would probably have needed an operation.

Then I have a word with Paul Scholes, because he has played only one senior game so far this season,. I'm concerned that I'm not giving him enough bites of the apple. I explain to him that when Eric goes, that's when he will emerge as a really key player. They play in similar positions, and I have him marked down as Eric's successor. Paul tells me that he is missing not playing in the first team, but I explain that if I sold him now I would only have to buy him back eventually. I have no idea how long Eric will carry on playing for us, other than that he still has a couple of years left on his contract. He can't go on for ever though.

I think young Scholes understands. He is one of the good guys. For a young player he is a man's man, and even while Eric is still at the club he's quite capable of getting into the team on merit.

### Saturday 28 September

It's Saturday, but for once I don't go to a game because I have to pick up friends at the airport. We train in the morning in preparation for tomorrow's match against Spurs at Old Trafford, and then I watch the youth team against Oldham.

### Sunday 29 September

Spurs have a few injuries and I expect us to win. Apart from a couple of squeaks, we get there comfortably in an open and entertaining match. We play in second gear and always look capable of upping the tempo – perhaps an understandable reaction after a midweek European tie, with all its mental and physical strains. You have to be fair to the players.

Ole Gunnar Solskjaer takes the headlines after scoring both goals in our 2–0 win. That boy is starting to make the hairs on the back of my neck stand up. I don't want to get carried away, but it's difficult to overestimate how good he could become one day.

# Into battle

*Premiership / Old Trafford / Att: 54,953*

**Manchester United 2**
Schmeichel, G Neville, Irwin, May, Pallister, Cantona, Butt, Beckham, Giggs (Cruyff), Poborsky (Scholes), Solskjaer
*Scorer: Solskjaer 2*

**Tottenham Hotspur 0**
Walker, Howells (Edinburgh), Calderwood, Fox (Rosenthal), Nielsen, Sheringham, Wilson, Campbell, Carr, Sinton, Allen

*Monday 30 September*

I need to get back into the gym. I've let myself down. Looking at all the dinners and functions I must attend this week I know I'm going to put on seven pounds. I've had good intentions in the past but they get wiped out by phone calls and administrative demands, so the answer is to come in very early, at around 7.30 am, when it's quiet and I won't be interrupted. The other advantage is that I can run through things with Ken Ramsden, who gets in early for a work-out. As well as being assistant secretary to Ken Merrett, he is our press secretary. As I torture myself on the treadmill, we can figure out how we are going to handle various things. We need to be in close contact and this seems an ideal way.

I start my week's social whirl by attending Brian McClair's testimonial boxing night at the Piccadilly Hotel. It's a smashing night with good honest boxers giving their all. The only hardship for me is sitting at the top table, right alongside Bernard Manning, who does his act before the boxing starts. There is no escape – he gives me absolute stick. My face is red as a beetroot as he slaughters me for supporting the Labour Party. I take my medicine and remind myself that it is all in good humour ... I think!

*Tuesday 1 October*

I was out tonight, speaking at a dinner for the Rainbow Trust, a charity which looks after seriously ill children at the St Francis Hospice. They do a marvellous job and these are the kind of dinners I'm happy to do. Earlier in the day Vince Miller, the MC, phoned to say that if on the way to dinner I called at the home of Joe Kennedy, a wealthy building and road contractor based in Manchester, he would make a big donation to the Trust. I agreed and his driver picked me up. On the way he put a tape on and asked me who was singing. It sounded good and familiar so I said I knew but just couldn't put a name to the guy. In fact it was Joe, who is not only a big United supporter but a man with a lovely voice. I met his family and then went off to the dinner. My speech was well received and they seemed pleased to see me.

*Wednesday 2 October*

Round three in a busy week. I'm at the opening of Manchester United's new restaurant, the Red Café. The idea is to give supporters a place to eat throughout the week and hopefully at prices comparable with similar venues.

It's a big night for the club, who have put so much work into the launch. Much of the advertising has centred round Ryan Giggs and Eric Cantona, but neither are going to be there. Ryan has been nominated for Sports Personality of Wales and feels he must be in Cardiff for the presentation so as not to let down his fellow countrymen. Eric's absence is more bizarre. He is double-booked and is due in France to shoot a television advert. I remember he had mentioned it and we had given approval without knowing the dates. He is so haphazard about that kind of thing and relies heavily on my secretary and his lawyer.

The clash is sod's law. We are in a hole, so by way of apology the two boys decide to do a video. Eric simply holds up a poem, a sequel to the trawler and seagulls epic, and just as incomprehensible. It starts with "What is an apology, but a cry for understanding from the heart of a man ... ?" I'm reminded that when you are in a hole, you should stop digging.

# Into battle

A lot of the Coronation Street stars were there; most of them seem to be United fans anyway and there were mutual exchanges of autographs. Mike Le Velle, who plays Kevin, sometimes plays football with us in our Friday evening team. Last time out he scored a hat-trick, but Nick Cochrane, who plays Andy McDonald, won't believe him and I was called as a witness. Warren Clarke who, among many popular roles, played the football club chairman in the television series "The Manageress", told me he was a messenger boy making cups of tea at the Manchester Evening News before he got his acting break.

# 3
## The blip

*Thursday 3 October*

Am I right or am I wrong? Along with David Davies of the FA, I've accepted an invitation to talk about football at a fringe meeting of the Labour Party in Blackpool. I'm pleased to do it, but a bit concerned about the other part of the evening's agenda – which involves politics. It's not my job as manager of Manchester United to flaunt my political affiliations, although people will no doubt draw their own conclusions from my background. I expect I'll get one or two letters saying that I shouldn't show my allegiance publicly or use my position in football to influence young voters. I have to consider those things. But when I did an article for the Labour Party magazine it was about football, not the merits of the party.

I have to say, though, that my experience of life still bites deep. In particular, the decline of the National Health Service still rankles. I can't forget how my mother died in one of Glasgow's biggest hospitals. There was no lack of duty and care, but there was a lack of money. Cladding was falling off the pipes and I'm thinking: "My mother is dying here. It's not right." They can't keep a hospital up to scratch without the funds to do it.

*Friday 4 October*

Despite my apprehensions, the day turns out quite well. I even tell Alastair Campbell, Tony Blair's press secretary, that I'm willing to be photographed with his boss and some youngsters. Labour's photo-opportunity is their response to John Major inviting the England football team to Downing Street. They don't miss a trick in politics.

I enjoy the meeting. David Davies speaks well, and I hold forth about the changing face of football. Naturally, the press pick up on my criticism of the way the fixture list is planned. I mean, who in their right mind would want to play Liverpool four days before a key European tie? And then Newcastle four days after? Every time an English team has a bad day in Europe, the press slaughter them – but the people who plan the fixtures bear some of the responsibility.

The journey back, in very bad weather, is horrible. I'm looking forward to a night at home after a very busy and social few days. Just as well it's an international week with no club fixtures, or I wouldn't have given myself a chance to prepare for the engagements properly.

*Saturday 5 October*

I travel to Scotland for a reunion dinner of Drumchapel Amateurs, probably the most famous boys' club football team in Britain. They changed the face of junior football in this country. The club was affiliated to a Boys' Brigade Company and used to travel abroad to play teams in Italy and Germany; commonplace now, but ground-breaking 40 years ago. They were funded by Douglas Smith, a truly remarkable man.

I am proud to have played for them. In fact, in the mid-1950s, 29 of us from Drumchapel joined professional clubs in the space of a year: players like George McLean, Bobby Hope, Asa Hartford and Jim Forrest. Kenny Dalglish played for them at one stage and around 14 of their players from that period became Scottish internationals. We used to wear the Celtic strip, not because we were connected with Celtic, but because it was the cheapest we could get. The club is still running, albeit along slightly different lines, concentrating on more senior teams. They even have their own ground now.

As well as being a reunion of old players, we're also here to celebrate Doug's 69th birthday. Having spent the journey up hoping that I recognise people I haven't seen since childhood, the first guy I meet says: "It's lovely to see you again" – and I don't recognise him. What makes it worse is that it turns out to be Joe Davin, a lad I was particularly friendly with who went on to play for Ipswich. What a bad start. Sorry Joe, but your hair is completely white now. It was a smashing night.

*Sunday 6 October*

I get a lift over to the Crow's Nest Hotel at Anstruther, where I am speaking at a dinner for a wheelchair charity, run by the family who owns the hotel. They are an amazing family of mother and seven daughters. All their names begin with the letter E. The father, Eddie, who's dead now, said after the seventh was born that if they had another girl she would be called Enough.

*Monday 7 October*

I learn that last night raised £10,500 for the wheelchair charity, which is great. I get away for nine holes of golf at St Andrews with Ian Birrell, the son of one of the sisters. He's a one-handicapper so I ask for a shot a hole. He wants to know my handicap but I tell him it doesn't matter, it's very windy and I need all the help I can get. Actually I surprise myself and play quite well to halve the nine holes. There's no time for the other nine though, because this isn't the end of my social commitments. I hurry back to Manchester in readiness for another charity dinner, in support of Muscular Dystrophy, at the Portland Hotel.

It's a charity which is close to my heart because of my friendship with a Scottish family whose son suffers from this cruel disease. Findlay Peterson and his wife had one afflicted son but wanted more family. They took advice and were told there was a one-in-a-million chance of a repeat. Sure enough, their second child was fine but a third had the disease as well.

So it's a special cause for me. However, my face falls when I arrive and find that Bernard Manning is on the bill again. I brace myself – and he doesn't disappoint me. I get some more fearful stick. He is a controversial character and not everyone likes his racist slant. If you become part of his comedy you have two choices: accept it, or walk out. One thing in his favour is that, for all his often offensive racism, he does an awful lot of charitable work. With any luck, the abuse he gives me can't go on for ever.

*Tuesday 8 October*

Another horrendous day in the life of AF. I get a call first thing from our physiotherapist to say there is a problem with one of the players. So I rush to the training ground to sort it out and then get a call from my secretary, to tell me the sixth form at Manchester Grammar School are waiting for me to talk to them. I had forgotten all about it, but Lynn tells me I can still redeem myself if I can get there by 11 am. I fly back home in my cosmic aeroplane to change into something more suitable than a tracksuit. Then I fly to MGS.

The school hall is fantastic and beautiful, quite daunting even. People talk about our theatre at Old Trafford but this is theatre, too, and I get a tingle. I speak for 10 or 15 minutes and make the point that I'm furious with myself for being late. I tell them that in my six years as an apprentice before joining a football club I was never late once. It's the way I was brought up. I hate being late. People ask me how I have become successful and, while it's obviously not the whole story, I always say that it helps if you have certain disciplines in life.

The boys receive me well and my biggest problem is

escaping to the sanctuary of the headmaster's study without having to sign 2,000 autographs. The first thing I see is a machine gun from World War One trained on me. I accept I was late for the presentation, but this is ridiculous! However, apparently the Head collects war memorabilia. Then I do an interview for the school magazine.

But that's not the end of it, because I go straight from the school to the opening of a firm of chartered accountants in Hale. I'm bang on time, and would even have been early if I had been able to find the place, but at least I'm not late. Being late twice in one day would have been too much to cope with!

*Wednesday 9 October*

Cathy's ready to leave me – she hasn't really seen me for four days – so I don't go to Wembley, but watch England play Poland on television instead. I think Glenn Hoddle has a problem in that the expectations of the media and the supporters are dangerously high after Euro 96. They're looking for the perfect team and the perfect performance. As I watch the Poles run England ragged in the first 20 minutes, I know it's going to be a hard night for the new manager.

Alan Shearer and Les Ferdinand are up front together. I have my doubts about playing two through the middle at international level. One of the problems that arises is that if, as well as two strikers, you play three in the middle across the back (which seems to be Glenn's way), they can be left marking just one man. In Europe, the opposition front players don't always play upfront. They drop deep and drift wide, leaving your central defenders picking their noses while your two midfield players run themselves silly trying to get the ball.

In this match, the Poles saturated the midfield, so I wasn't surprised they dominated the match. But then England got one of those slices of luck which change a game. A lot of the pre-match build-up focussed on Brian Clough calling goalkeeper

Jan Tomaszewski a clown before England's World Cup qualifier against Poland at Wembley in 1974. In fact, Tomaszewski subsequently played out of his skin to help eliminate England from the finals in West Germany. As I watch David Beckham's cross float to the far post to give Alan Shearer an easy goal with the keeper stranded, I can't help thinking that Clough's prediction about Czech keepers had come true after all, albeit some 23 years later! Still, people shouldn't dismiss luck. If you get lucky, appreciate it.

There was no disputing England's second goal. This one was typical Shearer. Ferdinand set the ball up nicely for him but Shearer hit it as if he meant to kill it. The keeper had no chance.


*Thursday 10 October*

It's collection time again, waiting for our ten internationals to return home. Solskjaer was taken off in Norway so I wonder about his fitness. Denis Irwin was away in Dublin, but it's not so much the match itself I worry about with the Irish as the game afterwards. A knees-up lasting into the wee small hours seems to be a part of their culture. I have spoken to Mick McCarthy, the manager, about my reservations, but will he be able to change a very old custom?

The particular problem I have this time is that our match against Liverpool on Saturday has an 11 am kick-off, which means even less recovery time than usual. We had to settle for a morning start because we play Fenerbahçe in Turkey next Wednesday so I didn't want a game on Sunday. But, because it's a live Sky fixture, that's how it was scheduled until I protested. We got a switch to the Saturday, but the police won't wear a night game and we can't be live on TV when everyone else is playing in the afternoon.

So morning it is. Nicky Butt might be another player short of sleep. He was with the England Under-21 team playing at Wolves when the floodlights failed. Kick-off was delayed until

# The blip

10pm. Most of the spectators had gone home by then and I went to bed myself after the first half. I talked to Nicky about it and he said the biggest problem for him was food. "I was starving," he said. I told him he was always starving, but I did take his point. How can you perform at your best at that time of night? The match should have been called off.

*Friday 11 October*
I want to try a different way of playing against Liverpool. I know their two midfield men, McManaman and Berger, will play off the front positions like old inside forwards, and I don't want them to come to Old Trafford and kill the pace of the game. I want our crowd to be up for it and excited, so I have a team meeting and explain how we are going to combat them. My intention is to play Pallister at the back and Giggs wide left, pushing Irwin up from full back into midfield against McManaman, while Butt picks up Berger. I'm confident we can prevent Liverpool getting the possession they need to slow things down. I contemplate taking the team away for the night, but decide that since so many of them have been away all week I'll let them sleep in their own beds. They'll report at 9 am.

*Saturday 12 October*
It's the morning of the Liverpool game, and Ryan Giggs reports in with a calf strain. Not only that, but David Fevre phones early to say he's had a call from Pallister, who's feeling his back again. All my best-laid plans have gone awry, but the worst thing I can do is show hesitancy. I dismiss the injured players from my thoughts because they are no use to me for this match. I call in Jordi Cruyff and ask him if he is willing to play a different role. He gives a keen response so I set out the same system, only with different players.

So to the game. Tactically I felt we got the first half right, although we were giving the ball away too easily in the last third of the pitch. Perhaps tiredness is creeping in – especially among those who played at Wembley, which is terribly draining on the legs. David Beckham still scores a terrific goal and never stops running, but I can see it is taking a lot out of him.

Liverpool play well in the second half and take the honours, although considering the amount of possession they enjoyed and the number of attacks they mounted, they never really cut us open.

At the press conference afterwards, I don't want to say that I thought our players were tired. That's not the message I want going out on the eve of our big European game against Fenerbahçe. Instead, I tell the press the players didn't follow my game-plan. It's true to a certain extent, but for me tiredness was the major reason for our disappointing second half.

Nonetheless I was very happy to have won. It's always important to beat your major competitors and Liverpool are certainly going to be that this season. Roy Evans has done a fantastic job for them. He has given them back their proper values. They all want to pass the ball and they are a good mix of experience and youth, with players like John Barnes and Mark Wright alongside youngsters like McManaman, McAteer, Fowler and Redknapp. They play the right way. I feel Liverpool and Manchester United are going to be big rivals in the battle for honours over the next few years.

It's been a demanding morning so I don't go to a match in the afternoon. I end up following the scores on Teletext – a pretty distorted way of watching sport.

*Premiership / Old Trafford / Att: 55,128*

**Manchester United 1**
Schmeichel, G Neville, Irwin, May, Cantona, Butt, Beckham, Cruyff,
Poborsky (Scholes), Johnsen, Solskjaer (Giggs)
*Scorer: Beckham*

**Liverpool 0**
James, Matteo, Scales (Redknapp), Bjornebye, Babb, McAteer, McManaman,
Thomas, Barnes, Berger, Collymore

# The blip

*Sunday 13 October*

The players are in to loosen off in preparation for the Fenerbahçe game, with running for those who didn't play yesterday. There are no new injuries, so it's just Giggs and Pallister who are making us sweat. Pally's the big worry. He is anxious about it himself, and maybe that's his biggest problem. I'll have to be careful how I treat this one. It's important we have him for Europe.

In the evening, I'm back at the dinner table. This time I'm at the Football Writers' Association awards at the Portland Hotel in Manchester, an annual event for all the northern-based managers who've had success the previous season. I'm receiving one of their crystal glass footballs.

It's an interesting occasion. But it's perhaps not as interesting for the journalists as a previous dinner, when I had a real go at Arsenal's directors for fining George Graham after a stormy game with Manchester United. I thought I was talking off the record, but they weren't having any of that. The story was splashed all over the next day's papers. Now when I get up to make a thank-you speech, there is always a great emphasis on putting pens away first before I begin; only then can I feel free.

The evening kicks off with an invitation to the Mail on Sunday's private room, where I meet Peter Reid, Frank Clark, Graham Barrow and Clare Tomlinson. Clare used to work as a press officer at the Football Association, and has just joined Arsenal.

People ask me why Manchester United doesn't employ a journalist as a full-time public relations officer, instead of relying on a part-time assistant secretary, as we do at present. The truth of the matter is that public relations officers are employed to get more coverage, which Manchester United hardly needs. Quite the opposite: we need to cut back on publicity, because at times it threatens to drown us and stop us doing our proper jobs.

*Monday 14 October*

Today my main concern is the state of the lads who played in their respective internationals, followed by the tough game against Liverpool. At lunchtime we are setting off on the four-and-a-half hour journey to Istanbul, so I decide on a nice relaxing morning. I'm satisfied this is the right approach. The only doubts are Gary Pallister and Ryan Giggs – until the moment we leave the ground, when Jordi Cruyff tells me he is feeling slight pain in his knee, which is a blow.

I've watched the game between Juventus and Fenerbahçe a dozen times, and certain aspects of the way the Turks play at home that interest me. In the last 20 minutes they could have scored three goals, all from the same move, launched from the same area and directed to the same area of the penalty box. They play a diamond shape in the middle of the park with Jay Jay Okocha pushed forward behind the strikers. He's important for them. I don't have Roy Keane to deal with that, so if Pally is fit I'll push Ronny Johnsen into midfield.

The journey's fine. We get a much nicer welcome than on our two previous visits to Istanbul, when we were greeted by fans chanting threats and shouting abuse. Then, it was real "Death to the infidels" stuff. I decide they must like us after all until I learn that the authorities shipped us in at another terminal while all the wild Turkish fans were waiting for us at the main airport. So things haven't changed much! We are staying in the Conrad this time, a fine modern hotel with excellent food in the Italian restaurant. All in all, a good start to the trip.

*Tuesday 15 October*

Graeme Souness and his wife Karen pay me a visit. Graeme is signing a player from Galatasaray and he speaks warmly of his time in Istanbul. The British managers who have worked here, like Graeme and Gordon Milne, all say they really enjoyed it and found the Turkish people lovely.

# The blip

Suddenly I'm thrown into an almighty panic as it hits me that I have forgotten Cathy's birthday, which was yesterday. Thank goodness Graeme's wife served as a reminder that I have a wife too. I dash off with our interpreter, Ahmet Kurcer, and his brother Kamet, who is a film producer, to one of Istanbul's biggest shopping malls. I get Cathy on Ahmet's mobile phone and ask her what she would like. It's the best I can do, but it's not a very good idea really ... as Cathy spells out when she shouts down the line, "Alex, this is pathetic." She's right, of course, particularly since I have also told an outright lie that the birthday card for her is still in my car. I end up buying her a nice coat. If she doesn't like it I'm afraid she's got rather a long trip to change it.

Never mind football, this is real pressure. I never seem to learn. I once forgot to get her a Christmas present. I remembered on Christmas Eve and pressed the panic button again, but it was too late; the shops were all shut. So I slipped a cheque in with her card on Christmas Day. That was another bummer idea; she simply tore it in two and dropped it in the bin. Of course I love her really, and I know she does deserve better. Oh, the agonies of married life; you would think after 30 years that I would have a system, wouldn't you?

Eventually, as we set off for our practice session at the Fenerbahçe ground, I get my mind focussed on football again. Giggs is struggling and I'm worried about Cruyff, but Pally has done a bit of work and feels comfortable. If we have him, and are defending properly, then we have a base from which to make an impact.

*Wednesday 16 October*
It's the morning of the match and we take the players for a walk. Cruyff declares himself fit so I decide to play him in the inside left position. Solskjaer will operate from the middle to inside right, and Cantona will sit behind them. My three in the

middle will be Beckham, Butt and Johnsen, whose particular role will be to shackle Okocha. We stress Okocha's role and I'm fairly confident the players have grasped the situation. I always ask if they have any questions; it's a good way of finding out whether the message has been received and understood. I tend to keep this kind of briefing simple and not go overboard tactically. That can be more confusing than constructive.

And so to the match. We put on a fabulous performance. The only problem is Okocha, who appears in a new role quite different from in the games we'd watched. For the first 15 minutes he played up front so Ronny Johnsen got dragged towards Pallister and May – unnecessarily, because they were quite capable of handling him as a striker. We got the message across from the touchline and once the problem had been sorted out we started to improve. Cruyff was unlucky with a shot which was deflected and saved by the keeper.

At the end of the first half, I didn't think there was a lot to be said. There were no real headaches and the players had solved their own difficulties out on the pitch. I just reminded them that because Fenerbahçe had to win, they would be taking more and more risks in trying to score as the game went on. Sure enough, that's how our first goal came about. Their left back was caught way forward and, from the free kick, Cantona sent Solskjaer away. The Norwegian waited for Beckham to come round the back of him and David scored a good goal.

Our second came thanks to marvellous bit of invention by Solskjaer who, instead of playing the obvious ball to Cantona, took the harder and more imaginative option of a backheel into the path of Cruyff. Cruyff squared it for Eric to score a really important goal.

It was a great night for us, made even better by the behaviour and manners of the players when our bus was stoned on the way back to the airport. A couple of windows were shattered but nobody was hurt. The players didn't make a fuss, just took it in their stride.

# The blip

The game was a perfect illustration of the way scoring away from home quietens a crowd. Our first goal completely knocked the stuffing out of the Fenerbahçe fans, and their team got little support in their efforts to get back into the game. I'll point it out to the players; it was an experience which should help them in the future.

Juventus and Rapid Vienna have drawn, so everything points to United and Juventus qualifying for the quarter-final stage.

*European Champions League / Fenerbahçe / Att: 26,200*

**Fenerbahçe 0**
Rüstü, Okechukwu, Høgh, Ibrahim, Ilker, Kemalettin, Tuncay (Aygün), Okocha, Bülent (Erol), Bolic, Kostadinov (Tarik)
**Manchester United 2**
Schmeichel, G Neville, Irwin, May, Johnsen, Pallister, Cantona, Butt, Beckham, Cruyff (Poborsky), Solskjaer
*Scorers: Beckham, Cantona*

## Thursday 17 October

We arrive home at 5 am in the morning, so everyone gets a day off in readiness for Sunday's match at Newcastle. We are all cock-a-hoop and I am delighted we've helped make this a much better week for English football in Europe. Liverpool put in a good performance to comprehensively beat Sion and Newcastle were a bit unlucky to go down 3–2 to a late sucker punch against Ferencvaros in Hungary. Our two away goals will be useful, and I'm sure Newcastle will win their second leg, which makes up for the ignomy of Aston Villa and Arsenal getting knocked out. But I'm still concerned with the recovery period and must make sure the players' legs are in the right condition for what will be a gruelling test at St James' Park.

## Friday 18 October

Back to clothes and porridge, as we say in Scotland. I hear a very disconcerting story from the Neville brothers which demonstrates the insensitivity of modern journalism. Apparently, they were woken up at 8 am yesterday by a reporter from the Manchester Evening News who wanted to question them about the stone-throwing incident on the bus. The newspaper car was spotted by their father, Neville Neville, who's commercial manager of Bury, as he left the house for work. It's obvious the journalists were waiting until he was out of the way before coming up to the house, despite the fact that the boys had only been in bed a couple of hours. It just shows you the crassness of today's media. What was even more ridiculous was that their own man, Stuart Mathieson, was on the trip with us and had presumably already filed the story at the same time as everyone else. We are not happy about it and will send a letter of complaint to the editor, although I doubt it will make any difference.

*Saturday 19 October*

We have a good training session before setting off for Newcastle – plenty of crossing practice done at a brisk pace. I wonder how some of the younger players are coping with playing midweek and at the weekend for a week or two now. I'm waiting for the reaction.

*Sunday 20 October*

I had every right to be worried. We crash to an embarrassing 5–0 defeat. The game started off at a frenetic pace, the atmosphere was fantastic and you sensed right from the off that the Newcastle players were up for it. They were flying into tackles and the referee was giving them a bit of help, which you often find happens up there. Yet I felt we were handling it and looking quite good until two controversial incidents which, in my view, decided the outcome. Our players claimed afterwards that the ball for Newcastle's first goal had not crossed the line, and Peter Schmeichel was booked for protesting. From where I was sitting it looked dodgy and the referee didn't seem to know. However, if the linesman was guessing, he guessed right – the replay on Sky proved it was a legitimate goal. But at the time it was a highly frustrating situation for our players to deal with.

The second goal certainly annoyed me. We should have had a penalty kick when their goalkeeper tripped Poborsky, but it wasn't given. To rub salt into the wound, Newcastle went straight up the other end where Ginola scored a fantastic goal. In that one move, he showed the kind of skill which justifies the import of foreign players. That's what people pay good money to see.

But it doesn't alter the fact that the penalty denied us by Steve Dunn, a referee new to the Premiership, proved very costly. As I remember, Dunn has refereed only one other of our games, a Cup tie I think, and it amazed me that he should be given this high-pressure match. How the hell could you expect him to referee well? Who decides to appoint an inexperienced referee for that kind of fixture? It baffles me. I'm convinced that a combination of inexperience and pressure from the home fans cost us a penalty kick and who knows, perhaps the game.

Great goal or not, it was a killer. We dominated the second half in attack, but it meant leaving our door open at the back. The third goal by Ferdinand finished us off. It didn't really matter, because by then I knew we were going to lose. All credit to the players, though, who kept trying to win the game, kept powering forward. The match stats showed that we had more shots on target than the home side. I must say that Newcastle's fifth was also a stunning goal. Philippe Albert showed great vision and subtlety to chip over Schmeichel's head – a marvellous finish for the Newcastle fans.

As I said at the post-match press conference, it was my biggest defeat as a manager. At times like that you just have to take your medicine and go home. It was a certainly a long journey. When you lose like that there is not much to be said. Everyone was in a very reflective mood. It was a very, very quiet bus ... and rightly so.

*Premiership / St. James' Park / Att: 36.579*

**Newcastle 5**
Srnicek, Watson (Barton), Peacock, Albert, Beresford, Lee (Clark), Beardsley, Batty, Ginola, Shearer, Ferdinand (Asprilla)
*Scorers: Peacock, Ginola, Ferdinand, Shearer, Albert*

**Manchester United 0**
Schmeichel, G Neville, May, Pallister, Irwin, Beckham, Butt, Johnsen (McClair), Cantona, Poborsky (Cruyff), Solskjaer (Scholes)

*Monday 21 October*

It's Coca-Cola Cup time. I'm going to tackle this competition as I did last year and select the fringe players and youngsters. I know it brought us a speedy exit at the hands of York City, but with hindsight that was because I made too many changes in defence.

I am going down that road again because there are players who need a rest and others who need a game. However, this time I'll exercise a little more caution at the back. I tell Johnsen and Solskjaer they can go home to Norway for a few days' break and I let Schmeichel, Beckham, Butt, Cantona and Irwin know they won't be playing. The group of players I will bring in is forming in my mind.

In the afternoon, I take a phone call from Norway inviting me over to make their Player of the Year presentation. Why me? Well, it emerges that Ole Gunnar Solskjaer is the winner and they think it would be appropriate. I explain that I'm really too busy to have another night away, but they offer to charter a private jet to fly me over for the ceremony and then straight back to Manchester.

I can't really say no to that, so I'm in Oslo by tea. After a terrific night, I get back home by 11.30 pm.

# The blip

I'm going to play the two Nevilles against Swindon tonight. They are both young and fit, and Philip in particular needs a senior game after his ankle operation. I'm keeping David May in defence but I'll give a chance to Chris Casper, who has been waiting a long time since he first got a look-in a year or so ago. Chris comes from a fine family and he's a great credit to them. Frank Casper, his father, had a tremendous career with Burnley and has brought up his boy to be a truly professional footballer.

Raimond Van der Gouw will play in goal. He is another fantastic pro, and a lively character in the dressing room. He's a wow with the girls in the office, too, who call him Van der Gorgeous. McClair and Scholes will play, and I'll bring in Ben Thornley and Michael Appleton. Ben had a knee injury so horrendous that at the time I worried for his career. But we put our fears to the back of our minds as much as we could and encouraged the boy. His response was great, and it will be a pleasure to see him in the first team this evening. Young Appleton has a great attitude too, and he's earned his chance.

We play with three central defenders and turn the defenders on the flanks into wing backs. We put in a good performance for a 2–1 win, which could have been more. Thornley and Poborsky both do well. After the match we learn we've been drawn away at Leicester in the next round. I look forward to that. There is always a good atmosphere at Filbert Street and they stick to sound footballing principles. But I'll continue to ring the changes; no disrespect to the competition or our opponents, but it's such a good opportunity to utilise the full squad.

*Coca-Cola Cup R3 / Old Trafford / Att: 49,305*

**Manchester United 2**
Van der Gouw, G Neville, May, P Neville, Casper, McClair, Poborsky, Keane, Scholes, Thornley, Appleton (Davies)
*Scorers: Poborsky, Scholes*

**Swindon Town 1**
Talia, Robinson, Elkins, Leitch, Seagraves, Culverhouse, Walters, Darras, Thorne (Cowe), Allison, Horlock
*Scorer: Thorne*

*Friday 25 October*

I make a late change of plan. We are now going to fly to Southampton, because it's a holiday weekend and the roads could be horrendous. The flight will cost £18,000, but we can afford it. Manchester United is a big club and it's important to get the preparations right. It makes for a speedy trip and we are soon ensconced at our hotel just outside Southampton. I have a full squad except for Ryan Giggs, whose niggling calf injury is beginning to worry me. We miss his penetration and speed on the left.

*Saturday 26 October*

What can I say after another horrendous result? Southampton register a cricket score against us at the Dell. We let in scrappy goals, lucky goals and good goals, but I am going to analyse every one to see if there is a common thread. One thing I am certain about: some players have spent too much time in the treatment room lately – and it shows. Players who miss training become dull and their reflexes lose sharpness. Fitness levels must be maintained and there must be proper preparation. I'm fed up with seeing one or two of them in the treatment room so often and I shall tell them it has to stop. Enough is enough. I intend to take a serious look at the whole situation. One of these days they are going to come up the stairs from their dressing room and find a bloody big padlock on the treatment room door. No reflection on physiotherapist David Fevre, who is first class, but I suspect it's too comfortable in there, particularly now that the days are getting wetter and colder.

Now I have got that off my chest, I have to admit that Southampton played well. Graeme Souness has them playing along the lines of Liverpool, in a system they all adhere to well. The Israeli, Berkovic, who looks a quality player, is difficult to pin down. Nevertheless, we were well up with the pace in the opening stages. We should have been two or three goals up before the incident which changed the course of the game.

22 July 1996: "There was only one club which interested him, and if it didn't work out with us he would be staying at Blackburn"

My summer signings: Van Der Gouw, Johnsen, Cruyff, Poborsky and Solskjaer

17 August 1996: "Already the Goal of the Season"

Ole Gunnar Solskjaer: "He's starting to make the hairs on the back of my neck curl"

September 1996: Talking tactics in Turin

Eric Cantona: "I suspect success in Europe had become very important to him, a personal Holy Grail"

11 September 1996 v Juventus (a): "The first half is just what I didn't want, and exactly the way I knew the Italians would play"

Contemplating defeat by Juventus in the Stadio Delle Alpi

25 September 1996:
A 2–0 win at home to
Rapid Vienna gets us
back on track

12 October 1996 v Liverpool (h): "Perhaps tiredness is creeping in"

16 October 1996
v Fenerbahçe (a):
"A fabulous performance"

26 October 1996 v
Southampton (a):
Roy Keane is sent off at
the Dell, scene of another
horrendous result

Dealing with the media: "The sad part is that, as time goes by, I instinctively try to protect myself which means being bland ... "

Youth and experience: Kiddo, Gary Neville and I at the Cliff

Ryan Giggs: "He has an electricity and balance that opponents just can't handle ... in two years he will be a truly wonderful player"

# The blip

After only 21 minutes, Roy Keane was sent off for a second booking. I feel bound to say that I disagreed fundamentally with Jeff Winter. The first booking was for dissent, after Keane protested at a foul in which Nicky Butt took a fearful clatter. Butt had to come off soon afterwards. Southampton certainly had the better of that incident.

Pallister was struggling as well and couldn't come out for the second half, so we had our problems trying to cope with the refereeing. I feel something must be done. When the League Managers' Association met the referees in London, as I understood it, the refs agreed to ease up on indiscriminate booking of players, which can so easily lead to dismissals. Some referees may have heeded the meeting, but perhaps Mr Winter did not.

Our lads were magnificent, and fought back to 3–2. At that point I honestly thought we could go on to win until Berkovic took the game away from us again. I was also impressed by Matt Le Tissier. His work rate is constantly criticised, but personally I feel we spend too much time worrying about what players can't do when we should be appreciating their positive qualities. Le Tissier has been Southampton's top scorer for the last seven years; what more does he have to do? I'll say this: if we didn't have Cantona and Scholes, then Le Tissier could play at Old Trafford, and if he can play for Manchester United he can play for England. He's a marvellous talent.

Le Tissier is not the main thing on my mind as once more we return home with our tails between our legs. I know I am in for a torrent of abuse from the media. I shall have to grit my teeth and take it. So will the players.

*Premiership / The Dell / Att: 15,253*

**Southampton 6**
Beasant, Dodd, Charlton (Potter), Dryden, Lundekvam, Van Gobbel, Oakley, Le Tissier (Watson), Ostenstad, Berkovic, Neilson (Magilton)
*Scorers: Berkovic 2, Le Tissier, Ostenstad 3*

**Manchester United 3**
Schmeichel, G Neville, May, Pallister (Irwin), Cantona, Butt (McClair), Beckham, P Neville, Cruyff (Solskjaer), Keane, Scholes
*Scorers: Beckham, May, Scholes*

*Tuesday 29 October*

The press conference to preview tomorrow night's European Champions' League match against Fenerbahçe at Old Trafford is lively. The press, of course, start to focus on our two heavy defeats in the League. I make it quite clear as soon as they try to start a post-mortem that I don't intend to dwell on the past. I had my say with the players after the game at The Dell and we discussed constructive points again yesterday. Now it's time to concentrate on the positive side for the next game. We don't forget anything at this club, but there's a difference between remembering and dwelling on things. You can only analyse so much, and I have done that. I tell the press that raking over our defeats was not on my agenda. I hope our run of League form is just a blip. Only Fenerbahçe matters now.

I've always felt that it's best to get things off your chest with players on a Saturday rather than wait until the Monday. Once a couple of days have passed, I could be in too good a mood, and that would ruin my image! My philosophy is to deal with the issue and then put it behind you. When I was a young manager, Jock Stein, the Celtic and Scotland manager I admired so much, advised me to wait until after the weekend before talking to the players. I tried it once and it was hopeless. It just didn't work for me, and since then I've concluded that you can't change the beast.

Eventually the media have to accept that I mean what I say, and that I'll talk about nothing but the European match. I have no real concerns about the outcome; I'm confident we will win. Fenerbahçe are a decent side. Their Nigerian, Okocha, is a skilful lad, and their two centre backs are fair performers. I am going to play Cantona on his own up front and I expect I shall be criticised again. People don't understand what I am trying to achieve. As far as they are concerned, we played this way against Juventus in Turin and lost, and the tactics make for an easy explanation for the defeat. They forget that we played the same way at Leeds and won 4–0. The idea behind playing Eric

on his own is that it pulls their central defenders out of position. Then we can get Cruyff or the midfielders, Butt and
Beckham, running through the middle. Roy Keane will make
sure the central area is covered.

*Wednesday 30 October*

Not what I had planned at all... Fenerbahçe beat us 1–0. It's
a major disappointment. We'd all assumed that tonight we
would qualify for the quarter finals and we've missed a great
opportunity. It's terribly ironic that the blow should fall just as
I prepare to celebrate ten years as manager of Manchester
United. As if failing to clinch a place in the next phase wasn't
bad enough, it is also the end of Manchester United's unbeaten
home record in Europe. That proud record stood for 40 years,
since Sir Matt Busby pioneered the way for English clubs on the
Continent. I am sad that it has gone under my management.
It's a reminder that life is a struggle and nothing can be taken
for granted.

I don't plead bad luck, but I must say we dominated the
match from start to finish. In terms of chances and strikes at
goal, we were the only team in the equation, and we didn't
deserve to lose. At the same time, perhaps we didn't do enough
to win. We had so much possession that we were almost too
comfortable on the ball, and certainly in the first half we fell
into an easy-going tempo which didn't extend the Fenerbahçe
defence enough. I'm not sure whether it was the low-key
atmosphere or too much caution on our part. Whatever the
reason, it was far too slow for Old Trafford. We did raise the
tempo in the second half and Cruyff came close when he rifled
one just outside the post. With 20 minutes to go, I brought on
Solskjaer and Scholes to replace Poborsky and Cruyff. The
changes were a bit of a risk, but I knew one goal would win the
game and take us through. Scholes was bright, but nothing
came of it; Solskjaer wasn't able to make a big enough impact.

Perhaps he was feeling drained by the two big defeats .

It wasn't the substitutions which lost us the game. With just 12 minutes to go, too many of our players got sucked into their half and we were caught on the break. It was a perfect example of the naïvety British teams so often reveal in Europe. The Turks knocked the ball to a front player and we were caught on the back foot, two against two. Our players were still getting back, so Bolic had a shot, which unfortunately took a wicked deflection off May to dip over Schmeichel's head. I think the Turks were as surprised as we were. It was a cruel blow; how many times do you see our teams conceding that kind of goal? You hope experience is the final message, but in the immediate aftermath, you do wonder.

The Turks came in afterwards to congratulate us on our sportsmanship. Their dressing room was really noisy with cele-bration and there was no denying them their hour of glory. They weren't gloating, and we congratulated them on their vic-tory. They're nice people, and they looked after us well in Turkey. You just have to bite the bullet and smile a lot.

Little did I know it, but that was only the beginning of my ordeal. It was late when I got home after all the press and tele-vision demands. As I drove up to the house with Gordon Campbell, a pal who was down from Scotland, Cathy was at the door to greet me with her own special welcome. She was chanting "Fergie, Fergie, for the sack."

It didn't surprise me – I've had 30 years of this. "Don't start," I told her wearily.

But she wasn't to be put off.

"Och, it's a stupid game anyway," she replied.

I looked at Gordon, shrugged my shoulders and said, "It's hopeless."

Still, I suppose her ribbing keeps my feet on the ground, and has done ever since our early days. I would get home from a match with Aberdeen in which everything had gone wrong, looking for a bit of sympathy ... but I was always easily outdone.

# The blip

"Never mind the football!" she would start. "What a day I've had – Jason's done this, Darren's done that, Mark's done this." And me, my head's bursting and I can hardly talk after shouting all day at the players!

*European Champions League / Old Trafford / Att: 53,297*
**Manchester United 0**
Schmeichel, G Neville (P Neville), Irwin, May, Johnsen, Cantona, Butt, Beckham, Cruyff (Solskjaer), Poborsky (Scholes), Keane
**Fenerbahçe 1**
Rüstü, Ilker, Uche, Høgh (Bülent), Kemalettin, Tuncay (Mustapha), Bolic (Tarik), Okocha, Kostadinov, Saffet, Bulut
*Scorer: Bolic*

*Thursday 31 October*

I'm still pondering how we could have lost such a match. The media are making a big splash about other issues as well, such as the loss of the 40-year record In my ten years as manager, that record has been a burden as well as a source of pride. The fact is that we've done well to protect it for so long, but I can think of a number of occasions when we rode our luck to keep it. We were lucky to get a 1–1 draw with Atletico Madrid in the Cup Winners' Cup in 1991, and I recall Peter Schmeichel rescuing us for a draw against Galatasaray last season. Red Star swamped us in the first half of the Super Cup in 1991 before Brian McClair scored the only goal of the game. I'm told by people like Brian Kidd that the club was just as lucky on a few occasions before my time. For instance in 1984, on Juventus' last visit, we only drew 1–1 thanks to a goal from our substitute, the late Alan Davies.

Luck may have helped us, but a 40-year record still has a good ring to it. The club can still be proud. It was always going to come to an end and, for the future of Manchester United, I am glad it has gone. Now we needn't worry about the record instead of concentrating on a win; we can be single-minded about our European ties at Old Trafford. And there's an added bonus. I won't have to suffer Brian Kidd winding me up by whispering "Remember the record" in my ear before every European match. He seems to think he set it himself, and I suppose he did help in his days as a United player. Last season, for instance, when we were on our way out of the Uefa Cup against Rotor Volgograd, Peter Schmeichel came up to score a last-gasp equaliser at 2–2. It didn't make any real difference because we were out on away goals, but that didn't stop Kiddo's mischievous whisper: "Never mind, the record's still OK." At least there'll be no more of that.

As for the troops, I'm on a recovery mission. It was a really bad night for us and I have to be careful how I handle them. After the Juventus match, I had a long talk about their need to express themselves, to remember who they are and to trust each other. One of my objectives at Old Trafford has been to build a squad in which players can look round the dressing room and say of each team-mate, "I'm glad he's in the team." We have achieved that, and I needed to remind them after their experience in Turin. But sometimes you just have to leave them alone to come to terms with the situation. I think that is the best option this time. There are too many areas of the game we could go into, but the priority is to get them out of the trough and in the right frame of mind for Saturday's match against Chelsea.

I know they are badly disappointed. They also have to live with the press reminding us that Chelsea have been very successful at Old Trafford. Last season, I dealt with Chelsea's record by acknowledging their good run and saying we had to do something about it. At least we got a draw. This time I'm not going down that road. I want the squad to start enjoying their football again. If they could get back the flow and return to more relaxed passing, it would unlock a lot of their problems.

I try to explain to them that they've been conceding all manner of goals – lucky ones, shitty ones, bad ones and great ones. We couldn't do anything about the lucky goals, because they either go for you or against you; all you can do is be thankful when fate is on your side and curse when it isn't. But we could eradicate the bad goals and even do something towards stopping the great ones. There have certainly been moments when one or two of the players could have done better, and there is an obvious need to recapture our concentration in defence.

This is all new to some of them. The youngsters like the Nevilles, Beckham and Butt have never lost two or three games in a row, not even when they were playing in the Reserves and junior teams. I imagine that four or five of them are asking themselves what to do now. Losing is new to them and so is criticism, which always seems to come in extra-large helpings when things go wrong at Manchester United. I have adopted a softly, softly approach and I shall continue on these lines at tomorrow's team talk.

I don't really feel like it, but I have another job to do today. Over the past few weeks I've been inundated with requests for interviews to mark my ten years as manager of Manchester United. It soon became clear that there wasn't time to see everyone individually, so I'm having two sessions today. First I'll talk to the Sunday newspaper people over a spot of lunch, and this afternoon I'll meet the dailies. It's unfortunate that the interviews coincide with our poor run of results, but I want to get them over this week because I'm taking Cathy away for a few days when we have our international break next week. The anniversary of my appointment falls on Wednesday of next week but my wife deserves a celebration after ten years, too!

So we put our present worries on the shelf and I talk to the media about what it means to be in charge of Britain's best club, and about our achievements. Presumably they will print their interviews this Sunday and then on 6 November, the actual anniversary of my arrival.

It all goes quite well. I make a special effort not to give any press men a blast.

*Friday 1 November*

There's a big turn-out for the press conference after today's training session. I have got to accept that if we lose a big game then we're front page news. I am questioned about tactics. A lot of English clubs have tried the old bulldog attitude in Europe in an attempt to steamroller the opposition. When it hasn't worked, the press have accused them of not being subtle, intelligent or inventive enough. It's said we have no patience, no composure, no technique, no this and no that. But when players try to be more sophisticated and it doesn't work in a particular match, there's still criticism. They can't have it both ways.

Winning a game of football can change a lot. If we had scored a goal on Wednesday night against Fenerbahçe, who would have been bothered by our tactics? We would have been in the quarter finals of the European Cup and everyone would have sung our praises. The bottom line is that the players still have ability. They have achieved so much together, and my confidence in the future is my theme at the press conference.

I also have to deal with a veiled hint that Eric Cantona, because he is a quiet man, is not a good captain for times like these. But, I tell them, there are different kinds of captains. Bobby Moore wasn't a shouter, but a player who led by example, just like Eric. It's amazing the angles journalists come up with. Eric captained us to the Double last season and no one complained then. The players adore him. So he has suffered a loss of form and confidence lately, but there's nothing strange about that; it happens to everyone. You just have to trust in your ability – and I'm sure that's what Eric's telling himself at the moment.

Chelsea will be without a major player tomorrow. Matthew Harding, their vice-chairman, was killed in a helicopter crash returning from Chelsea's game against Bolton. He was obviously held in high esteem not just by his fellow directors and staff, but by ordinary supporters. I met him only once, and then briefly, but you can judge by the reaction of the club's followers that here was an exceptional man with an extraordinary passion and love for his club. He devoted money and commitment, a powerful combination which certainly appealed to fans. I can understand their feelings. He was an important figure in the movement, led by Ken Bates, which has seen Chelsea emerge as one of the most talked-about and adventurous teams of the season.

*Saturday 2 November*

So much for the kid-glove treatment. Despite all the talk about proper defending, we fail to stop the goals and go 2–1 down to Chelsea.

The first goal is ridiculous, a free header bouncing in front of Schmeichel which everyone left. The uncertainty is still there and the lack of concentration has surfaced again. We are one down at half time, but I don't dwell on the goal because it is more important to work on improving our attack. I speak about the way Leboeuf isn't running back with the strikers but depending on either offside or his goalkeeper, and about dropping in angled balls for late runs. But it's just not our day.

Chelsea enjoy coming to Old Trafford and it shows in their play. They are well up for it. They are very strong up front, Mark Hughes and Vialli. The second half is an uphill struggle for us. Their second kills it, another bad goal from our point of view. Until we get better concentration at the back we don't stand a proper chance.

Until this season, Gary Pallister and Steve Bruce played together in defence, and were affectionately known at the club as Dolly and Daisy. Their partnership didn't gel overnight; it took time to became the solid foundation on which our successes were built. Now that Steve has left the club and Gary is injured for a lot of the time, we have a new centre-back pairing. It's asking a lot of David May and Ronny Johnsen to immediately hit the same heights. Individually, both have done well, but they need more time to reach that kind of understanding.

I have abandoned the idea of buying Nadal from Barcelona. Now that he has played in Europe for Bobby Robson, he is ineligible to play for anyone else in Europe. I had him in mind for the knock-out stages of the European Cup, but we'll have to do without. I don't see him as a long-term buy for our League – he is around 30 and we have our own players – but he could have done a job for us in Europe with his experience and strength.

I am still on the look-out, and the Continent is the most likely place to find the right talent at the right price. I don't feel pressed to buy; only the very best could improve on the good young squad we already have – and the best are not always available, for obvious reasons. If we qualify for the European Cup quarter finals, I will definitely buy someone to insure against injury and to be better prepared to play on the wider front which Europe demands. Les Kershaw, our chief scout, is out and about all over Europe with this mind.

*Premiership / Old Trafford / Att: 55,198*

**Manchester United 1**
Schmeichel, Irwin, May, Cantona, Butt, Beckham, P Neville, Keane, Scholes (Poborsky), Johnsen, Solskjaer
*Scorer: May*

**Chelsea 2**
Hitchcock, Petrescu, Leboeuf, Clarke, Vialli, Hughes, Wise, Duberry, Burley, Matteo, Minto
*Scorers: Duberry, Vialli*

*Sunday 3 November*

I have to grasp the nettle and be honest about the areas where we are failing. This is no time to fudge issues or make excuses. In the past I've always been a better manager in adversity; we'll have to see whether that's still true.

At least I have plenty of thinking time. Thanks to the international weekend, we have a fortnight's break. I'm flying first thing to Turin with Brian Kidd, to watch Juventus at home to Napoli in preparation for our next Champions' League fixture.

# The blip

It's a non-stop day. We travel out via Frankfurt and come back straight after the match through Paris. Everything clicks into place and I'm back in the house by 9.30 pm, which isn't bad.

Watching Juventus confirms my opinion that they have hardly any chinks in their armour, but the more pressing problem on my mind is what to do about our own team, and Eric Cantona in particular. There is no doubt he has lost his touch and confidence and I am sure it has a lot to do with his fitness. He is a big man who needs to train, something he didn't do much of during our last international break. Eric, of course, wasn't playing since France continue to ignore him, and we let him have an easy time. He had a nagging hip injury so I thought the rest might do him good and, with that in mind, I let him go home to France to deal with some commercial ventures.

When he got back there were hardly any other senior players around so he was working with the kids on his own, which I think he finds difficult. I had a chat with him about how to plan the next break better. He agreed, so now I must consider how best to use him over the next fortnight. I shall suggest he starts by playing in Bryan Gunn's testimonial match at Norwich tomorrow night.

## Monday 4 November

Eric is happy about playing tonight. There will be a big crowd at Carrow Road, but also a relaxed atmosphere, and I think the responsibility of playing with the youngsters like Terry Cooke, Chris Casper and John Curtis will help him. I also make plans for the following week, when the international players return. I explain to Eric that we are going to train morning and afternoon to get our fitness levels right.

I could use Ryan Giggs this evening because he has just about recovered from his calf injury, but if I do he might well get called up by Bobby Gould for Wales and that would be too much for him. I've already had Bobby on the phone. I can understand his eagerness to have Ryan – he has a small squad and limited resources – but I explain to him that the lad is nowhere near ready for international football. With the fitness and pace required these days, players need seven to ten days' proper training before going into an international.

We travel to Norwich. It's a good night for me – and for Bryan Gunn. I am delighted to do him a favour by taking a team to Carrow Road because I had him as a young goalkeeper at Aberdeen. In fact, he used to babysit for our boys. Cathy would leave them all plates of food, and Bryan had an enormous appetite. I remember the next morning Jason often saying, "Big Bryan stole our sandwiches again."

I enjoyed meeting Christine Anderson again. She's the widow of Chris Anderson, a director at Aberdeen who died tragically early in 1986. Their daughter lives in Norwich, so she was at the match too. Years ago, back in 1980, Chris used to predict the advent of satellite television. At the time I had no idea what on earth he was talking about. He was such a great visionary, an innovative man who was determined that Aberdeen would be in the forefront of Scottish and European football again.

All in all, it was a most enjoyable night. Our boys played well in a 3–0 win. I was proud of the way they behaved afterwards towards the autograph hunters and the crowds wanting to talk to them and take their photographs. The older players like Brian McClair, Van der Gouw and Cantona set a good example for the likes of Curtis, Cooke, Thornley and Appleton. The Norwich crowd started off by booing Eric every time he touched the ball, and by the end they were applauding and cheering him. He took a couple of whacks, but he enjoyed himself. He wouldn't come off when I suggested a substitution.

The dark cloud hanging over us seems to lighten a little.

It was good to see Steve Bruce again. He played for us against his old team and he hasn't changed, still demanding every ball with all his old enthusiasm. We have missed him and

# The blip

I would have loved him to have stayed. I would have got 20 or 25 games out of him, which would have meant something; but he knew that given his age I had to start thinking of phasing him out. He wasn't ready for that. He still wants to play every game and you can't fault him for it. He decided, and I couldn't disagree, that his Old Trafford rainbow was coming to an end so he set off for another challenge at Birmingham.

I heard him telling our young players, "You make the most of it while you are with Manchester United, because there's nothing like it. When you leave it's the end of life as you know it."

One day I guess I'll understand what he means.

# 4
# Ten incredible years

Ten years to the day since I took over at Old Trafford and, judging by the events of the past fortnight, my sense of timing is rubbish. What a way to celebrate an anniversary ... but two crazy weeks mustn't take the gloss off a fantastic decade.

It's been a great time. I feel privileged to have worked with some players who were outstanding not only in their talent, but as men. Overall, despite the recent blips, I can be proud of my achievements. The pressure of recent weeks will prove a small hiccup in the grand scheme of things. Anyway, the current problems are nothing compared to six years ago, when things were not going well. Season 1989/90: now those were really dark days.

The chairman, Martin Edwards, has always insisted that my job was never in jeopardy. But it didn't feel like that at the time. We had to play Nottingham Forest in the third round of the FA Cup with an injury-hit team, and everyone tipped us as victims of a Cup shock. But the fans were superb, the players rose to the occasion to pull off a 1–0 victory, and we went on to win the Cup. Who knows what would have happened if we had lost? As it was, that first trophy proved the catalyst for all our subsequent success. First it inspired me to success in Europe in 1992, then to make a determined bid for the Championship after all the years – and all the managers since Sir Matt Busby – that had gone by without winning the League.

The absence of the Championship had been like a millstone round the neck of everyone connected with the club. I was so proud when we finally did it in 1993. The day we actually became champions, I went off on my own for a game of golf at Mottram Hall in Cheshire, not far from where I live. I was playing the 17th hole when a total stranger raced up, threw his arms round my neck and told me that Oldham had beaten Aston Villa. Manchester United were champions after 26 barren years.

I will never forget striding up the 18th fairway. I had a picture in my mind of Arnold Palmer receiving thunderous acclaim from the hundreds of people lining the final hole at Troon for the Open Championship of 1962. There wasn't even a squirrel applauding me, but it didn't matter because we were champions. We've been on a roll ever since, winning back-to-back Championships and that unique double Double.

I've had offers to move on, but I've never felt the urge to leave. I was told a year ago that the job at Inter Milan was mine if I wanted it, but you don't walk away from a club like Manchester United until you are told you're no longer wanted. I'm 55 now, with a contract that takes me up to 58. I have no desire to work for any other club. If I ever feel depressed, or we have the kind of run like the one we've just had, all I have to do is walk round the magnificent stadium and recall all the high points of the last five years.

In football they say you're only as good as your last result, and I've certainly been through a low point of my career over recent weeks. Never in my worst nightmares did I think it was possible, in such a short space of time, to lose by five at Newcastle, have six put past us at Southampton, and forfeit our unbeaten home record in Europe. I have agonised as much as everyone else who has Manchester United's cause at heart, but I will not panic. I know we will come through OK. Our base is too solid, our players too good, and my management too experienced.

It's experience which is the great advantage. I may have mellowed as I've got older, but my main thrust in management hasn't changed. I still believe strongly in the work ethic, in discipline. Obviously, I have to subscribe to modern trends, but my beliefs in how the game should be played are still the same. They're manifest in the current United side, though perhaps I rely more on my senior players these days. I have made a habit in recent seasons of inviting them into our coaches' room for tea and toast when we are discussing things. From my point of view, it builds up a better understanding. It also introduces them to the management side of the game; for instance, Bryan Robson and Steve Bruce have both benefitted from being in on our discussions.

You always hope to be friendly with players, but meals with wives and so on are not on my agenda. That kind of socialising just doesn't work. All I ask for is respect, and with that respect come high standards and professionalism. In any case, a Manchester United player must have something extra in terms of character. We always assess that side of a player, junior or senior. Sometimes it's obvious, but I've also seen a player develop the necessary character, and that potential is something you must always take into account with either a schoolboy or a new signing. United players certainly need strong characters to handle the demands at Old Trafford: the standards we expect of them, the expectations of the fans, the attention of the media, and playing what amounts to a Cup final every game.

People may have been writing us off lately, but we'll be there when it matters. That's down to character. Endurance, perseverance, a refusal to give in – those are the qualities which will see us through. I've had some bad results in 22 years of management, some real shockers, but they've been superseded by the fantastic days.

Would I change much if I had my time over again? Not a lot, because you're always going to make mistakes. The important thing is to learn not repeat to them. So much for the last decade ... Now it's time to put football on one side for a few days and take a break in London with Cathy. But I do hope she stops singing "Fergie, Fergie for the sack!"

*Tuesday 5 November*

We've set a training programme for Eric Cantona, which Brian Kidd will supervise. Personally, I'm glad I'm away. If I was around, there would have been a media circus to mark my 10th anniversary which would just add up to a lot of hype.

We're invited to a party at Mick Hucknall's house in the evening. There's a firework display and Mick is in the kitchen himself making the pasta. He is such an ordinary guy, so down to earth for a pop star, with no airs and graces. He also says what he thinks, which is refreshing – there's never a hidden agenda. It's a good night.

*Wednesday 6 November*

Today is the actual anniversary of my arrival as manager of Manchester United and guess what ... I'm taken out shopping. You would think a man of my experience would be able to find a way out of it. We are soon in Harrods where Cathy takes a fancy to a newfangled cooking pot for pasta, complete with strainer. But of course we don't buy just one ... I find myself carrying four, one for each of the boys as well.

Relief arrives at lunch time since Cathy has arranged to meet Tessa, our daughter-in-law. I'm due to have lunch with Ian McShane but he can't make it because of a delayed recording. So I phone a friend and tell him I'm desperate to get tickets for Albert Finney's new play, Art, and am having no luck. He comes back to me eventually with good news. I don't ask how he got the tickets; we're just delighted to have them.

The manager meets us at the theatre and asks if we we'd like a drink with Penny, Albert's girlfriend. She tells us Albert is very nervous because he knows I'm coming. I can't believe such a mega-star could be worried by a football manager, but it shows what an amazing impact the game has on people.

It's a powerful play, which also stars Tom Courtney and the Scottish actor Ken Stott. Afterwards we're invited backstage, where it's my turn to feel embarrassed and nervous about meeting Albert.

However, the first thing he does is produce a bottle of champagne to congratulate me on my ten years and toast the next ten! Tom Courtney and Ken Stott then appear, as does Joan Plowright, who still looks fantastic.

In different company I can really put football out of my mind for a short while.

*Saturday 9 November*

I've been back at work for a couple of days now. Yesterday we trained at The Cliff; this morning I give Eric Cantona and David May a good session. Brian Kidd is away watching the Switzerland v Norway Under-21 international, but there's no more resting for Eric, and David knows he has to keep working, too. The Reserves are at Nottingham. It's an important match because Ryan Giggs is making his comeback.

In the afternoon I drive up to Glasgow to take part in the Great Scot Awards, which are run by the Sunday Mail to honour Scotsmen who have done something special in business, medicine, sport or entertainment. I'm given a great reception as one of three nominations in the sporting category. I'm delighted to say that I win an award. You get a lot of these kind of presentations in football, but recognition from your own country is extra special. It's why Ryan Giggs preferred to go back to Wales for an award instead of attending the opening of the Red Café, a new restaurant at Old Trafford. The overall Great Scot award goes to the parents of the Dunblane children killed in that terrible shooting tragedy. It was received on behalf of the mums and dads by the minister of the church in Dunblane, Colin Mackintosh, and it was a very emotional moment. We were all visibly moved.

Afterwards, while we were photographed, I talked with Colin Mackintosh. I'm always telling Cathy – and anyone else who will listen – about people from Govan, my part of Glasgow. Sure enough, the Minister not only comes from round the corner from where I lived, but his house was on my paper round in Birkenhead Drive. Cathy's not going to believe this when I tell her.

Chris de Burgh, who offered to help the Dunblane fund, sings a couple of numbers, and then my brother's wife wins the star prize in the raffle: a holiday in New York and Boston. To think I actually paid for the raffle ticket!

On the drive up to Glasgow, I listened to commentary on England's World Cup qualifier in Georgia. I'm impressed with Glenn Hoddle's start in international management. It's clear he's prepared to change his tactics for each game and try something different. I like his thinking. For instance, he played Alan Shearer and Les Ferdinand together in attack against Poland, but injury to Shearer forced him back to the drawing board for the Georgia game. There were all kinds of suggestions flying about beforehand, but his final selection was for Teddy Sheringham to drop in the hole and make space for Ferdinand. To protect Paul Gascoigne, he brought in David Batty. It was something of a surprise because Batty is your proverbial terrier, but it worked brilliantly – he rattled the opposition, performing a little bit like Nobby Stiles did for England in 1966. With Paul Ince sitting in front of the back four, Gascoigne had great freedom. England won again and are on course to qualify. Glenn deserves great credit for his start.

*Monday 11 November*

The international players are back. We've got a clear week to prepare for Arsenal's visit next Saturday, and then of course for the big one against Juventus at Old Trafford four days later. With the visit of the Italians in mind, I must try and rev up the fans. On our last European night the atmosphere was so low key it did absolutely nothing to rouse the players from their already comatose state. I shall devote my notes in the programme for the Arsenal game to the problem, and I'll back an appeal from the Independent Supporters' Association to stage a flag night. Representatives from the Association came to see me the other week worried about the lack of atmosphere and suggested promoting flag-waving to try and whip up more enthusiasm.

Recently, Old Trafford has not been the same daunting place for visitors it once was. There certainly isn't the kind of atmosphere that made the stadium quiver with excitement and tension when we played Barcelona here, for instance. It doesn't seem as vibrant as in the old days when Liverpool, then the dominant force in the game, found the atmosphere at Old Trafford so frightening that more often than not they couldn't handle it.

There are several theories about the cause of the problem. One view is that the growing number of hospitality packages has attracted a different type of audience. A visiting party might come to Manchester for a nice weekend, sit and admire the ground and then wait to be entertained, just as if they were at the theatre for a musical. No passion, no commitment, just a lovely day out.

Some people believe that the removal of terraces put a dampener on the cheering. But I also believe that success breeds contentment, and that fans forget how to show anger when things are going wrong.

I'm sure there is an element of truth in all these theories somewhere along the line, but whatever the reasons I'd like to see a return to a more hostile stadium.

We botched up one chance of qualifying for the European Cup quarter finals when we lost at Old Trafford to Fenerbahçe. I have every confidence that we will make it to the next stage, but our fans have a part to play, too. So I shall make my appeal in the programme: ask them to bring their flags, wave them and shout their heads off.

*Tuesday 12 November*

We may have come in for some fierce criticism during our downturn in fortunes but, as I remind the players, nobody goes through life on silver wings. We are not vain enough at Manchester United to think we can go through our careers without suffering bad times as well as good.

There have to be disappointments and set-backs – although being prepared for a bad patch does not mean we accept it, or that it doesn't alarm us. This week, I drum it into the players that it's imperative we put matters right. Losing can become a habit, just as winning breeds success. I shall make them well aware of the need to get our house back in order again. This is where a manager earns his money, and where the players earn their reputations and reveal their true character.

I'm confident that we'll pull out of our nose dive. Only four weeks ago, our two-goal win against Fenerbahçe in Istanbul was hailed as the best English performance in Europe for 15 years. Yet now the same bunch of players are being pilloried as abject failures and their manager called worse than useless. A month is a short time in which to fall from heaven to hell, and clearly what is needed is a sense of perspective. Certainly, the present situation is one of the great challenges that regularly come along in football. We must get back to playing the way people expect us to play, and the fans must bring Old Trafford alive again. It's bad enough hearing the manager and players are useless without being told our fans are rubbish as well!

*Wednesday 13 November*

We have a great desire to do well in Europe and the match against Juventus next week is never far from my thoughts. But after our poor performance against Fenerbahçe and the two heavy League defeats, the Arsenal game has become much more significant. We have simply got to win – and I'm determined that we will. I usually do better in adversity. The hackles come up and I can focus on what needs to be done.

I plan the whole week very carefully. On Monday I talk to the players and outline the week's schedule. On Tuesday Kiddo gives them an intense physical work-out to get their edge back, so they're fit and fresh again. The players are coming in for two sessions a day. I keep emphasising that we need better concentration when we are defending. For instance, if we are going to play the opposition offside at times, we must all be sure when and how. It doesn't matter so much what system you play, as long as everyone is doing the same thing. It's better to push up when someone is pressing the ball, but only if there is one striker against our centre back – otherwise we risk a late run from a second striker.

We practise defending against set-pieces to avoid the kind of goal we conceded against Chelsea. It was unusual for us to lose a goal from a corner kick. In the afternoon we have another practice match with the same theme, as if we are playing against Arsenal. It seems to work quite well. There is a far better level of concentration and the game is played at a hell of a pace. Sometimes in a practice match the Reserves are nervous or the first team idle, but today I am pleased with the tempo. Everyone shows great commitment.

I make it clear to the players, especially the younger ones, that they all have to rest in the evenings, and that if they step out of the house I'll chop their legs off. The older ones have got their responsibilities; their lives are more consistent since their families are a steadying influence. You know the pattern of their lifestyles. It's the younger ones you have to watch, and they're the ones who particularly need the rest – players like the Nevilles, Beckham, Butt, Scholes and Giggs.

It's at times like this that I think back to the year we were pipped for the Championship by Leeds. We had just lost to Nottingham Forest on the Saturday and had a midweek match against West Ham, yet on the Monday in between Ryan and Lee Sharpe decided to go for a night out in Blackpool. I didn't know at the time, but I soon found out; it's amazing how these things come to light. We lost to West Ham on the Wednesday and the following night I was in Morecambe to make a presentation at an England Schools' function. I was having dinner when a chap casually mentioned that he had seen Giggsy and Sharpey in Blackpool on the Monday. I told him he must have been mistaken because of the West Ham match in midweek, but he insisted that he'd spoken to them. He even described Lee Sharpe's jeep. He was just innocently making conversation and had no idea of the significance of what he was saying, but by then smoke was coming out of my ears. I couldn't wait to get away and I made my excuses as quickly as possible. I tore down that road back to Manchester, straight to Sharpe's house, and I couldn't have timed it better. I caught them all having another party. The place was bursting with music and girls. They even had the apprentices there. It didn't go on much longer, not after I'd kicked a few doors and a few backsides. Talk about a party pooper!

They were only young lads then, of course, and kids will be kids. You always get prank situations, they're part of growing up. But it's also part of growing up to learn just how far you can go. A manager, like a parent, has to put his foot down pretty firmly when things get out of hand. Anyway, my parting words to Ryan these days when I feel he should be taking it easy are invariably "And don't be going to Blackpool." I smile now, but he knows and so, I hope, do all the others!

I don't shelter them all the time. I try to protect them from too much exposure and too many social functions when they are just emerging into the big-time, because they need to concentrate on football and their careers. But gradually I give them more freedom and I expect them to take on more responsibilities towards the fans and the public.

Tonight, for instance, Ryan Giggs and David Beckham are the star guests at the 150th anniversary dinner of the YMCA, which has had close links with Manchester United for many years and which we are pleased to help. The dinner is in our new North Stand and there will be around 700 people there. The boys are in for a tiring night, signing autographs and all that, but they're older now and must play their part in fulfilling the club's obligations.

*Thursday 14 November*

My main objective all week has been to remind the players what the club requires of them: in particular hunger, determination and pride. Build on those foundations and you build to last. The strength of our team comes from the ability of the players, of course, but also from our preparations and our desire for success. It's built on the ambitions of myself, of Brian Kidd, of the supporters and of all the players we have had over the years. We haven't got to our present position through drawing winning lottery numbers. We done it step by step, getting better and better, never standing still.

But it's time to lighten up, at least physically, and today we are at Mottram Hall for massage and relaxation. The major work has been done. Last week's programme, along with the matches played by the international players, will ensure everyone is physically and mentally up for it. Andy Pinkerton does a great massage job at the hotel. He reminds me of Jimmy Steele, the former Celtic and Scotland masseur, who used to say after a session with the players, 'Their muscles are like the strings of a violin now ... perfectly tuned by James Steele.'

*Friday 15 November*

At the Friday press conference today I let fly at the tabloid newspaper which had us supposedly signing yet more players this week. This time they linked us with a deal for Patrick Kluivert and Ronald de Boer, the Ajax strikers. They are both accomplished players, but this kind of story – if people believe it – makes us look foolish. There is no way the Dutch champions are going to sell while they are still in the European Cup and aiming, like us, for a place in the quarter finals. It's also common knowledge that Kluivert, who becomes a free agent at the end of the season, is pretty well lined up for AC Milan. Linking us with him flies in the face of all logic.

However, the story must make our supporters wonder what is going on, especially when nothing materialises. The fact is that we have made no inquiries for any player (other than Nadal) since our close-season signings. I must admit that if I hadn't been so sure Alan Shearer was joining us, then I might have been looking at other strikers. When the Shearer deal fell through we were left in mid-air, but you don't just rush out and buy someone else just for the sake of it. I like to investigate my signings thoroughly, and that takes time, especially when it involves foreign players. You have only to look around at the number of imports who have failed to understand my reasons.

In any case, we are far from desperate. We already have one new striker in Ole Gunnar Solskjaer, who I happen to believe is going to be a very good player. We also have the luckless Andy Cole waiting in the wings. A broken leg and then illness have put him out of sight, but he is certainly not out of mind. Getting him back will be like signing a new player. And if we qualify for the quarter finals of the European Cup, I shall try to sign someone else to give us even more strength in depth.

In the meantime I wish the papers would stop linking us with every name being pushed by some agent or another for a transfer.

*Saturday 16 November*
  Thank goodness we play more like our real selves against Arsenal. They've got that dour, uncompromising determination which means you never get an easy game against them. For me,

# Ten incredible years

their key player is Tony Adams, who is a real handful. And you have always got to be alive to Ian Wright. He's such a sharp beggar and his goal awareness is second to none. His goal against Newcastle at Highbury last season was unbelievable. Winterburn played the ball in and Wright showed such calmness, such audacity, such cheek as he nonchalantly chipped the goalkeeper, as if to say, "Hey, I do this every day!" He's got that cocky arrogance about him.

For the first 20 minutes, Arsenal look like a team who are on a good run: confident, positive and getting forward a lot. In contrast, we look like a side having a barren time and grappling to get in touch with the game. But as the minutes go by we improve, and the first half is pretty even. At half-time I tell the players they have done the hard part and urge them to keep playing the ball in behind the Arsenal defence, who were not handling that kind of situation very well. That was how we got our winner.

If you can create panic in the Arsenal defence you know you are doing well. They have such vast experience – the average age at the back is around 32. Our goal had panic written all over it. The ball was knocked back to David Seaman by Lee Dixon and the goalkeeper failed to gather it properly. Nicky Butt came in along the line and squeezed in a shot, which was deflected in by Winterburn. At that point everything changed for Manchester United. It was like walking into another world: our play was transformed. In the last 25 minutes we were excellent. Wright had one great chance but Peter Schmeichel made a fantastic save. But the main thing was that we were more like our old selves. It was good to see.

*Premiership / Old Trafford / Att: 55,210*

**Manchester United 1**
Schmeichel, G Neville, May, Johnsen, P Neville, Butt, Beckham, Cantona, Poborsky, Solskjaer, Giggs
*Scorer: Winterburn (own goal)*

**Arsenal 0**
Seaman, Dixon, Winterburn, Vieira, Bould, Adams, Platt, Wright, Merson, Bergkamp, Keown

*Sunday 17 November*

The players are in to loosen off in preparation for Juventus on Wednesday. Ryan is stiff after playing his first game at this level for a month, but that's normal. There are no complications and he will be all right for midweek. There is a bit more spice about the training ground. The best cure for a man is a good victory, and I am much more confident about our prospects after yesterday's win.

*Monday 18 November*

We had a training session to work on keeping possession.

A flare-up on Saturday between Schmeichel and Wright has spilled into the newspapers. There's been a complaint to the FA that our goalkeeper racially abused the Arsenal man. The incident happened just before half time, when Wright challenged Schmeichel with his foot up and was booked. The two players clearly had words but it seems someone has alleged, after watching television, that Peter called his opponent a "black bastard". I'm disappointed. Both men have tempers and for someone to complain is ridiculous. The next thing we know, a United fan is going to report an Arsenal player for something. I hope the FA throw the complaint in the bin where it belongs.

The whole business of racial abuse seems to have got out of hand these days. A few years back, when Paul Ince was involved in an incident at Wembley once, I asked him why he got so upset when someone called him black. After all, he frequently referred to me as a Scottish so-and-so, so what was the difference? He told me the Scots aren't a race; naturally I had to remind him that we are in fact the master race!

More seriously, I come from an environment in the west of Scotland where prejudices reign, and where there's always been bigotry between the Catholics and Protestants. Time has diluted the sectarianism, and inter-marriage has overshadowed people's ignorance, but there are still extremists. It will be a long time yet before the rivalry between the Scots and English is removed, but that's only natural when set against a history of the English taking land away from us Scots. Earlier generations were born to hate, but though political resentment might linger, I'd like to think most of us have moved on. I joke about the rivalry and the superiority of the Scots but I don't hate the English. In fact, I've come to enjoy living in England and the people I live and work with.

Of course we should never forget dreadful events like the Holocaust, the nationalistic wars of Eastern Europe and the genocide in Africa, but I think we are past all that in this country. It doesn't help when people manufacture so-called racial incidents out of an everyday clash between two strong-minded players in the heat of a match. I hope no one at the FA is going to pander to this complaint, which is simply someone trying to make a mountain out of a molehill. As I say ... away into the wastepaper bin with it!

*Tuesday 19 November*

I call a team meeting to stress the same thing we said before the first Juventus game: in the early part of the match they try to overpower you. In Turin that's exactly what happened, and we can't afford to play second fiddle this time. We have to impose ourselves physically and tactically, and not just because of the situation in our Champions' League group. We're playing against the best, and it's time to put our credentials on the table.

*Wednesday 20 November*

The start of the match worries me, not so much because of the way Juventus play, but more because of the nervousness we show in clearing our lines. We are poor at bringing the ball out of defence and, after seven minutes, we suffer a huge blow when Philip Neville comes off with a pulled hamstring and I have to put on a substitute.

With Irwin and Pallister already injured, the strain on our resources forces me to switch Roy Keane into the centre of defence. The other option would be to keep the partnership of May and Johnsen, and let Keane play right back with Gary Neville crossing to the left. But Juventus' primary threat is down the right, with Alen Boksic spinning out down that flank, so Johnsen's pace on the left is more important to us. Keane is a great centre back anyway, and I know he can handle everything that comes through the middle. It means taking our main thrust out of the middle of the park, but there is no other option. I just want to get through the first half without conceding a goal.

For the first 25 minutes, Juventus are undoubtedly the better side. They work well together, their attitude is good – everything I expected, really. It doesn't surprise me; they are good professionals and every player earns his corn. But as we approach half time things start to change a little in our favour and we create a few chances.

Cantona has a great opportunity – the confident Eric of old would have buried it. David May goes close with a header and there are a couple more half-chances besides. We have one or two squeaks ourselves, but just as I feel we have really begun to impose ourselves, the hammer blow comes, ten minutes before half time.

Nicky Butt concedes a penalty which reflects his immaturity. He really knows the risks of challenging inside the box. It surprises me, because although he is a young player he has been in the first team for a couple of seasons now, and has been fantastic, But once he makes contact there is no way he's going to get away with it. Del Piero goes down as if he's been shot. The Italians are brilliant at that, and though it is undoubtedly a penalty, Del Piero makes sure the referee gives it.

It's disappointing because we have just started to make our presence felt; it's as if we aren't meant to win this match.

# Ten incredible years

At the break, all I ask them is whether they want to win the game or be second best. I remind them how we've been speaking all week about imposing ourselves. We still aren't forceful enough and we're not using our strong point, which is switching play.

But oh, what a glorious second-half performance. This is Manchester United, the Manchester United I love, playing the kind of football that makes everyone want to watch us. It is so exhilarating. The shackles come off, the players express themselves and have a right good go. Juventus have a couple of chances from what I reckon are offside positions, and our goal opportunities certainly outnumber theirs. We get six or seven clear-cut chances.

Eric Cantona, for all the hard time the press are giving him at the moment, could have scored five by himself. Their goalkeeper makes one fantastic save from Eric, who also hits the top of the bar. It is then that I have to admit he has lost a wee bit of confidence. I would normally expect him to do better, though he wasn't the only one.

Giggs could have scored with a back-post header from the kind of position that saw him score against Nottingham Forest – same position, same cross. Solskjaer is so unlucky with a header which couldn't be closer and then Beckham, our jewel in the crown when it comes to hitting the ball sweetly, has a golden chance but knocks the ball wide.

You could say that there is anxiety about our finishing, but I still feel the players are absolutely brilliant. I can't look at one player and say, well, you had a nightmare – or even been disappointing.

*European Champions League / Old Trafford / Att: 53,529*
**Manchester United 0**
Schmeichel, G Neville, Johnsen, May, P Neville (McClair), Beckham, Butt, Keane, Giggs, Cantona, Solskjaer (Cruyff)
**Juventus 1**
Peruzzi, Torricelli (Juliano), Ferrara, Montero, Porrini, Di Livio, Deschamps, Zidane, Jugovic, Boksic, Del Piero (Tacchinardi)
*Scorer: Del Piero (penalty)*

*Thursday 21 November*

I start to meet supporters and they are down, flat with disappointment. I'm disappointed, too, but my overriding feeling is one of pride in the players for their magnificent performance. I am far more disappointed with the press and the load of crap they wrote about how we had been outplayed.

I know we are taking it to the wire and that everything now depends on the final round of matches in our Champions' League group. To go through to the quarter finals in March, we must win or draw against Rapid Vienna in Austria and hope that Juventus beat or draw with Fenerbahçe in Italy, depending on our result. We are cutting it fine. This is the price for home defeats against Fenerbahçe and Juventus. But I still cannot come to terms with the media reaction.

The majority of the critics have savaged us for a lack of technique and class but I'm having none of it. I shook the hand of every one of my players as they came off the pitch at the end and was proud to do so. Our performance against the champions of Europe was superb. With first-class backing from the fans, it was one of those fantastic European nights at Old Trafford which we will look back on in years to come with pride and a thrill.

I know we lost and and that our big European dream is on the line, but I'm still confident of success. That second-half display against the Italians gave me great heart. We showed what we were capable of, and I simply don't go along with the critics who seem to think we swamped Juventus through endeavour rather than skill. Determination versus class, they said, which is rubbish. I am sick of reading that Juventus had all the technique while we were supposed to be playing kick-and-rush stuff.

It's a nonsense. You don't create so many good chances to slaughter the most powerful team in Europe by simply charging around. Some of our football against Juventus was top drawer stuff in terms of skill, control, passing and vision. I was impressed at the time, and as I study the videos of the game today I'm even more convinced that we had just as much class as the opposition.

When you lose a game of football, it's never easy to take. You go over and over where you went wrong to try to determine how to avoid your mistakes in future. But this time I couldn't fault either the individuals or the team-work. Both were magnificent. Juventus took off their attacking full back and a midfield man in order to put on a centre back and an extra defender to try to stop Ryan Giggs. What does that show, other than their alarm in the face of some devastating play?

One wonders what the outcome would have been if we hadn't had that early injury to Phil Neville which meant I had to pull Roy Keane out of midfield to play at the back. We adjusted, and by the second half we were irresistible. We've had our problems, thanks to injuries and loss of form; but I'm convinced that if we get through in Vienna and qualify for the knock-out phase we will do extremely well.

Now it's recovery time for the players. There is a price to pay for the great effort against Juventus. We've got an awful lot of strains and pulls. It looks as if Keane, Butt and Beckham are OK, so I will have a decent enough midfield to get a grip of the game at Middlesbrough on Saturday. The problem will be in defence, where we are without both Nevilles, Irwin and Pallister. It's a similar problem as we had last December.

My first move is to recall John O'Kane from a loan spell with Bury and then bring young Michael Clegg into the picture. O'Kane has played a few times at senior level in other competitions and he was one of the boys in the outstanding youth team of 1992. He'll be fine. Clegg is new to the first-team squad but is doing well in the Reserves and his attitude is first-class; a great example to any aspiring young footballer. It'll ensure him a good career in the game, hopefully at Manchester United.

I'm bringing Ben Thornley into the team in a left-sided role. Jordi Cruyff is only just back after injury and his confidence is not a hundred per cent. Like Karel Poborsky and a lot of other foreign players, he needs time to adjust. They often reach a plateau before moving forward again.

I feel more for Karel because he can't speak English yet. I can't sit him down and explain things to him, tell him when he is doing well and when he isn't. I hope he will soon settle down; he's a great pro and fantastic trainer. He is having English lessons twice a week and things will improve a lot once he has come to terms with the language.


*Saturday 23 November*

We're on our way by bus to Middlesbrough and I'm thinking about Emerson. His Brazilian wife is having problems coming to terms with the North East and its weather. It's cold today, and seems to get colder the nearer we get to Middlesbrough, so we tease Karel and ask him if it is warm in the Czech Republic.

"No, no," he says. But I don't know whether he understands what we are on about.

Considering the changes I've had to make for the game, with O'Kane, Clegg and Thornley all playing, I'm delighted with a 2–2 draw. In fact we almost snatch it. We would have done, but for a soft penalty given by our old friend Alan Wilkie, he of Eric Cantona and kung-fu fame. Let me add that Middlesbrough would have had cause for complaint if they hadn't managed a draw, but that's not the point. We were in control at the end when the ball was driven at Paul Scholes – straight, smack, bang at his face from six yards. What player wouldn't have put his hand up to protect his face? It was hardly as if he meant to play the ball. But the referee gave another of his unexpected decisions and said it was hand ball.

We also had an indirect free kick in the penalty box, and I've not seen one of those given in the area for ten years. I didn't like the way Ravanelli chased the referee around appealing for penalty kicks, either. It was all done in the best Italian tradition too, which can be so effective. They're such demonstrative people.

Sometimes we have benefitted from Mr Wilkie's decisions ourselves. For instance, there was the soft penalty we were awarded against Manchester City after the Cantona sending-off. But for his own good I think Mr Wilkie should be kept away from Manchester United! We clearly affect the guy; he is ashen-faced when he gets one of our games! Of course, I can't help feeling that if he had punished the players who kicked Cole and Cantona at Selhurst Park in that fateful match against Crystal Palace, we wouldn't have had the Cantona dismissal and the subsequent clash with the fan, but that's only my opinion.

So there's plenty to mull over on the trek back, not least our heartening performance and a good debut for young Clegg. It was nice to see Thornley doing well, too. He tired towards the end and I brought Cruyff on to take over, but he made a good impact. O'Kane did all right too.

The other results have gone in our favour. Both Newcastle and Liverpool have drawn their matches.

*Premiership / Riverside Stadium / Att: 30,063*

**Middlesbrough 2**
Walsh, Cox, Vickers, Whyte, Hignett, Mustoe, Beck, Moore, Juninho, Ravanelli (Stamp), Fleming
*Scorers: Ravanelli, Hignett (penalty)*

**Manchester United 2**
Schmeichel, Clegg, O'Kane (McClair), May, Johnsen, Butt, Keane, Beckham, Cantona, Scholes, Thornley (Cruyff)
*Scorers: Keane, May*

## Sunday 24 November

Sundays can be quite entertaining for a football fan, provided you have an understanding wife.

Today, for instance, there is an Italian match, then Arsenal against Tottenham followed by the Scottish Coca-Cola Cup final between Rangers and Hearts, with a Spanish League fixture tonight. As I say, it does require some tolerance from the family. Either that, or someone like Cathy, who surrendered and waved the white flag many years ago.

*Monday 25 November*

Prompted no doubt by our visit to Middlesbrough, some of the papers are linking us again with Fabrizio Ravanelli. It's a bit naughty, because there's no way I'd complicate Bryan Robson's management by trying to lure away one of the players he only signed this season.

Don't get me wrong: I admire the striking qualities of the White Feather. He's not the youngest – he's been at the top a long time – but he is a fabulous player, up there with the leading scorers in the Premiership. In fact at the moment, he's scored as many as Alan Shearer, which says it all. But Bryan Robson gave too much to Manchester United in his time for me to do the dirty on him. I don't forget that kind of thing, and he deserves to get on with a very innovative signing without any interference from Manchester United. All credit to him for going for a striker who had just helped Juventus win the European Cup, and good luck to him.

Maybe I should have thought of Ravanelli myself, but at that time I was so convinced Shearer was a Manchester United player that I wasn't considering anyone else – especially in view of what Shearer was going to cost us! I've already been on the phone to Robbo to assure him that the talk in the papers suggesting Ravanelli is unhappy at Middlesbrough and is ready to come to Old Trafford is none of our doing.

In the evening I have one of those rewarding and satisfying obligations: helping to judge a painting competition for primary school children, organised by the Rainbow Trust in aid of the St Francis Hospice. It's at Manchester Town Hall in Albert Square. Along with a local artist, Michael Brown, we pick out winners for the different age groups. It's amazing how brilliant kids are when they are encouraged to express themselves. They also contribute poems about a rainbow and their ideas and imagination are terrific. Our players and staff have supported this charity for some years because it is so worthwhile, one you can really get your teeth into. I'm loaded with flu but I was never going to miss this engagement.

The bonus is that we finish fairly early, so I zoom across to Old Trafford to catch our youngsters playing Wrexham in the FA Youth Cup. I don't like to miss our Youth team in action. I'm delighted to find that by the time I get there we are four goals up. I stay to see them score another three and then leave early. I don't think they are going to lose now!

Away to my bed after a smashing night, feeling rotten, but glad I made the effort.


*Tuesday 26 November*

The youngsters finished with a 7–0 win last night. They're a promising bunch. It would be too much to expect them to emulate the lads who won the FA Youth Cup in 1992, and who are now such a key part of our first team squad – after all, the class of '92 has produced eight internationals at Under-21 and senior level. Nonetheless, you won't get a better defensive youth partnership than John Curtis, the former England Schools' captain from Nuneaton, and local boy Wesley Brown. We also have some exceptional midfield players in Richard Wellens, another local youngster, and Mark Wilson from Scunthorpe. And I'm glad to say Scotland is represented – and well represented too – by Alec Notman from Edinburgh. He scored four of the goals against Wrexham and has also been doing remarkably well in the Reserves. Our other promising strikers are Jamie Wood from Salford and David Brown from Oldham.

I'm sure some of those boys will go all the way. In the meantime, they'll give a good account of themselves in this season's

youth competition – though in the next round they play
Liverpool, the current Cup holders. A big test.

I need to plan a team for tomorrow night's Coca-Cola Cup
tie at Leicester, but instead I am caught up helping Ryan Giggs
make a film for a Japanese company. When I first agreed to do
it two months ago, it didn't seem a problem. But now I've got
all sorts of problems with injuries and I can't concentrate. At a
club like ours, you've got to be careful you don't get distracted
from the core business of football. I only have a bit part putting
Ryan through some training exercises, but it's still time
consuming.

Once we're through I start to juggle with the squad. The
Neville brothers are both injured, Giggs is still bothered by his
ankle, Pallister is not ready and Johnsen has flu. I want to rest
Beckham and Butt in readiness for next week's European
crunch game. It adds up to quite a big hole in our playing staff.

No matter, it gives me the opportunity to give other players
a game. Van der Gouw will play in goal, with Clegg and
O'Kane at full back again. Chris Casper and Ben Thornley
will get another chance, plus there are starting places for Cruyff
and Poborsky.

*Wednesday 27 November*
There were a few familiar faces missing against Leicester.
The team was a lot younger than I'd have liked, but that's
no excuse. We should have done far better. It was a terrible
performance, and what disappointed and annoyed me was our
ball control. The pitch was hard with frost but wet on top,
which made the short passing game almost impossible. Even
so, these boys have been brought up on control and passing.
We deserved to go out 2–0. The only bonus was Paul Scholes
missing a penalty which might have given us a draw – a replay
was definitely not on my agenda. It was win or bust, thanks to
all our other commitments.

On the coach back we hear the other results. I'm pleased for Bryan Robson, whose Middlesbrough team have beaten Newcastle in their North East derby . That's a significant result for him. When I hear that Bolton have beaten Spurs 6–1, I decide that perhaps our result wasn't so bad after all and feel a bit perkier. Stockport draw with West Ham – David Jones has done a good job at Edgeley Park. Then we listen to the draw. With all the big clubs now missing and two Premiership clubs drawn together in the quarter finals, this competition is really there for the taking.

But the future of this League Cup competition is still open to question. There is talk of eliminating automatic entry into the Uefa Cup for the winners and if that happens, there must be a different formula. We were seeded for the third round ... maybe they should consider excusing Premiership sides until the fourth? There is the chance of a Wembley appearance in the final, so I would not like to be out of it altogether. The sponsors deserve commitment, which I have always borne in mind. But you have to weigh that against the structure of English football, the number of games we play and our European involvement. It's really a matter of balance.

*Coca-Cola Cup R4 / Filbert Street / Att: 20,428*
**Leicester City 2**
Keller, Grayson, Whitlow (Watts), Prior, Walsh, Izzet, Lennon, Taylor (Lawrence), Claridge, Parker, Heskey
*Scorers: Claridge, Heskey*
**Manchester United 0**
Van der Gouw, Clegg, O'Kane (Appleton), May, Keane, Casper, Poborsky (Cooke), McClair, Scholes, Cruyff, Thornley (Davies)

*Thursday 28 November*
We play Leicester again on Saturday, this time in the League at Old Trafford.

I hope Pallister is fit because he needs a game before we play in Vienna next week. I'm hopeful for Gary Neville and Denis

Irwin and I must check on Johnsen, who has had an Achilles strain as well as flu. It looks as if we will have a full-strength midfield again, with Beckham, Butt, Keane and Giggs all fit.

I'm going to play Jordi Cruyff up front through the middle because I want to see how he fits in alongside Cantona. It may provide me with another option. The lad has been a bit down lately and it will give him a lift. He knows he's had a little dip in form, which I'm sure is all part of coming to England.

*Saturday 30 November*

I remember Leicester taking a point off us a couple of years ago when they were at the bottom of the table. Quite a few of the same players, like Walsh, Whitlow, Parker and Grayson, are still in the team. I know they'll make it hard for us again this time, but I do expect to win.

In fact, we run out comfortable 3–1 victors, but we have to wait until the last 15 minutes for our goals. Leicester play five at the back and retreat to the edge of their box with their three midfielders working their tails off to live with our guys, so they're not easy to break down. They leave the big boy, Heskey, up front. He is massive, and his pace is a threat too. Claridge drifts and can dribble.

It takes a long time to win the match but we give a determined performance. Once Nicky Butt scores the opener, the goals come with a rush from Solskjaer and then Butt again. In the end we could easily have scored five or six.

The expansive mood and talent of our players were evident in the final stages, although Eric Cantona was disappointing. This has happened two or three times on the eve of a European match and I wonder if Eric's concentration is focussed on next Wednesday. But I can't brood because it's still a win which helps us back up the table and allows us to turn our minds on to the big European night in Vienna.

# Ten incredible years

*Premiership / Old Trafford / Att: 55,196*

**Manchester United 3**
Schmeichel, G Neville, Irwin, May, Pallister, Cantona, Butt, Beckham,
Giggs (Poborsky), Cruyff (Solskjaer), Keane
*Scorers: Butt 2, Solskjaer*

**Leicester City 1**
Keller, Grayson, Prior, Watts, Izzet, Lennon, Parker, Campbell (Lewis), Marshall,
Claridge, Heskey
*Scorer: Lennon*

*Sunday 1 December*

In for a loosener, and everyone is bright and breezy in anticipation of our clash with destiny in Vienna on Wednesday.

One or two of the press have jumped on the bandwagon,
trying to make me highlight the importance of the match. Well
of course it's important. Our performance, coupled with that of
Juventus' against our group rivals Fenerbahçe, will decide
whether we go through to the quarter finals of the European
Cup. But at a club like Manchester United, how do you put one
match above another in terms of importance? We're involved
in an unending succession of key fixtures.

What I do know is that our experience of mega-matches
over the last five years will serve a purpose next week. I know
we go into any big game capable of winning it. We have no
injuries from the Leicester game and everyone is ready.

*Monday 2 December*

In training, I decide to concentrate on the finishing. The
main aim is to make sure Cantona and Solskjaer get plenty of
strikes in on goal. Kiddo puts on a good session and I keep
close to our strikers, constantly reminding them of the value of
early shots and making sure they hit the target. I've got to get
them back to thinking more about scoring. A player like
Cantona improves as the season goes on. When he is not
playing as well as he can, he needs to think more about his
scoring ratio. We know he can pass the ball and do many other

129

things extremely well, but goals are a team's meat and drink and essential to victory. If things are not going that smoothly for a striker, he should focus on the main part of his game. Scoring can bring back overall form, so I want Eric to concentrate on his finishing.

I have this gnawing fear that Rapid Vienna, who are already out of the competition and have nothing to lose, could still make things very difficult for us on Wednesday. They play with a sweeper and have not lost at home in Europe for 15 matches. They are also the only team to have taken points off Juventus, so there is substance to my anxiety. A goal from anyone would be welcome, but I have got to think mainly in terms of Cantona and Solskjaer.

We have a good session and the atmosphere is upbeat as the players go about their work. They are looking forward to the match and I don't sense any apprehension, which pleases me. The players know that when we get back to our strongest side we are capable of taking on anyone. They are comfortable in the knowledge that Keane and Giggs are back, and especially glad that Pallister is fit again. Pally came through the Leicester game superbly – as if he had never been away, in fact. His presence will give us that much-needed feeling of security. Maybe he will be our foundation for a victory.

*Tuesday 3 December*

We set off accompanied by forecasts of bad weather in Vienna, ranging from one foot of snow to ten. When we get there we are greeted by a lovely crisp, sunny day. We settle into a hotel called the City Club which features an underground pyramid complete with tropical conditions and a huge sports development. There are four tennis courts, about three swimming pools, saunas, a magnificent gymnasium and all the trimmings. It's our kind of place, and the players quickly start to relax.

# Ten incredible years

In the hotel, I hold the usual press conference for the English journalists who have travelled out with us, plus the Austrian media. It's quite straightforward. I leave as soon as I can; I have a lot of thinking to do and I want to finalise my thoughts before we train at the stadium in the evening. Some of the English press lads are surprised when I send Solskjaer, Gary Neville and David Beckham, into the conference. Normally I'm quite protective of our young players, but these boys are in Vienna to do a man's job and they might as well realise it. You don't want players shooting their mouths off, but you do want them able to talk responsibly about the game, the club and their careers. From all accounts I gather they acquitted themselves well.

Later we go to the Ernst Happel Stadium for our permitted training session. The pitch is in magnificent condition, just like a bowling green. My mind drifts back to 1980, when I brought Aberdeen here to play Austria Memphis in the European Cup. We got through ... and now I'm hoping for a repeat.

The stadium is covered now and holds around 40,000, but when I was last here there were open terraces and a 80,000 capacity – it had a fantastic atmosphere. But it's still a good football theatre and they tell me it will be a full house. It should be a terrific occasion. The players will love it.

*Wednesday 4 December*

I pointedly tell the players in my pre-match talk that they are going to enjoy themselves. I don't want them apprehensive, and I am trying to send out the right vibes so they will be bursting to get out there. I urge them to concentrate on playing at speed. If they can achieve that, Rapid won't be able to live with them.

It turns out to be a sensational night. We achieve exactly what we set out to do. When Ryan Giggs scores our first goal from Eric Cantona's pass, I immediately start wondering what Fenerbahçe are doing in Turin. There had been all this talk about Juventus resting five players, but in my mind I knew they would not let us down. I reckon that even if they do leave a few players out, the reserves will be fresh and eager to do well, so it might benefit us. At least, that's what I try telling myself! I also tell myself that Marcello Lippi, the Juventus coach, knows what he is doing. He's not the type who wants to relax. His whole psyche is geared to the work ethic. I really don't think he is going to betray those beliefs by allowing his players to ease up.

At half time I'm told Juventus are 1–0 up on the Turks, but we decide not to tell the players so that they keep focussing on their own job of winning. We play well in the second half and my only worry is that we have to wait until 20 minutes from the end to get a second goal. By that time we should have had two or three; when it does come it's a good one, engineered by David Beckham and scored by Cantona. I'm pleased for Eric. If you can get a player thinking about scoring, the other things will fall into place. In fact Eric gives a good all-round performance, though they are all splendid tonight.

Once we have got the second goal, I ask ITV's Gary Newbon, who's standing near the dug-out, for the score in Turin. He tells me Juventus are still winning 1–0. I'm quite relaxed; I can't see Fenerbahçe scoring twice in the last 15 minutes.

The only downer of the night comes when Roy Keane demonstrates his determination by chasing back after Kühbauer to retrieve a lost cause. He makes a great tackle to knock the ball away, but in doing so catches his leg on his opponent's studs and sustains a horrible gash just below the knee. Later, we discover it needs 19 stitches.

When the players first wave for a stretcher, we fear a broken leg. But bad as the cut is, thankfully there's no break. Nonetheless Roy will be out for a month, and it sours the atmosphere somewhat. The other results start to come in and I can't believe Rosenborg have beaten AC Milan in the San Siro. It must be the most amazing result in the European Cup for years.

# Ten incredible years

FC Porto win 2–1 in Gothenburg to finish with the same group record as Juventus: won five, drawn one, lost none. They will be our quarter-final opponents over two legs in March. They are a strong side, but the three-month gap can change things. It could be a different ball game by then, and I know that we always do well in March and April. We have won Championships at that stage of the season and I predict now that the Portuguese are in for one hell of a tussle.

*European Champions League / Ernst Happel Stadium / Att: 40,000*
**Rapid Vienna 0**
Konsel, Ivanov, Schöttel, Stöger (Mandreko), Stumpf (Penksa), Kühbauer, Prosenik, Ratajczyk, Wagner, Zingler, Heraf
**Manchester United 2**
Schmeichel, G Neville (Casper), Irwin, May, Pallister, Cantona, Butt (Poborsky), Beckham, Giggs, Keane (McClair), Solskjaer
*Scorers: Giggs, Cantona*

# 5
# Back on course

Everything is going to plan. My strategy at the start of the season was twofold. I wanted us to concentrate on the Champions' League, and make sure we finished in the top two of our group and qualified for the quarter finals in March. At the same time we had to do well enough in the League to keep pace with the leading pack of Championship contenders.

Well, it's going according to plan. Europe is safely on the back-burner for three months. Knowing we have that exciting challenge to look forward to will surely be an inspiration as we concentrate fully on the Premiership.

There is nothing – bar injuries, of course – to cramp our style in the League now. I'm hopeful that without the distraction of Europe we'll be able to put together the kind of run that puts pressure on our rivals. There is the FA Cup of course, but we are used to battling on the two fronts of League and Cup from January onwards. It's lucky that we usually thrive on these twin demands!

To my mind, our real achievement so far has been not so much actually qualifying for the quarter finals, but doing it with depleted resources. A quick glance at our line-ups for the European games shows the extent of the changes forced on me by injuries to the squad. Pallister, Keane, Giggs and of course Cole all missed matches, and they are key players. A lot of people would have been pessimistic in those circumstances; all credit to the players, then, that we made it. Of course we rue those two home defeats – and losing our unbeaten home record in Europe. I'd rather have lost against a great team like Juventus; there's not the same dignity in losing it to Fenerbahçe, I'm afraid.

But I'm pleased with our improvement away from home. The players are handling the test of foreign combat away from Old Trafford much better. In the long run, that's an important indication that we're getting to grips with European football.

*Thursday 5 December*

There's an air of quiet satisfaction on the plane straight after the game, as we fly home from Vienna in the early hours. Admittedly, there's also a tinge of relief. We'd looked almost assured of our place in the last eight relatively early in the competition, before those successive home defeats against Fenerbahçe and Juventus put us on the rack. It may have gone to the wire, but we made it in the end.

It takes me back to when I was manager of Aberdeen and we reached the quarter finals of the European Cup for the first time. It felt as if we had actually won the Cup, because it had been so important to get to that stage of the competition; the three-month build-up, the anticipation and the excitement were what the fans craved.

Those are our sentiments now. Everyone's talking about Porto. We could take 20,000 with us to Portugal if our ticket allocation was big enough.

*Friday 6 December*

We are transfer news again. This time we're supposed to be poised to buy the Brazilian striker Ronaldo from Barcelona.

It's true that Ronaldo's agent asked me a little while ago if I would be interested in the player. My first reaction was to wonder why Barcelona would sell such an important player after paying £13 million for him only last July. The agent said that was no problem; there was a clause in his contract which allowed him to move if an offer came in above a certain sum. He told me I wouldn't even have to talk to the club, I could go straight to the Spanish FA. So then I asked him about money. I soon told him he was talking to the wrong guy, and that he should go and see the Chairman and frighten the life out of him, not me!

It transpired that the fee would be around $32 million, with a salary of $4 million a year. We are talking here about a £20 million transfer fee plus a pay packet of well over £2 million a year.

Now I would love to see Ronaldo playing for Manchester United. I have a gut feeling Old Trafford would be his kind of stage. But can you really justify that kind of outlay when you are a public company? Perhaps I could steal the Crown Jewels... but how would the rest of our players feel? And what if he did an Emerson and didn't take to life in Manchester? And what guarantee would we have that the same agent wouldn't be hawking him around again in six months' time?

It's a big problem these days. There's so much wheeling and dealing, no deal is sacrosanct. There's always a loophole or a get-out clause, so you have little assurance that a player will complete a contract. In my view, you can't build a team on that kind of foundation. I get agents coming to me all the time saying they can get us such-and-such a player because there is a clause in his contract which allows him to move. I also get messages that certain top players would like to play for Manchester United. Naturally, when an agent asks if you're interested, you've got to say yes. What else could you say if, say, when Pele was at his peak, you were told he wanted to join your club?

But I suspect the real truth is that, having got an expression of interest, the agent then goes back to the player and tells him he can get him a move to Manchester United if he wants.

What you have these days is a transfer marketplace created by agents. Of course, they work the media as well. It's a fact that many agents do business with the tabloids. Sometimes you get several agents all claiming to represent the same player. Another popular ploy is for an agent to come to you and say, "I've been authorised by the president of this or that club to buy one of your players." It's invariably a con trick, but there's so much money about these days that they're all trying to get a slice of the action.

They remind me of market makers in the Stock Exchange. There's a lot of jiggery pokery, but you can't afford not to listen; at some stage you might be interested in one of their propositions. There's a whole network of agents to cut through – home and abroad, they often work together. It's not easy to deal with.

### Saturday 7 December

Now we've got to practice what we preach and make sure we get some points at West Ham tomorrow. People say we have a bad record there, but in fact we've only lost once at Upton Park – though that was an important defeat in the run-in for the Championship we failed to win. They'll certainly give us a hard game, and their fans are among the most volatile in the country. I'm not sure whether they are as hostile to everyone, but I know I'm always glad to get out of the place. We're not frightened – we can handle it – but it's not my favourite ground.

### Sunday 8 December

I don't know whether it was tiredness or just relief at qualifying for the next stage in Europe, but we didn't perform well and the Hammers deserved their point. I was by no means a happy bunny. When you're two goals up with 11 minutes to go, you shouldn't end up drawing the match. We threw it away with rubbish defending.

Events before the game should have given me an inkling it would end up being a frustrating day. Because the police had warned us about traffic congestion, we went to the ground very early and I held my team talk in the dressing room. At Upton Park, the fans can almost see in. We could hear them, especially one fellow who shouted, "What's the difference between a Scotsman and a coconut?" My spiel came to a stop because I knew the players weren't listening to me; they were waiting for the answer. Sure enough, it came: "At least you can get a drink out of a coconut." Of course the players just fell about after this crack aimed at their boss. There wasn't much laughter afterwards when I told them I was fed up with the way they were repeatedly losing sloppy goals. I told them enough was enough.

David Beckham did score a marvellous goal, but he looked tired. Eric Cantona put in a terrific pass for Ole Gunnar to score the second, but overall it was a poor performance. My forebodings about the place were borne out when our coach stopped at traffic lights shortly after we set off for home. We were sitting there helpless outside this pub where West Ham fans were drinking, and they let loose with a fusillade of bottles. The police moved in quickly but before they arrived we were gridlocked, and I had visions of the fans setting fire to our coach. As I say, not my favourite place to visit, and the experience capped a disappointing day.

*Premiership / Upton Park / Att: 25,045*

**West Ham 2**
Miklosko, Dicks, Bilic (Potts), Bowen, Reiper, Bishop, Moncur, Dumitrescu, Rowland (Raducioiu), Hughes, Dowie
*Scorers: Dicks (penalty), Radicioiu*

**Manchester United 2**
Schmeichel, Irwin, May, Pallister, Johnsen, Beckham, Giggs, McClair, Cantona, Poborsky (Neville), Solskjaer
*Scorers: Beckham, Solskjaer*

## Monday 9 December

I'm very conscious that it is other teams' performances which are keeping us afloat. Fortunately for us, while we were dropping points at Upton Park, Newcastle muddled through a goalless draw at Nottingham Forest. Liverpool lost at home to Sheffield Wednesday and Arsenal could only draw at home to Derby County. Soon we're going to have to put our own house in order.

I tell David Beckham that I don't want to see him for another five days and that he is to take a complete rest. He's a restless soul, a lad who likes to get round the shops – clothes and music mainly, I guess. He himself admits that he finds it difficult to stay in the house, that he just can't sit still. I let him know that if I hear he is even thinking of going out shopping in Manchester, I shall fine him a week's wages.

It's important he understands how crucial rest is. He has done fantastically well this season and played in virtually every match, bar a couple of Coca-Cola Cup ties. That's 23 club games in all, plus three World Cup qualifiers for England, and we haven't even reached the half-way point of the season. Eric Cantona has played about the same number of games, but he is experienced, and a powerful man besides. David is still young, has some growing to do, and is the type of midfield player who covers a lot of ground in a match.

We have a 10-day break now with no game on Saturday, so the rest of the players get a couple of days off as well.

*Tuesday 10 December*

Andy Cole's got the all-clear to start training again. He's been laid up since breaking his leg earlier this season, and the latest scan shows the break has completely healed. It's good news at just the right time. We could do with a reserve fixture for him, and I'll try to rearrange the Derby County Pontin's League game to give him a run before Christmas.

Andy has had some shocking bad luck. To go down with pneumonia over the summer was bad enough, but then to find himself up against Neil Ruddock in a reserve game was really unfortunate. Surely his luck must change.

# Back on course

*Wednesday 11 December*

I read that Brian Clough has gone into a hospital which specialises in drink problems, which reminds me of the pressures on all football managers. Turning to drink is an obvious escape from stress, both for managers and players. I remember when I first took over at Old Trafford, I found that a number of players were a bit too fond of a drink (or two) for my liking. At the time, I wondered if the pressure of playing for such a big club was threatening to turn the place into more of a drinking den than a football club.

I wish Cloughie well. There's no doubt he has been a major figure in post-war management. Perhaps the game took more out of him than we realised at the time.

A lot of people find escape in a bottle. It's a retreat to a world where they feel safe, oblivious to events which may be stressing them out,where they can tell themselves that the next day will look after itself. I remember once getting a request from the visiting team for a bottle of whisky. The coach explained it was known as "the team spirit" and was for their manager, only they'd forgotten to pack it with the rest of the kit.

People occasionally ask me how I cope with stress. I take a drink when I feel like it, but happily I don't need it to cope – not yet, anyway! I tend to withdraw into myself when I feel the pressure mounting. Kiddo will be talking to me sometimes and then complain, "You're not listening to me, you're in another world." He is half right. I'm certainly not concentrating on what he is saying (no reflection on the wisdom of his words), but I am listening. Most of what he's saying goes in one ear and out the other, but if there's something I need to note, I switch right back on. It's not just Brian Kidd who gets this treatment; it's all the people who want a slice of my attention. If their demands come at a stressful time, then for the sake of my own well-being I have to put down some kind of a shutter.

There is always going to be gossip at a big club like Manchester United, and I have to try and blank it out when things get hectic so I can concentrate on the important issues. I think people who are leaders, be it in industry, politics or sport, need to be able to withdraw into themselves at times. It's my safety valve, a knack I have cultivated.

Only the other day the Chairman was reminding me not to take on too much. But as I said to him at the time, I do set limits. I may at the training ground well before 8 am, but I always try to be back home by 4 pm – especially if I'm out again in the evening. I'll try to get in an hour's sleep, practise the piano for a spell, or absorb myself in a film or a book.

All football managers have to take a step back at times, or they'd never survive.

*Thursday 12 December*
Our plans for a new training complex are finally coming to fruition. The issue has been an obsession of mine for a few years: a club of our stature must have facilities in keeping with our achievements and ambitions, and I want a site which will see us into the next century. We have looked carefully at our existing sites, including Littleton Road in Salford next door to The Cliff training ground on Lower Broughton Road. The drawings we had made showed that the area was simply not big enough for everything I had in mind. Michael Edelson, a director of the club, suggested we buy Heaton Park, and we also looked at a site near Wythenshawe before we eventually found the ideal place.

We've bought 100 acres from Shell at Carrington, subject to planning permission. It's near a motorway link on the Cheshire side, where most of our players live. We're at the final planning stage and I hope the work will start this summer.

We will have eight pitches, one specifically for the senior squad, backed by half-pitches for training exercises. Then there'll be various smaller sized pitches for the youngsters. The pitches will have under-soil heating and there'll be a swimming pool and a rehabilitation centre as well as gymnasium, medical rooms and dressing rooms. It will cost between £10 million and £12 million, but it will be money well spent. We'll keep The Cliff as a Centre of Excellence because it's convenient for all the kids who live on the north side of Manchester.

In its day, the Cliff was an admirable training ground, but we have outgrown it. Sir Matt Busby had a playing staff of around 40; we now have 60 players and our whole operation is much more sophisticated. You can't afford to stand still in this game and other clubs are catching us up in an area Sir Matt and the board pioneered. Howard Wilkinson's last major contribution at Leeds was to oversee the opening of a new training ground. Middlesbrough and Wolves also have new training centres. Liverpool, who were (until recently at any rate) a buying club rather than interested in youth development, have plans for a new training complex for coaching at all levels.

Youth development is a big, big part of Manchester United, and has been since the Busby Babes. People like Brian Kidd and Les Kershaw have travelled all over Europe in the last few years to look at what the big Continental clubs are doing in this area. They have studied the facilities at Panathinaikos, who have a fantastic set-up, as well as clubs like Bayern Munich, Auxerre, AC Milan, Inter Milan, Ajax and the French National School. We've now incorporated the best of their ideas into our own plans to provide top-rate facilities for our players.

*Saturday 14 December*

I flew to Spain this morning to watch their national team play Yugoslavia in Valencia. I wanted to have a look at the Yugoslavian centre back Djukic. He was recommended to us, but I'm afraid his team were a shambles. They lost 2–0, and the defeat didn't show him in a very good light. We'd need to watch him again. Actually, I was more impressed by Mijatovic, the Slav centre forward who played in Spain with Valencia before getting a transfer to Real Madrid. He was a classic case of a player returning to play in front of one-time fans and being given the bird in a big way. Every time he touched the ball the noise was incredible. It made Paul Ince's returns to West Ham sound like auditions for a church choir.

The match was a lesson in how English clubs are targetting European players at the moment. There are more agents in the Yugoslav team hotel than residents – I must have come away with about 50 calling cards. I'm staying overnight and aim to be back on Sunday in time to watch the Sky Premiership match. Kiddo will take training in the morning.

*Monday 16 December*

David Beckham came to see me to say he's had a good rest. He insisted he hadn't been out shopping and he was ready to play at Hillsborough on Wednesday. I said, "Thank you very much David, it's nice of you to volunteer your services, but you'll still be a substitute." His face dropped a mile, but I meant it when I said he must get proper rest at this stage of the season. I want him to be a star still in ten years' time.

I already have my line-up in mind, and it includes Paul Scholes. The wee lad's been brilliant in training and it's time to give him his head. I explained that he mustn't judge his career on what has happened to him lately; he's been on the sidelines so I can give the new foreign players a chance to show what they can do. I tell him he'll have his chance at Sheffield Wednesday, when he can play for a jersey. I'll put him in midfield.

*Tuesday 17 December*

Wednesday have gone undefeated for about 10 games. It'll be a hard game, but we've got to win, so as to show that without the distraction of Europe for three months we intend to make an impact on the Premiership. We can't leave it any longer.

The only thing going on at the moment is me talking big in the papers. The players must produce performances that back up what I've been saying, and I hold a meeting to get this message across. I tell the players that if we win, we put everyone on the back foot and our rivals will say, 'That's them started off again.'

*Wednesday 18 December*

So much for my inspired talk ... The first half against Sheffield Wednesday was abysmal. I've never seen us defend so badly. We were quite good in attack, incisive at times, and could have scored three. But I wasn't happy with what was going on at the back. I was hopping mad at half-time. After the interval we were more like ourselves, but we still gave away a bad goal. Paul Scholes got an equaliser, but our poor defending has to stop. I keep saying this lately; it really isn't good enough.

Mind you, all credit to David Pleat and Peter Shreeves, who are getting the best out of their players at Hillsborough. I could not dispute the result: a 1–1 draw was fair.

*Premiership / Hillsborough / Att: 37,671*

**Sheffield Wednesday 1**
Pressman, Atherton, Nolan, Pembridge, Walker, Whittingham, Carbone (Blinker), Booth (Hirst), Hyde (Trustfull), Nicol, Stefanovic
*Scorer: Carbone*

**Manchester United 1**
Schmeichel, G Neville (Beckham), Irwin, May, Johnsen (P Neville), Pallister, Giggs, Cantona, Butt, Solskjaer, Scholes
*Scorer: Scholes*

*Thursday 19 December*

Yet more speculation about players we are supposedly interested in signing. The papers are wrong about Stefan Schwarz, the Fiorentina midfield player; I must confess I've never even thought about him. But they're nearer the mark with Gabriel Batistuta. In fact, I made inquiries about him last summer after the collapse of the Shearer deal, but there was nothing doing. Fiorentina said their fans would shoot them if they even thought about selling their star centre forward.

*Friday 20 December*

Tomorrow we entertain Sunderland. Last season they slaughtered us at Old Trafford in the third round of the FA Cup, before we managed to salvage a 2–2 draw. I think they got wind of our line-up that day and knew we were going to play with three centre backs, because they played a striker out wide and dragged our formation all over the place. In the first half we were a shambles. It wasn't until I took off Paul Parker and reverted to a flat back four that we turned the game round. We played well in the replay and eventually won 2–1.

But Peter Reid has done a great job at Roker Park – with the help, I might point out, of two of my staff. He took one of our coaches, Bryan "Pop" Robson, back to his native North East, and also signed up Jimmy Hagan, our scout in the area. Peter is a good manager and obviously adept at "tapping" as well.

Last season's Cup tie is still very much in my mind, but that won't deter me from playing three centre backs again tomorrow. If Peter Reid counters with a wide striker, then Denis Irwin will go wide to pick him up.

My major concern, however, is our defensive performance. Look at the averages over the years: teams which concede no more than 33 or 34 goals in a season are in the frame for the Championship. Yet here we are with 25 already in the back of our net after only 17 matches. At this rate we'll end up with a goals-against tally of around 55, and I doubt if anyone's ever won the League with that kind of defence.

There's every reason to be concerned, and I decide it's time to put on my psychology hat. I call in the experienced players like Cantona and Schmeichel, along with the defenders, for a chat. I know big Peter doesn't like playing with three centre backs, simply because he thinks we are good enough to play with a flat back four. But I tell them that until I have sufficient confidence that they can go through a game without conceding a goal then we'll keep playing three in the middle.

Schmikes has a big frown on his face, which is exactly the response I wanted. I hammer home the message that if we can't get it right at the back then we won't win the League.


*Saturday 21 December*

My plans for Sunderland held good for all of 10 minutes of the game, then Gary Pallister ricked his back and couldn't get up against anyone.

It threw us into disarray. My counter was to switch Gary Neville into a marking role, give Denis Irwin a normal full-back position and then let Pally operate as the free defender. With the help of an excellent display by Gary Neville, who did a good job on Alex Rae, we got our shape back. Scoring the first goal to open up the play is so important for us, and Solskjaer did it after 35 minutes. From then on everything flowed. We got a penalty, which Cantona took – never for a moment did I think of taking the penalty responsibility off him after his miss at Leeds earlier in the season.

Eric also scored a magnificent goal 10 minutes from the end. From the dug-out you could see the line of the ball as it curved inside the post. The cameras caught it well, too, but what remains most vividly in my mind is Eric's response. It was the look of him, as if he was saying, "Don't ever doubt me. I know I haven't been playing as well as I can, but I'm back, and here's to the memories."

We picked up the speed of our play in the second half and it was first class. Sunderland are one of the hardest teams to play against because they work extremely hard to close the ball down, so this was a fine result. Scoring five without reply is always healthy for all-round morale.

# A Will to Win

*Premiership / Old Trafford / Att: 55,081*

**Manchester United 5**
Schmeichel, G Neville, Irwin, May, P Neville, Pallister (McClair), Giggs (Thornley), Butt, Cantona, Scholes, Solskjaer (Poborsky)
*Scorers: Solskjaer 2, Cantona 2 (1 penalty), Butt*

**Sunderland 0**
Perez, Kubicki, Hall, Bracewell (Agnew), Ball, Melville, Gray (Bridges), Ord, Russell, Kelly, Rae (Stewart)

## *Monday 23 December*

Brian Kidd and I get down to looking at our busy holiday programme over Christmas and the New Year. It's the same for every club of course, but the schedule requires some thought. For instance, we have to discuss when to bring in the masseur; which player to take off if we go ahead; which players might be fresher and who could come in for a game. Playing this number of fixtures is hard enough physically; what is even more important is to keep the players mentally fresh. So we plan nice light sessions with plenty of the work they enjoy, like practising their finishing.

If there's a game on Boxing Day, we usually let the players have Christmas Day with their families before they come into the Cliff at around 5 pm. Then if it's an away fixture we travel to the venue, or to a local hotel if we're at Old Trafford. This year we're playing Nottingham Forest and we'll stick to the usual routine.

Gary Pallister's back injury will keep him out, possibly for two or three weeks. Fortunately it doesn't seem to be his previous disc bother but a muscle strain. Just as much of a problem is that he does worry, often unnecessarily. We'll send him to the specialist again for reassurance that it's not something really serious. Gary might hide it well, but I know he's a worrier, and anyone who has had back trouble knows it can be a painful experience.

David May, who is struggling on with a hernia, will play through the holiday programme in view of Pally's absence. We

Kevin Keegan: "I told him that he shouldn't have allowed the media to become his master"

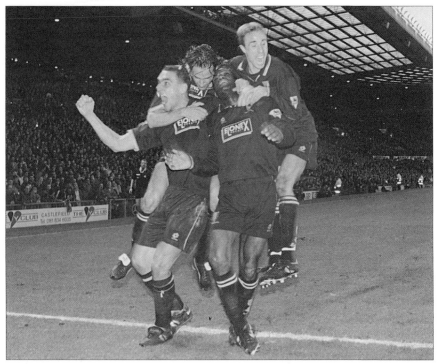

25 January 1997 v Wimbledon (h): "I honestly admire what Wimbledon have achieved. They call themselves the Crazy Gang, but they don't seem crazy to me"

4 December 1996 v Vienna (a): Anxious moments as Roy Keane is stretchered off ...

... but we qualify for the European Cup quarter finals

5 March 1997 v Porto (h): A 4–0 win was beyond my wildest dreams

19 March 1997: A relaxed press conference in Porto

David Beckham: "A restless soul ... I keep telling him I'll phone his house to make sure he's resting"

Andy Cole: "If he can just get the demons out of his head and simply enjoy his game, he could be the best striker in the business"

8 April 1997: Final preparations in Dortmund's Westfalenstadion

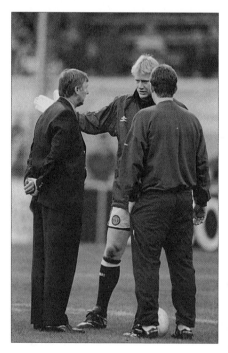

9 April 1997 v Borussia Dortmund (a): Peter Schmeichel fails a last-minute fitness test

"Nicky Butt hits the post after a great run"

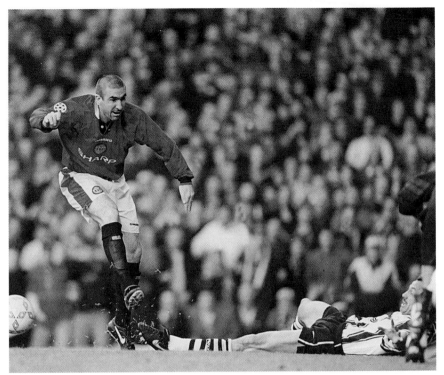

23 April 1997 v Dortmund (h): "Jurgen Kohler made some remarkable clearances and interceptions"

European Cup elimination: "It's a devastating blow, and I just don't know how long it'll take me to get over it"

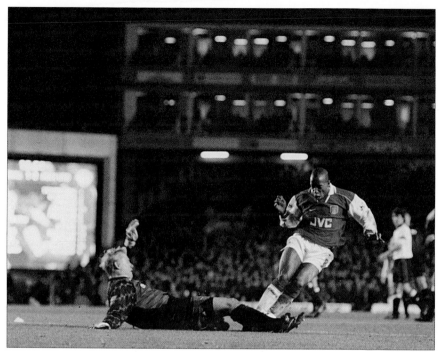

19 February 1997 v Arsenal (a): "If Eric Cantona had done the same, he'd have been locked up on Devil's Island"

22 March 1997 v Everton (a): "The game was won on the plane back from victory in Oporto. Not one player took a drink"

# Back on course

hope to get David an operation in the New Year, which will give him a couple of months to recuperate before the European quarter finals in March.

I'll leave Ronny Johnsen out again to give his Achilles injury more rest. It looks like May and Gary Neville at centre back, with Phil Neville and Denis Irwin the full backs.

Meanwhile I'm grateful to Jim Smith for rearranging our Pontin's League fixture. He's going to bring his Derby County reserve team to Gigg Lane tonight so I can give Andy Cole a game. Christmas week is difficult because all clubs try to squeeze in staff parties and team lunches, but I explain to Jim that unless his lot come over we haven't a reserve match until well into January. I'm desperate to give Coley a run out.

It's a bitterly cold night and the park is nice and flat, though a bit flinty. That doesn't stop Cole. I'm delighted to see him score a goal – and a typical one at that. As soon as the ball is played towards his chest he has it down and delivered in a twinkle. He has the quickest feet imaginable. I can see he is not bursting his sides, but he is not the kind of player who sprints around madly to prove he is fit. He's a predator who only comes alive around the box.

I have great faith in Andy. He's had a stop-start season so far, what with illness and injury, but we'll soon have him back – with luck, to somewhere near his best. I was surprised to read recently one journalist refer to "the reviled" Andy Cole. I just don't understand that. The fans have been fantastic, and have kept right behind him all the way. The key is definitely his confidence, and if he keeps remembering that the fans are backing him then I'm sure he can go on to be a top striker at Old Trafford.

Players like Andy can sometimes pick up on one small piece of criticism and magnify it. They get to the point where they believe that one jibe is representative of everyone's view. I can sympathise; Andy cost a lot of money, but he has to trust the people who bought him. I was delighted to pay £7 million, didn't hesitate at all, because he has so much in his armoury. If he could just get the demons out of his head and simply enjoy his game, he could be the best striker in the business. The next stage on his road back will be the subs' bench at Forest.

*Wednesday 25 December*

I really enjoy Christmas Day. The whole family – all 15 of us – sit down for lunch. How many people have three mothers-in-law at Christmas dinner, I wonder? That's how it works out at our place: Mark, his wife and her mother from France join Darren, his wife and her mother from Manchester. My mother-in-law lives with us, and I suppose if you count Cathy as a mother-in-law, there are four of them round the table. Jason and his wife are there with our three grandchildren, plus my niece from South Africa. Oh, and the dog too!

The wine flows, as you can imagine. The only sadness is that all three of the grandchildren, Jake as well as the twins, are in the throes of flu, snuffling away and looking so helpless.

It's a lovely day until, like everyone else in the football business, I have to take my leave and report to the ground – courtesy of a lift from Brian McClair, the highest-paid chauffeur in the country. We travel over to our hotel in Nottingham and have a light buffet in the evening. I guess we've all done plenty of eating earlier in the day.

*Thursday 26 December*

I come down to breakfast to be greeted with the news that Philip Neville is desperately poorly with flu. It means that I'll have to risk Ronny Johnsen, although he's not a hundred per cent fit.

It looks a gamble early on in the game, when Nottingham Forest's Kevin Campbell storms through and Peter Schmeichel is forced to block his shot. But once the defence settles down and the team pick up the rhythm, we do very well.

I had asked our players to keep switching the play from one side to the other, so that Forest's three centre backs would be forced to defend the wide areas. Giggs attacked the space on the left and caused them a lot of problems, and we ran up another big score to win 4–0.

Everyone will remember the game for its goals, especially the one from David Beckham. He is getting quite a reputation, thanks to the spectacular strikes he's been putting in from long-range shots and sweetly hit free kicks. I play David after giving him a two-match break – a rest of 18 days – and he looks all the better for it. I think he relished the time off once he realised how insistent I was that he should rest.

Forest put us under pressure again in the second half. Ian Woan is a particular threat; he rips us open with a string of vicious corner kicks, whipped in with that great left foot of his. But our third goal kills them off – and it's a worthy goal with which to clinch victory. Ole Gunnar Solskjaer's finish is easy enough, but Cantona shows fantastic control and balance between receiving the ball from Beckham and shooting against the bar.

I bring on Cole for the final 20 minutes. Within five he scores a superb goal which is typical of his play. With hardly any draw back, he skims his shot into the far corner of the net. Every player is so pleased for him, as are the fans, and with good reason: in my 10 years, this is only my second or third win at the City Ground. It is emphatic as well. Following the Sunderland match, it will have the media saying Manchester United are back.

*Premiership / City Ground / Att: 29,032*

**Nottingham Forest 0**
Crossley, Jerkan, Pearce, Cooper, Chettle, Allen, Woan, Haaland, Saunders (Gemmill), Campbell, Clough (Lee)
**Manchester United 4**
Schmeichel, G Neville, Irwin, May, Johnsen, Scholes, Cantona, Butt (McClair), Solskjaer, Beckham (Cole), Giggs (Poborsky)
*Scorers: Beckham, Butt, Solskjaer, Cole*

*Friday 27 December*

We're on a high. I told the players after the Sunderland match that they should take advantage of the attractive 7–1 odds being offered by the bookmakers and back themselves to win the League. If ever there was a bet of the century, that's it. If they had any conviction at all they should have put their money on while the going was good.

I don't know whether they jumped in or not, but a great chance has gone. Today the odds shortened to 3–1. The bookies know the significance of our recovery!

We can't afford to be complacent. Tomorrow we entertain Leeds, and it'll be one hell of a match. Over the years I've found it difficult to come to terms with Leeds United. Last season summed them up: after some abysmal displays in the run-up to their match with us, they produced a Herculean performance at Old Trafford with just 10 men. Was it because they knew their supporters would never forgive them for flopping against the hated Manchester United? If so, do fans have more power than a manager to motivate a team?

It's a sobering thought, particularly given a manager with the pedigree of Howard Wilkinson. He brought Leeds back from the dead, won them the Championship and gave unstinting commitment to his players. Did they give the same back to Howard? With the money the players get nowadays, the least one can expect is full commitment from them for every match.

Now Leeds have a new manager in George Graham. I'd hate to think things could go the same way again; I'm sure George is aware of what became of Howard and will make sure he doesn't succumb to the same fate. It will be good to see George walk through the front door tomorrow as manager of a Premiership club once more. He contributed too much to the game when he was at Arsenal to be squeezed out for good. He's paid his dues and I shall welcome him to Old Trafford, even if I found the way Howard Wilkinson left Leeds distressing. It seemed like one day they were talking about him moving upstairs to become director of football at Elland Road, then almost overnight everything changed. Modern football is an impatient business.

*Saturday 28 December*

I mustn't get too introspective; we have a game to win today and it's going to be a tough one. Leeds went five games without loss before their shock defeat by Coventry.

Our problem will be set pieces, which they will have practised long and hard – that's George's way. They will also set out their stall to man-mark Eric Cantona, and every one of their players will be given an individual job to do. I can't see Tony Yeboah lasting the game, though. He's been complaining in the papers that he wants a proper chance, but he looks a stone overweight.

I'm right. Yeboah is pulled off after 70 minutes and looks glad. He's knackered. We win the game 1–0, although not as comfortably as I'd like given that we were the home side. Considering the nature of the opposition, it's a good result.

The style of our early goal is also satisfying: great football between Giggs and Cantona before Giggs is brought down for a penalty. Eric missed against Leeds earlier in the season, but obliges this time, as I know he will. The really significant thing is that we didn't lose a goal. That tells me we might just be back in gear. Thinking back to the number of important 1–0 victories we enjoyed last season reminds me it was the recipe which won us the League.

*Premiership / Old Trafford / Att: 55,256*

**Manchester United 1**
Schmeichel, G Neville, May, Johnsen, Irwin, Beckham, Keane, Giggs, Cantona, Scholes (Butt), Solskjaer (Cole)
*Scorer: Cantona pen*

**Leeds United 0**
Martyn, Kelly, Palmer, Radebe, Halle, Dorigo, Jackson, Bowyer, Deane, Rush, Yeboah (Gray)

*Monday 30 December*

Andy Pinkerton, the masseur, comes in: I know the effects so many games can have. We use the jaccuzi too. I take the opportunity to have individual chats with the senior players. It's a time to give credit where it's due, and emphasise what happens when we get back into the groove. Players like Eric, Denis Irwin and Peter Schmeichel have the greatest responsibility. I tell them they've been more like their old selves and that's what we expect from them. Long may it continue!

*Wednesday 1 January*

Scarcely time to draw breath, and another game is upon us. This time it's against Aston Villa at Old Trafford. The fixtures – and the pressure – come so thick and fast these days that it's easy to forget that there's another life going on out there. I'm sure some very important things are happening in the big wide world, but I'm not really aware of what they are. My only lifeline to reality is via the grandchildren. Jake's flu is a bit better but the twins are still full of cold. When they're just seven months old, there's not a lot you can do to comfort them. It takes me back to the time when Mark and the twins, Jason and Darren, were that age.

But I can't afford to dwell on life elsewhere; my world is football, and we shall have to be at our best to beat Aston Villa this afternoon. They're so determined and dour.

Actually, we're unlucky: we miss three fantastic chances. Ryan Giggs knows he should have scored with a header. In the end we have to settle for a goalless draw after shackling Dwight Yorke, who is a handful. I said at the start of the season that Villa were my dark horses for the League, and I'm not changing my mind. A 0–0 draw is not the kind of result you expect from Manchester United, but you get these goalless games. Some are good, some bad. This is certainly better than the first-half towsing we got at Villa Park last season when we lost 3–1.

# Back on course

*Premiership / Old Trafford / Att: 55,133*
**Manchester United 0**
Schmeichel, G Neville, Irwin, May, Johnsen, Keane, Butt (Scholes), Beckham, Cantona, Giggs, Solskjaer (Cole)
**Aston Villa 0**
Bosnich, Nelson, Staunton, Tiler, Ehiogu, Townsend, Taylor (Johnsen), Draper, Milosevic, Yorke, Wright

*Thursday 2 January*

After his missed opportunity at Villa Park, the first thing I say to Ryan Giggs today is "What's happened to diving headers these days? You know, the kind of goals you used to see the likes of Denis Law, Tommy Lawton, Nat Lofthouse, Dixie Dean and Alex Ferguson score?"

I get a wry smile, probably at the mention of the last name.

However, at last I feel we're back on course. We're starting to get some consistency and we seem to have stopped the rot at the back, with four clean sheets. One key factor is the return of Roy Keane. He got that nasty leg wound in Vienna and missed four games, before coming back against Leeds in place of Nicky Butt, who was seedy after having a wisdom tooth out on the morning of the match. Keane had only had two or three training sessions but he was outstanding, just as he was against Villa. The way he's just picked up from where he left off tells you just how great a player he is.

I feel much more at ease with myself. With the midfield back to top strength we have a chance against anyone. Other teams have had mixed results, which go in our favour: Liverpool lost to Chelsea and Arsenal went down a couple of times. It's all starting to tighten up.

*Friday 3 January*

It's the third round of the FA Cup tomorrow, and right on cue the bad weather arrives. The outdoor pitches are frozen and icy, which restricts what we can do. Happily, we're not doing much anyway because of the quick succession of matches. After such a hectic programme you expect a few injuries and look for signs of tiredness. But Beckham has had his rest and, given that some absences have been forced through injury, players like Keane have come back refreshed. I hope we shall see Pallister all the better for his present break.

Philip Neville will be having a longer rest than we anticipated. What we thought was flu on Boxing Day developed dramatically and he became quite ill. It was obviously something more serious; the doctor diagnosed glandular fever. Phil has been ordered to take a complete rest and he will be monitored very carefully before he is allowed to train again. He could be out for several weeks. But overall we are looking quite fresh, which at this stage of the season, after a busy period, is a definite bonus. It's an encouraging sign for tomorrow's Cup tie against Spurs at Old Trafford.

*Saturday 4 January*

I read the morning papers and can find only one writer tipping Manchester United to win the Cup, plus another pundit who says the winner of our match this afternoon against Spurs will go all the way. So in my team talk, I tell the players that everyone seems to think we are only interested in Europe and that we won't be giving one hundred per cent in the League or Cup. Prove them wrong, I say, because there's nothing better than walking out at Wembley on FA Cup final day. We're not exempt from being victims of a Cup shock, as York City proved last season, and that will happen again if their attitude is not right. I add that if I thought Tottenham could out-battle us in front of 55,000 people on our own ground, then I would head for the River Irwell, never to be seen again. I finish by mocking them once again, telling them that no one fancies them for the Cup, and leave them to it. I say, "Get yourselves sorted out, I do enough talking at this club."

Schmeichel is delighted. I think he sees it as his chance to be manager for the day and is soon busy organising the corner kicks and such. I'm away for a cup of tea. Then I sit back to see the repercussions of one of my shortest ever team talks.

I'm not too disappointed. Spurs have a lot of injuries and some familiar faces missing, but their young players give their all, much as ours would in the same situation. Spurs' two youngsters up front find it difficult to find a cutting edge against defenders like Pallister and May. Roy Keane has another unbelievable game. He's simply got better and better since his return. Their 7,000 fans make for a good atmosphere, too.

We're the better team, but we still need to reshape at half-time. Young Scholes, playing in midfield, has been operating in an area he doesn't particularly enjoy, so I tell him not to be afraid to get into the opposition box; we have plenty of others who will defend. Sure enough, after a few minutes he's in the right place at the right time to open the scoring with a very well-taken goal. But it is our second, 10 minutes from the end, which sets everyone talking – and deservedly so. David Beckham's beautifully curled free kick leaves Ian Walker helpless.

Into the hat we go, and come out with another home tie against either Crewe or Wimbledon. I think it will be the Dons; I simply can't see Crewe being strong enough to handle them.

*FA Cup R5 / Old Trafford / Att: 52,495*
**Manchester United 2**
Schmeichel, G Neville, Irwin (McClair), May, Johnsen, Keane, Cantona, Scholes, Cole (Solskjaer), Beckham, Giggs
*Scorers: Scholes, Beckham*
**Tottenham Hotspur 0**
Walker, Carr, Nielsen, Howells, Calderwood, Edinburgh, Sinton, Allen, Austin, Campbell, Fenn

*Sunday 5 January*
Our Cup tie against Spurs, and the fact that we are down there next weekend in the League, reminds me of Alan Sugar's

views on players coming here from abroad. He's made no secret that has he is not particularly enamoured with them, after Jurgen Klinsmann left the club after only one season.

Sugar felt Spurs had been left in the lurch and, as they say, once bitten, once shy. The problem is that managers are forced to look overseas these days. Our home transfer market has become so inflated that players from abroad are better value. And obviously, after my summer signings of two Dutchmen, two Norwegians and a Czech Republic international, I don't completely share the fears of the Tottenham chairman.

But I do agree you have to do your homework very carefully to make sure you are getting not just a good player, but a character who will settle and adjust to the English game and the English way of life.

Bryan Robson has been very adventurous in bringing in players from Brazil, but it's given him a few headaches as well. Knowing Bryan, I'm sure he will make going for such skilful players pay off in the long run. But his experience underlines the need to think long and hard. It's a matter of balance: if you look at the Manchester United team, you'll see not only a combination of youth and experience, but a balance of home-grown players (many of them local) working alongside the foreign visitors.

Everyone at Old Trafford has benefitted from Eric Cantona. His contribution in that first Championship success was decisive, and he's been a great positive influence since then. Peter Schmeichel has been so successful on and off the field that one almost forgets he's a Dane.

I'm also very happy with the summer arrivals. Raimond Van Der Gouw hasn't had much chance to show his ability in the first team, but I assure you his goalkeeping in the reserves and in training has been sensational; I'd have no hesitation playing him if Peter was injured.

Ronny Johnsen has been a great success, especially considering this is his first season. He's already made an impressive number of senior appearances. As for Ole Solskjaer, he has been nothing less than a revelation, bearing in mind he'll get even better. Jordi Cruyff and Karel Poborsky are taking longer to adjust, but they perhaps peaked in the European Championships and we won't see the best of them again until next season. I'm certainly satisfied with them. They are quality young players who can only get better in time, unlike some of the better known stars who have come into our game from places like Italy. You can't beat the clock, and I wonder how long some of them will continue playing.

I have to build, not just for today but for the long term. I must admit I have a tinge of regret at rejecting Ruud Gullit when he became available. I'm afraid his age and record of injuries put me off. Perhaps I shouldn't have allowed myself to be sidetracked; in retrospect it might have been a mistake. No matter, I am quite happy with what we have as we head into 1997 and, I hope, more success.


*Monday 6 January*

At last a break, and it's very welcome after five games in 14 days. We have a clear week before we play at Spurs on Saturday, which fits in well with today's trip to London for the announcement of Howard Wilkinson as the FA's new Director of Coaching. I have been called to Lancaster Gate, this time for the right reasons. I'm pleased to support Howard, who I worked with on the committee of the League Managers' Association. Other committee members, including John Barnwell and Dave Bassett, are also there.

Howard was fantastic as our chairman. He gave our relatively new organisation the kind of stability and respect which at one stage I thought were impossible to achieve. He did more than anyone to put our association on a firm footing after other people had tried to build on shifting sands. I have long felt that the football authorities somehow regarded managers almost as an irrelevance because they're here one minute and gone the next, passing like ships in the night.

The position of chief executive at the League Manager's Association is more settled too. Frank Clark did the job part-time for a while. He was followed by Steve Coppell, Jim Smith and Gordon Milne. Now John Barnwell is at the helm. John has experienced the ups and downs of life in football, both as a player and manager, and I think he will help consolidate what Howard did so much to establish.

Glenn Hoddle and all his England staff were at Lancaster .Gate today to support the start of a new era for English football. Without wishing to get too political, I can see a light at the end of the tunnel after the long reign of Charles Hughes as Director of Coaching. It always felt to me as if Charles lived on this remote island to which there was no means of transport. You certainly didn't bump into him at matches, though Charles was a leading light in the game for 20 or 30 years and I'd have thought he'd have wanted to see what the standard was at the sharp end of the professional game.

It's a bit like a quote I read the other day claiming that Mark McGhee, the Wolves manager, had said that their game at Bolton was one they could afford to lose. In my book, the job of a manager is to win every match, and talking about losing is well nigh treason. A manager should be the eternal optimist; if I was a supporter, I would wonder about a boss who entertained the thought of defeat.

Mind you, some managers build a gallows for themselves. One manager I knew in Scotland said that such-and-such a player would never play in his team again because he wasn't a trier. Three weeks later the boy was back in the team, which left the fans entitled to ask why he was being played if he didn't try. The first step to the gallows had been laid!

Anyway, at the start of the FA meeting I felt the media were a bit edgy, but they mellowed after hearing Howard's outline of his plans and ideas. His appointment heralds a new beginning for English football. Now we've got someone we managers can go to with problems about youth policies and the like. Howard will certainly give them an opinion. My only advice to managers who consult him is to make sure they have plenty of time available. He can go on a bit.

On the journey back from London I weighed up our situation at Manchester United. I always take a pad with me on the train, and there are certainly plenty of thoughts winging round my head at the moment. We are coming to the stage of the season when we have to show our mettle and step up a gear if we're to win the League. We're not playing well enough yet. We're getting nearer, in that we're more consistent and defending properly again, but we need to produce more.

It will be a good run-in. The three or four teams I expected for the final chase are all there – except for my dark horses, Aston Villa, who have had too many draws lately. They drew 0-0 at our place on New Year's Day and it was obvious that their uppermost thought was to make sure they didn't lose. Their tactics should have been designed to win the game.

Liverpool and Newcastle are there in the leading group, and Arsenal have come through strongly, considering they had a succession of managers before the arrival of Arsene Wenger, who has got them playing their best football for a long time. I rate Chelsea the new dark horses. They have started winning at home and could be on a roll.

*Tuesday 7 January*

I'm looking forward to tonight's FA Youth Cup tie at Liverpool. They've been working hard at this level at Anfield for a couple of years now. In fact, I've been stung, because I believe they nicked three boys from under our noses after sponsoring a team in the Manchester area. That's bold for you. Imagine us trying to sponsor a club in Liverpool... we'd be run out of town. Anyway, their poaching has been noted, and serves as a little warning that other clubs have stepped up their youth activities. Which reminds us not to get complacent about our own youth set-up.

Liverpool beat us in the Youth Cup final last season. They have a few bright players I'm interested in seeing, especially a Welsh youngster called Michael Owen who we had for coaching from the age of 11 or 12. We wanted to sign him but we weren't prepared to meet his father's requirements, so he signed for Liverpool. You always have to be extremely careful when you are dealing with the future of young players. My policy is to tell parents they must trust us and assure them that if their boys make the grade, then we'll look after them appropriately and fairly.

As for the match itself, we win 2–1 but I'm disappointed in our players. They didn't do themselves justice. What I look for in a Manchester United player is his readiness to stand up to pressure, intimidation, provocation and bad breaks of fortune. I look for someone to take a game by the scruff of the neck and show the determination to change its course if things aren't going right, and those things were lacking. In the first half Liverpool were the superior team, first to every ball. Young Owen proved a handful for John Curtis, and that tells you he has a good chance. We rate John, who's a year and a half older, very highly.

We didn't become the better team until the last 20 minutes when we changed tactics and went to playing with two wide players, whereupon Liverpool tired because they had to chase the ball more. We also got a good break, winning a penalty soon after they'd scored with a penalty of their own.

Nonetheless, we have four, possibly five, players in this season's youth team who I expect to make the grade for Manchester United. The rest will certainly get careers in the game. Wes Brown, John Curtis and Mark Wilson all looked Manchester United players. Richard Wellens and Ryan Ford can do better, and all Alex Notman has to do is grow a bit!

## Back on course

We are through to the next round, but I don't think we have heard the last of Liverpool as a force at youth level. Old Trafford and Anfield have always been great rivals at League level; I can see it extending to the kids now.

# 6
# Keegan quits

*Wednesday 8 January*

This is a day I will remember for the rest of my life. It's the funeral of my old friend Jim Rodger, the Scottish sports writer, and I've not been looking forward to it.

The morning started badly when I overslept – perhaps because of our busy Christmas – and blew my chances of catching the plane to Scotland. I was due to fly with Bobby Charlton, so I had to call him at the airport to rearrange the trip. We agreed to drive up. We were talking about Jim when my mobile went.

"Have you heard?" asked my son Jason. "Kevin Keegan has resigned." My first reaction was disbelief, but when I switched on the radio, the news was confirmed after about a minute .

I imagine it's pretty difficult to put together a programme at short notice which does justice to such a shock event, but what I heard on the radio was utter drivel; a terrible effort. Throughout the day I listened to countless interviews with managers and supporters, all trying to explain why Kevin had turned away from football at a time when there was still so much to play for. One Newcastle caller on a phone-in even blamed me, as if I'd somehow been responsible for his team losing to Arsenal and Blackburn.

But what really angered me was that the issue of media pressure – and its effect on Kevin – wasn't addressed once.

Three years ago I offered Kevin some advice. He told me that he met the press every single day at the training ground, and I said he was off his head. Did he really believe he'd be able to think of something different to tell them every day? I advised him to put a stop to it immediately. I don't think he did.

To a football manager, pressure doesn't just mean producing a winning team and satisfying the fans. These days, it's a question of feeding a hungry media, too. The press, in my view, has become a monster, not least because of the growing ego of many of its writers. How many times nowadays do you see an article written by "the Sportswriter of the Year", or "Britain's number-one columnist"? This is the level of ego a manager has to satisfy, and I tell you, it's not easy. They know all the answers, right or wrong; they want exclusive stories and confidential background; they want their cards marked; they want gossip. And believe me, if they don't get it, you're in trouble.

I believe I should go into a press conference to tell the truth. Yet if I do, and if I'm critical, the media jump down my throat and accuse me of moaning or whingeing. I think many of them look for me to step out of line because I have never wined and dined the press. I have a great respect for a lot of journalists but I've never really socialised with them, or cultivated them and used them for my own ends like some managers do. The sad part is that, as time goes by, I instinctively try to protect myself – which means being bland and saying nothing that really means anything. Only the other day a writer, one of my closer associates in the media, reported my comments in a press conference as "grumbling". I was disappointed, because what I had tried to do was give an honest opinion.

I certainly don't get the press coverage I think I'm entitled to. I know the reporters have a job to do, but I no longer see it as part of my job to fulfill their interests. Kevin Keegan obviously looked at it differently, and they protected him, even loved him. He was the king of the media. But, in the long run, I don't think it helped him do his proper job. He made a rod for his own back and they caned him with it as they slowly but surely destroyed his peace of mind.

# Keegan quits

So was I myself responsible in any way for Kevin's resignation, as that Newcastle fan suggested? I went over the events which prompted Kevin's outburst last season, when he accused me of trying to wind up the Leeds players to have a real go at Newcastle. I'd like to put that matter straight. To start with, I didn't criticise either Newcastle or Kevin Keegan. In fact, when we beat them 1–0 at their place last year I phoned the Newcastle local paper to pass on my appreciation of their team and fans. I've always been impressed by the way their fans concentrate on their own team instead of goading the opposition. They never go in for chants like "If you hate Man United clap your hands", or the arm waving which signifies the Munich air crash. I admire them for that; I'm embarrassed to admit that our own fans tend to taunt rivals. I've taken them to task about it once or twice in my match programme notes, pleading with them to concentrate on their own team rather then get involved in vendettas with visitors. To their great credit, Newcastle fans are not like that. I went out of my way to pay tribute to them after our victory in March, which I sensed was a very significant step towards us winning the Championship.

Kevin ignored all this when he had his go at me. It was as if I was trying to undermine him. In fact, I think I had more cause for complaint at that time than he did. It seemed like every man and his dog was against Manchester United winning the League again. The papers dug out as many ex-pat Geordies as they could find to write pieces saying how much they hoped Newcastle would take the title. If Kevin was annoyed with me, how did he think I felt, hearing time and time again how much people wanted Newcastle to pip us at the post?

At times, trying to win the League is a bit like trying to win a war, and nobody ever won a war without tactics. I started to analyse one or two of hurdles facing us, and one of them was Leeds and their poor run of results. The Leeds players were no longer playing for their manager, which I thought disgraceful.

The day before we played Leeds at Old Trafford, David Walker of the Daily Mail rang and asked me if I would say something in support of Howard. I refused to speak before the match because it could have come over as patronising, but I agreed to talk afterwards. In the event we won 1–0, but Leeds played out of their skins, despite being down to 10 men. Their performance was in complete contrast to their form at the time. In my view, their players knew their fans would never forgive them if they died with their boots on against Manchester United.

As we came off at the end, I told Howard I thought it was diabolical the way his players were treating him, and I asked if he minded me having a pop about it in the press. He replied that if I thought the cap fitted, I should wear it. So I did. I addressed the question of how Leeds intended to play in their vital next few games not because I wanted them to stand up to Newcastle in particular, but because I was worried for Howard. I wanted them to carry on playing with the commitment and passion they had shown against us. That way they might have given Howard a chance of survival.

That was all I had in mind. But Kevin took it completely the wrong way ... and they say I'm paranoid!

I noticed that after Howard had been sacked, Gary McAllister, who was Leeds captain at that time, admitted the players had let their manager down. His concern came a little late in the day.

As I heard the news of his retirement, I felt sorry for Kevin. He's a man who I believe is his own worst enemy, but also the sort who always had to get his own way. Maybe it was because he'd always known success. Once he'd left Scunthorpe it was silver lining all the way, both as player and manager. His career flew on gossamer wings.

He also gave me the impression that if he didn't get his own way, he was liable to pick up his ball and go home. Let me quickly add that he is such a bubbly and likeable character that one can't help but admire him. The amount of his time he was prepared to give to others was selfless, and that was reflected in the way he agreed to see the press every day. That's Kevin: a generous man who perhaps gave too much in the wrong places.

When I was manager of Aberdeen, we ran a tournament in Pittodrie and I invited clubs to send representatives up to help publicise it. Manchester United sent Mick Brown, West Ham sent Tony Parkes, and Kevin Keegan came from Southampton. On that particular day I had a lot of schoolboys in for coaching and thought I'd surprise them by asking Kevin to spend a few minutes with them at lunchtime. I asked Kevin if he would do me the favour, and he duly came along. He was absolutely fantastic. He spoke to all the kids, asked their names, their clubs, their positions and if they practised. It was the best public relations exercise I ever had at Aberdeen.

You could see then what kind of man he was; a natural born giver of his time and energy. He is an emotional man, too, and his outburst against me was pure emotion. I think it was unfair but, by that time, the press had probably created demons in his head, which is sad.

I worried about our relationship after that. We teamed up for television work for the European Championship during the summer, and that went smoothly enough. But before the FA Charity Shield in August he came up and told me he had decided to ask his assistant, Terry McDermott, to lead out the Newcastle team in his place. I couldn't help wondering if he intended it as a snub. I simply told him that I enjoyed taking my team out at Wembley and that I thought he deserved to lead his players out, too. I wonder if he now regrets missing the opportunity for, as things turned out, it was his last chance. I just can't see him coming back into football management.

With hindsight, it's not surprising he walked out. I saw the change in him this season – no doubt caused by the disappointment of last year – and I didn't enjoy watching him starting to show the strain. Once he has recovered, I hope he will do two things. Firstly, that he remembers I told him that he shouldn't have allowed the media to become his master; secondly, that he analyse what I actually said at the time of the Leeds affair. Then he will realise that I never criticised Kevin Keegan, his club or his supporters. I hope he finds it within himself to accept that I have nothing but the greatest respect for him.

All this went through my head as I chatted to Sir Bobby on our way to Jim Rodger's funeral. Jim was one of the most influential and powerful sports journalists in Britain. I first met him when I was only 15 and playing for Glasgow Boys against Edinburgh, and he went on to play a key role right through my career. We all knew him as "Scoop". He was a newspaperman, but so deeply involved in football that he negotiated my transfer to Rangers. It was Jim who brought the manager, Scott Symon, from Ibrox to my house one Saturday lunchtime. Later, he organised my move to Aberdeen as the club's manager – and I was just the tip of the iceberg.

Gigi Peronace, the agent who masterminded Italy's first raids on the English market, used him as his main contact, so he was heavily involved in the transfers of Denis Law and Joe Baker to Torino. He was a master of networking before the word had even been invented. Former Spurs manager Bill Nicholson was a close friend, and Jim had a hand in the transfers of Dave Mackay and Bill Brown from Scotland to Spurs. In fact, it would probably be quicker to list the Scottish transfers in which he was not involved.

He might have played the role of an agent, but he never took a penny for his trouble. For example, after he'd overseen Ian Ure's transfer from Dundee to Arsenal, a grateful Ian asked how much he owed. "Nothing, son," Jim said. "Just tell your mammy and daddy how proud you are to be joining the famous Arsenal."

He knew everything that was going on in the game, but he kept it all to himself. I shall miss his Sunday morning phone calls and his invariable greeting: "How's things, son?" You would somehow find yourself telling him everything, partly because you knew he probably knew anyway, but mostly because he was the soul of discretion. If you asked him what was happening with such-and-such a transfer, he would say, "I'm not sure, son." As far as he was concerned, it was a matter of trust. Of course, he eventually used all his information for a story in his newspaper, but only at the right time – after the deal had been done, for instance.

My abiding memory of him was from 1984 when, as manager of Aberdeen, I got an invitation to dinner at a big function at Holyrood Palace in Edinburgh for the Queen's visit to Scotland. We were playing a midweek game some weeks beforehand when Jim came into what he used to call "our office". I told him I wouldn't be able to go because I had booked a cruise on the Canberra with the family and couldn't afford to waste a £10,000 holiday. He immediately asked for my ports of call. A week later, he was back to tell me that Lord King, the chief of British Airways, would send his private jet to fly me from Gibraltar to Edinburgh for the dinner, and then back out again to rejoin the ship in Tel Aviv. Jim always had contacts in high places – Sir William Armstrong, the former Treasury chief, was his cousin. I imagine he badgered Lord King into this amazing bit of generosity.

Two weeks later, Jim was in Aberdeen again for our European semi final against Porto with bad news. Israeli security would not allow anyone to board a ship in Tel Aviv. All I could do was ask Jim to convey my thanks to Lord King.

"We must let Her Majesty know," Jim declared. Before I knew what he was doing he was on the phone to Diane Morgan, the Queen's secretary, at Buckingham Palace. I was so embarrassed as Jim announced: "Hello hen, I'm phoning to ask you to let Her Majesty know Alex won't be able to come to dinner with her in Edinburgh.'

You can imagine the reply ... "Alex who? Oh well, I'll let her know anyway."

A few days later I got a letter, signed by the Queen, saying how sorry she was that I wouldn't be able to make it. Such was the influence of Jim Rodger!

It's a funny thing about life. As you get older and lose friends and people you've known a long time, you start to evaluate the people who have made a mark on you, start to recognise who the truly great people were. I went through a period like that, starting with the death of my father, then Sir Matt Busby, and now Jim Rodger, a unique man who touched many lives for the good. The turn-out at his funeral demonstrated the respect he built up over decades. Sir David McNee, the police chief in Glasgow who became the Metropolitan Commissioner at Scotland Yard, gave the address. I told David afterwards that the last line of his tribute really melted me. He simply said Jim Rodger was "a truly great Scot".

I had to turn down an invitation from Jimmy Steele, the old Scottish masseur I sometimes invite to our training ground, because I had to call on Jim's wife, Cathy. Bobby and I still had to drive back to England to get to Wimbledon's Cup tie at Bolton. It was with great regret, too, because we hadn't eaten all day and I would have loved a bowl of Margaret's mince and tatties with Jimmy. On the way out of Glasgow I bought a local paper and read that Peggy Herbiston, the Labour MP from Shotts, had died. Ironic that one of Jim's heroes should have gone just the day before.

The match at Burnden Park was very competitive. Wimbledon were aggressive and positive, qualities well matched by Bolton. But it had been a long, emotional day and I was too drained to enjoy it.

*Thursday 9 January*

This afternoon's board meeting is to plan for next season, and specifically for Europe. We have to be prepared. It's no use waiting until the competition is upon us and then having to rush to beat the transfer deadlines. I've got a fine playing staff, but if we are going to progress we have to beat the best Italian teams. To compete with the likes of Juventus we need maybe two more top players.

So I've got my eye on three players, two of them defenders, one a striker. However, I think I can predict the board's reaction. The salaries, if not the transfer fees, are going to be astronomical. One of the problems nowadays is that all the salaries quoted by agents are what they want net. There is no mention of income tax; all they are concerned about is the cash their player gets clear, and I just don't know how they expect us to arrange it. It's not how we do things in this country.

I know I can be a dreamer and an optimist, but I have two remaining ambitions for Manchester United. One is to win the Champions' Cup; the other is to play in an 80,000-seat stadium. Those two things would put us three or four steps ahead of everyone else. It would be like climbing Everest and looking down on the rest of the world, a really powerful feeling. Nobody would be able to match our power base for revenue and resources.

There is no question in my mind that we could fill an 80,000 all-seater stadium – provided, of course, that we are competing at the very top. Which brings me back to the need for another couple of world-class players. The search goes on.

This evening I'm at a premiere of *Evita* at Arena Cinemas. A lot of the players are there too, and the proceeds are going to charities. It's a pleasant, relaxing night watching a marvellous movie. Madonna was tremendous.


*Friday 10 January*
You would think that a quiet night at the cinema would pass unnoticed, but David Beckham is in the headlines again. They photographed him watching the film wearing glasses, which explains some of the scoring chances he has missed! Of course,

they're asking questions in the dressing room. His latest girl-friend wears specs, and someone unkindly wonders if David was posing and trying to portray himself as such a good player, he doesn't even need to see the goal. I don't mind him getting ribbed. With all the publicity he is getting, it will help keep his feet on the ground – and that's before I rip into him!

Anyway, the general consensus is that we all enjoyed *Evita*. Until, that is, Gary Neville suddenly declares, "It's the worst film I've ever seen." I ask him how he could possibly come to that conclusion after the rubbish videos he watches on the team bus, but he's adamant. I tell him I must have a word with Glenn Hoddle and explain that one of his international players is no longer rational.

I make time to see Alan Austin today. He's done a fine job with the club's Development Association, but ticket sales are under pressure these days, not just from the national lottery but from sweepstakes run by the bookmakers. Alan has come up with ideas which involve the players helping to boost the fund-raising. He is so dedicated, he needs all the backing he can get.

I also go to the holiday exhibition at G-Mex with Gary Pallister. The club has a stall there and we spend a couple of hours signing autographs and talking to visitors.

All these distractions after such an emotional week make it hard for me to focus on our game at Tottenham in two days' time. We are without Denis Irwin and Phil Neville, so I decide to risk bringing Pallister back, but to help him by playing with three centre backs. Somehow we squeeze in a little practice match. Ryan Giggs will play wing back; he's a good defender and great tackler. I'd prefer to have him in the last third of the field, but with the players available, this is the best of the options open to me.

I remind the players that it will be a difficult game after beating Spurs in the FA Cup. They must watch their discipline – there were one or two personal confrontations at Old Trafford. They must not get sucked into any feuds.

# Keegan quits

*Saturday 11 January*

I watch a little of the A-team match at The Cliff before the first team have a short training session. Then we travel to our hotel just outside London. I very rarely leave the team the night before a game, but I make an exception tonight to have a meal with David Gibson, head of Sony Europe. He tells me that Kevin Keegan has flown to Paris on his way to Miami. I shall keep that news to myself. Everyone is hunting Kevin, but he deserves his privacy at a time like this.

*Sunday 12 January*

Lots of people said they enjoyed the game at White Hart Lane because it was end-to-end stuff, but I was disappointed. Technically it was not as good as I had expected, and for me it dragged. In the first half we looked like a jigsaw with all the pieces hopelessly mixed up. We were all over the place, and our three centre backs were finding it difficult to come to terms with their roles. Tottenham hit our bar twice in the space of a few seconds, but we scored with our first concerted attack of the match: Scholes, Neville, Keane, Cantona, and into Solskjaer for a splendid goal in keeping with the free-flowing football. Giggs should have made it 2–0 and we paid for his miss by conceding a goal right on half time. Roy Keane had left his man: a lapse of concentration, but he knew it.

I never thought we would lose the game, but I still had to figure out the best way of winning it. I had the option of bringing on either Andy Cole or Karel Poborsky, and plumped for the winger with a return to a normal back four. It worked. Karel won the ball off David Howells and fed Ronny Johnsen, who played in David Beckham to score one of the fantastic long-distance goals that are becoming his hallmark. Spurs backed off David – and you do that at your peril. It won the game for us.

In the evening, David Beckham and I are among the guests

at the Sky television awards. On the way to the studios, David tells me that he was headbutted during the game. It had apparently been caught on camera, but wasn't shown. I wonder if there would have been similar discretion if it'd been a United player offending? If it had been Cantona, for instance, it would have been tin hats all round and head for a bomb-proof shelter.

That, however, turned out to be the least of my concerns. Throughout the night I had to face a barrage of kids screaming abuse at Manchester United. Every time we were mentioned there were boos and cries of "wankers". Perhaps the sound technicians were able to doctor the transmission so that people watching at home were not aware of it, but for those of us there it was insulting and unnecessary. All kinds of show business stars, along with club chairmen, managers and players were at the awards, so why did they need a public, especially the rabble they let in? In fairness, they did the actual programme extremely well. But if they think I shall be there next year they have another thing coming. I just had to sit tight-lipped and console myself with the thought that it would be one experience I will not repeat.

The other thing that rankled was the decision to give Matt Le Tissier the Goal of the Year award ahead of David Beckham. Pelé's attempt to score from the halfway line has been shown regularly on television for the past 25 years; now Beckham comes along and does it ... and still doesn't get the award, despite Anna Walker describing it at the time as the Goal of the Decade. But I've got to say that no one was more embarrassed than Matt himself, who sought out David afterwards to apologise. He had no need to do that, because there's no denying the quality of Le Tissier's goals – although he certainly hasn't been the only one to chip Peter Schmeichel!

Some managers were kind enough to say that I was ignored as well and that I should have been Manager of the Year in view of our League and FA Cup double, but missing out doesn't worry me. I voted for Joe Kinnear myself, and was the first to congratulate him afterwards. I honestly believe Joe's achievements with Wimbledon deserve every bit of recognition that comes his way. There were no sour grapes from me. I thought it was nice that all his players, chairman and staff were there; it was indicative of the club spirit at Wimbledon. They might not have their own ground, but they certainly have their own special quality, and that's even more important.

*Premiership / White Hart Lane / Att: 33,026*

**Tottenham Hotspur 1**
Walker, Edinburgh, Howells, Calderwood, Campbell, Carr (Fox), Sinton, Allen, Vega (Austin), Wilson, Iversen
*Scorer: Allen*

**Manchester United 2**
Schmeichel, G Neville, May, Pallister, Johnsen (Casper), Scholes (Poborsky), Cantona, Beckham, Keane, Solskjaer (Cole), Giggs
*Scorers: Solskjaer, Beckham*

## Monday 13 January

I read the reports of yesterday's match and found myself in the press conference described as "doleful" and "unrelenting". What's that got to do with the match? I really do wonder about the point of meeting the media after a game if all they're interested in is a character assassination of the manager. How do they want me to be? Sure, I've just won a game, but it'd be totally tactless to come in all smiles. The last thing I want to do is gloat over another manager's misfortune. A post-match press conference might suit the reporters, but we're coming to the stage where it is of no benefit to us managers. So why do we accept it? And why can't they just accept me for the way I am, rather than constantly analysing my manner and temperament?

## Tuesday 14 January

The transfer deadline is upon us, so we make a second inquiry about Henning Berg, the Blackburn Rovers defender. The chairman has already spoken to Robert Coar, his opposite number at Ewood Park, and got the same kind of reply they gave us about Alan Shearer.

The fitness of our central defenders is still giving me concern, and Berg would have been an excellent signing. Apparently he's a United fan who'd have loved the opportunity to join us. I haven't totally lost interest, but the lack of encouragement from Blackburn forces me to turn my attentions to Roberto Rios, Real Betis' Spanish defender. I've been to watch him already and I thought he was excellent. He's young, tall and pacey. Like many Continental players, he has a clause in his contract stating that he can move on if the bid reaches a certain figure. The only snag, again, is that the price on his head is £10 million, a prohibitive fee for a centre half. However, I'll definitely keep an eye on the situation because I have a feeling that he might eventually go for a lot less. The Real Betis president is wealthy, but he recently bought Alfonso from Real Madrid for £6.5 million plus other players from Holland and Croatia, so he might need to recoup some cash.

I give an interview to Paul Hince of the Manchester Evening News after much badgering. He wants a half-term report on the season so far, but I don't feel our local paper does us any favours these days so I'm reluctant to do them any in return. I'm still outraged at the editor conducting a phone-in asking if I should be sacked after I decided to make a few changes to the playing staff a couple of seasons ago; he thought he'd add a little more fuel to the controversy. After what we'd achieved, surely I was entitled to expect a little more faith in my judgment, especially from people I've always worked closely with?

I relax later, though, when I go to the Stretford Arndale to support the Dr Banardo charity. There are several hundred people waiting for autographs and photographs. I find that meeting ordinary people, many of them faithful supporters, can be a release. Some people in the public eye escape from stress by wrapping themselves in a cocoon – Mark Hughes, for example, was idolised at Manchester United but didn't enjoy it. He was always last into the training ground and first away back to his castle where he no doubt drew up the drawbridge. But I can be quite comfortable at a charity bash, and I feel I'm helping a good cause.

*Wednesday 15 January*

The match-fixing allegations involving Bruce Grobbelaar, John Fashanu, Hans Segers and a Far East betting syndicate man have finally come to court. One of the fixtures being discussed is our 3–3 draw at Anfield three years ago. It was an amazing match; we were three goals up in 24 minutes, but by half time Nigel Clough had clawed it back to 3–2, then Neil Ruddock got an equaliser 10 minutes from the end. The idea of the match being fixed never crossed my mind, but I do remember saying that Grobbelaar looked like he was struggling when Ryan Giggs chipped him. Although, to be fair, it was a good chip.

We launched our new blue strip today with the usual squad photograph. Umbro have done a good job, but I'm very conscious that only last week the FA came under fire for bringing out a new England kit so soon after Christmas. I must admit I always get the heeby-jeebies when we bring out fresh gear. The last thing I would want people to feel is that we were exploiting children. But provided they know in advance there's a new strip coming out, we shouldn't feel guilty; I was always buying my boys a new strip at Christmas when they were young. Most youngsters get great wear out of their shirts. Some never have them off their backs in holiday time and even use them as pyjamas.

Every team has always had three versions; in our case a first choice of red, then blue for playing the likes of Arsenal or Southampton, and white for matches against the claret and blue of, say, Aston Villa and West Ham. But it's a good idea to put a sell-by date on each garment so that fans know exactly when a replacement is due. The FA have said they will introduce the rule for the England strip, and I'm sure Manchester United will examine this possibility for our kit, too.

*Thursday 16 January*

Now I know why I had my doubts about that Evening News interview. It was supposed to be a review of the first half of our season, and in the course of the conversation I mentioned that I hoped I still wouldn't be doing the more menial tasks, like putting the cones out, in three years' time. So imagine my surprise when I read that I have set my retirement date and intend to bow out at the age of 58 for the new millennium. What's more, it was splashed all over the back page, taken out of context and turned into "news".

The truth is that you can't possibly set a time to leave a job like this one, because nobody can predict what will happen in three years' time (which is when my present contract is due to run out). Maybe I will have had enough of Manchester United, perhaps Manchester United will have had enough of me ... who knows?

It's just as possible, though, that I will be just as ambitious and hungry for success as I am now. My health and family would obviously come into the equation. Maybe I'll be happy and grateful just to be able to get out of bed in the morning. But I could do without the speculation or people setting me a time limit. I now have supporters coming to the training ground pleading with me not to leave. We are at a very exciting stage of the season and frankly, retirement is the last thing on my mind – even if certain scribes would have you believe that my nerves should be jangling at the prospect of the competition, now that Kenny Dalglish is back in football as the manager of Newcastle. Now I respect Dalglish immensely, but I can't believe such piffle! How gullible do they think their readers are? Even in England they are not that daft! Kenny showed his qualities when he took over from Joe Fagan as manager of

Liverpool, and demonstrated he could be just as successful bringing in a club from the cold when he led Blackburn to the Championship. But how does all that measure up to the success we have had at Old Trafford in the last six years? Why should we suddenly become nervous? Why should I start to tremble?

In any case, a manager's role is limited. He can buy players, pick the team and decide the tactics. But come the run-in, the final burst for a trophy, it's all about the players and their ability to produce under pressure. The manager can talk himself blue in the face, but if his players aren't up to it, if they haven't got the bottle, there's little he can do. I am under no illusions about a manager's influence, and I don't expect Kenny Dalglish considers himself a magician either.

But of course it's good media fodder to regurgitate the supposed personal rivalry between us. Sorry to disappoint, but there's little foundation for it. Kenny asked me to write a foreword for the book he published recently and I was pleased to oblige. When he was out of football, he phoned me quite a few times. I certainly sympathised with the way his position at Blackburn was terminated – by letter, with a request for his club car to be returned.

Kenny's final year at Ewood Park was always going to be awkward after he handed over the management reins to Ray Harford and became director of football. I think he found it difficult to take a back seat, and one wonders whether Harford really wanted him there in the background. It was reminiscent of the time Sir Matt Busby "moved upstairs" when he retired from the front line at Old Trafford, and his successors found themselves not really knowing how to handle things. Silly really, because they should have drawn on his experience to help them.

When things started to go wrong at Blackburn, Kenny got a lot of criticism. People said he spent too much time on the golf course. But if he felt he wasn't wanted around, what else could he do but distance himself? I suppose the criticism shouldn't surprise me because the media love building people up to knock them down again. Kevin Keegan is the victim now: once hailed as the great Messiah, they're chipping away at him, saying he lacked defensive knowledge, criticising his gung-ho approach. I even read one critic suggesting that half the dressing room wanted rid of him anyway. Were they saying that kind of thing at the time? Of course they weren't. This is the manager who befriended the media – and they fed off him. Now they've turned on him, the same people I'm sure Kevin looked upon as his friends.

The cycle of media emotion at Newcastle is incredible. First it was all doom and despair with the Keegan resignation, now they're trying to rubbish him as the build-up for Dalglish gets underway. Everyone predicts Kenny will cultivate a more defensive, pragmatic approach at St James' Park, but I think Blackburn's style was more Harford than Dalglish. I associate Dalglish with the Liverpool method: good possession, hard work and class players (witness his cultivation of players like John Barnes and Peter Beardsley). Certainly a lot of the pundits now believe Newcastle are certain to win the League, but I don't think it will be quite as easy as that. If Kenny makes them more defensive, they won't win as many games as they did. They may lose fewer goals and fewer games, but that isn't necessarily a recipe for winning Championships.

In any case, no one can change things overnight. The rebuilding could take two or three years of trying to retain the good elements while introducing a more defensive awareness. Kevin realised he needed to do something in this respect, which is why he signed David Batty. Kenny is wise enough to have analysed everything – and he certainly won't be taken in by all the hype.

Meanwhile, theories as to why Kevin packed it in are still flying around. They range from his relationship with Sir John Hall, his chairman and benefactor, to the club's proposed flotation, and of course the saga of missing out on last season's

Championship followed by this season's disappointing results. But we won't really know until Kevin himself chooses to tell us. Perhaps he simply felt it was time to go.

*Friday 17 January*

We organise a game this morning to test David Beckham's ankle. It will also maintain our momentum as we prepare for the weekend's fixture against struggling Coventry. It's vitally important to keep a winning run going.

At Coventry we're met by the usual barrage of autograph hunters. It's amazing how the dedicated hunters find out which hotel you're going to use, even when you change the venue. Actually, the ones we see regularly, the ones who always come laden with sheaves of photographs for the players to sign, are beginning to bug me. They just sit in the hotel all day and bring 30 or 40 pictures for signing; I'm convinced they must be selling them. When we were last in Sheffield I'm afraid I let rip. I've no objection to the kids who often come to the hotel with their parents – we all grow up with heroes and I like the players to contribute to that tradition. But grown men making a business out of signatures is a different ball game altogether, and it's irritating. They couldn't possibly be collecting autographed photographs for a personal collection because they wouldn't have room for all the ones we've given them. Somehow or other, I'm going to put a stop to it.

*Saturday 18 January*

For the first time this season, I feel as if we are really up to winning the League. The resilience and determination of the side shone through against Coventry; Roy Keane is fitter now, and he and

Paul Scholes were magnificent. Scholes seems to have overcome his chest problems. He suffered from some kind of asthma last season, so we sent him to a specialist during the summer and he was prescribed an inhaler which he uses before games and at half-time if necessary. He used to tire in the last 15 minutes of a match, which worried us, but he's doing really well now. He's had to be patient, but even when he's been out of the team he was never out of my plans. He's a grand little player.

Coventry ran themselves into the ground – we always seem to bring the best out of the opposition. Darren Huckerby, for instance, was on a high, and should have had a penalty, but penalties don't seem to be on referee Steve Dunn's agenda at the moment. Our control was probably too pedantic, but in the second half we stepped up the tempo and the sheer intensity of our football had Coventry struggling.

Ryan Giggs scored – worth mentioning because it was with his right foot – and Solskjaer got the other for what was, in the end, a very comfortable 2–0 win. It convinced me that, when the end of the season comes around, we'll be knocking on the title door again.

It was interesting to see Gordon Strachan in his role as manager. As one of my players, first at Aberdeen and then at United, he never gave any indication that he would want to stay in the game. But as his playing career nears its end, he's obviously realised how much he will miss being involved in football. It happens to a lot of successful players. Gordon is following stars like Kenny Dalglish, Ray Wilkins, Bryan Robson, Trevor Francis and Glenn Hoddle in making the move into top management lacking only experience.

It's a rocky road, and I just hope that Gordon will avail himself of the vast experience of Ron Atkinson. He should never be too proud to ask for advice; he's jumped into management at the deep end without the having learnt the ropes at a lower level. When you come into the job like that, you need either a very good chairman or plenty of money – and preferably both.

# Keegan quits

*Premiership / Highfield Road / Att: 23,085*
**Coventry City 0**
Ogrizovic, Shaw, Williams, Richardson, Jess (Hall), Whelan, McAllister, Salako, Telfer, Borrows, Huckerby
**Manchester United 2**
Schmeichel, G Neville, Irwin, Pallister, Johnsen (Casper), Keane, Cantona, Poborsky, Scholes, Solskjaer, Giggs
*Scorers: Giggs, Solskjaer*


## *Sunday 19 January*

A relaxing Sunday for a change, though my intended long lie-in was interrupted by my two granddaughters climbing into bed to help me read the papers. I enjoyed my day until I watched Everton play Arsenal on television and was infuriated by the inadequacies of the linesmen.

Calling them referees' assistants doesn't appear to have made them any more aware of players running from on-side positions. Nick Barmby made a great run and scored with a tremendous finish, but was flagged offside. The number of times this happened was embarrassing, and I could imagine Joe Royle jumping up and down in rage. It's not funny when results are going against you and the pressure's on. The fans, too, are entitled to see as many goals as the rules allow, yet there is still this tendency to flag offside regardless of where an attacker has run from.

Arsenal impressed me. I noticed an improvement in their passing ability and their third man runs. The players seem to be enjoying the system Arsene Wenger has introduced, which is important. They weren't among the four teams I originally thought would be Championship contenders, but they are making me change my mind.


## *Monday 20 January*

We have an important staff meeting this morning to decide the immediate futures of 24 of our boys. These are last year's schoolboys who have been coming for coaching, and we have to choose which ones we take on to our junior staff as YTS boys for full-time training. It's invariably a long debate which involves us listening carefully to the opinions of people like Paul McGuinness, our youth development officer, who has an insight into the background, family and character of the boys. It's not just ability with a football that counts.

I recall the day we were making a decision on Mark Tinkler, a Middlesbrough lad who's now doing well at Leeds. Mark had a disappointing trial match here, after which our Middlesbrough scout Joe Brunskill (who's sadly now dead) played his part in reminding me that you must always listen to your staff.

"If you would just give me a minute of your time, Mr Ferguson," Joe said in his usual way, "I'd like you to know that I would put my life on this boy. He's going to be a good player and it would be unwise to drop our interest in him." Sure enough, Mark gave an outstanding performance in the next practice match. Though he ultimately chose to join Leeds, as was his privilege, he's lived up to Joe's judgment.

Brian Kidd is in Madrid on one of his missions studying coaching methods abroad, which means I had to take training. The meeting delayed me and the waiting first-team squad players were not happy bunnies. I immediately asked Eric Cantona to take the warm-up, so at least I cheered him up.

*Tuesday 21 January*

Training was difficult because the pitch was crisp with frost. Gary Pallister in particular found it a problem with his back injury. But we got through it, and after they had showered and dressed the players went across to our indoor arena to meet the handicapped children who we invite to the ground once a year for a special day out.

There were about a hundred kids there and the players were marvellous with them, showing lots of patience as they gave autographs and had their photographs taken with the kids. They really entered into the spirit of the occasion and the visitors seemed to get a lot out of it. We get a lot of requests for visits from young disabled people and find that if we concentrate them into one day, we can do it properly and make sure there is plenty of time for everyone.

I prepare my manager's piece for the weekend match programme. I want to address the controversial habit of fans who stand up in their seats for long periods. This irritates lots of the other fans, so I feel I must make my position clear. It's not an issue which will go away in a hurry.

Sure, the battle cry which goes round the stadium impresses me. In fact, when that chant of "Stand up for the Champions" rings out, the hair on the back of my neck curls. However, it's being taken too literally. Standing up at exciting moments like the scoring of a goal is one thing, but standing throughout a game is quite a different thing altogether.

One problems is that not everyone is able to stand for 90 minutes: the elderly, the disabled, and of course those who are just not tall enough to see if the people in front are on their feet. We all know the history of all-seater grounds, and I think we all understand that the reason they were introduced was to achieve better safety after the tragedy of Hillsborough.

There might be a case at some stage in the future for reintroducing small but safe standing areas for those fans who still feel uncomfortable sitting down throughout a game. What concerns me now are complaints about people who habitually ignore perfectly good seats to stand up for the entire game. I'm sure there's an element of defiance here, but it's clear that the stand-up brigade are making life miserable for a section of our fans.

I want as much vocal support and encouragement as possible – the effect was obvious in the Juventus match, when the crowd helped us all they could. So I'll appeal for everyone to sing, shout and cheer ... but to do it sitting down.

*Wednesday 22 January*

I had planned to watch Stockport County's FA Cup tie against Southampton at Edgeley Park tonight, particularly since we play Southampton in 10 days' time. We applied for a directors' box ticket last week, but I found out today that we haven't got one. Now I don't want to be a prima donna, but it's impossible for me to watch a match sitting in the stands. I know I'll have to spend more time signing autographs than watching the game, and there may well be someone nearby who doesn't like Manchester United – yes, it does happen!

I'm a bit miffed, especially because we loaned Ben Thornley to Stockport for two months. I'm even more disturbed when Bobby Campbell brings a couple of Portuguese agents along to Old Trafford to meet me and they have to leave soon afterwards to get to Edgeley Park, where they have tickets for the directors' box. It's a bit worrying when agents can get tickets at the expense of a local manager, and tells you something about the way agents have an increasing influence over our game.

So instead of going to Edgeley Park, I travel to Tranmere to watch our reserves in action. It's an awful game, which does little for my regard for agents. In fact, it's so bad that I abandon it at half time in favour of going home to catch the second half of Stockport's game on the television. They really played well in what was a tremendously exciting game.

*Thursday 23 January*

Kiddo is back from his coaching trip in Spain, and we are worrying about whether Pallister will overcome his hamstring strain to be fit for our Cup tie against Wimbledon at Old Trafford in two days' time. It'll be a testing match against a team enjoying their best ever spell in the League: they're currently fifth, with three games in hand on the leaders. They are also in the semi finals of the Coca-Cola Cup, and play us in the fourth round of the FA Cup. They have a lot on their plate, but they're handling it well.

However, the last time I said something complimentary about Wimbledon, Joe Kinnear accused me of trying to soften them up with kind words. I seem to have acquired a reputation for psychological warfare these days – shades of Kevin Keegan's outburst – but it isn't kidology. I honestly admire and respect what Wimbledon have achieved. They refer to themselves as the Crazy Gang, but they don't seem crazy to me. We are in for a pounding Cup tie.

*Friday 24 January*

I'll leave my final decision on Pally's fitness until tomorrow, but in the meantime I must have an alternative plan of action. So we practise for 20 minutes with a back five in which Roy Keane plays as a central defender. In the absence of Pallister, this should give some purpose and resolve in defence. I have already told Chris Casper he can expect to start after coming on in the last two games as a substitute. I also bring young Michael Clegg into the picture. He's a local boy who did well at Middlesbrough and in the Coca-Cola Cup earlier in the season. He has worked hard at his game, he's very determined, and I'm quite confident that he'll do well playing as a wing back on the right flank. Denis Irwin has a similar role on the left.

I know a lot of managers would gamble with Pally for a Cup tie on the grounds that you only get one chance in a knock-out competition, but I take a different view. Any side I put out for a Cup tie will be up for it, so the personnel doesn't worry me. I'm more concerned that Pallister be fit for the League game with Wimbledon the following Wednesday. I'll have to depend on our Cup tradition to see us through if Pally doesn't make it.

*Saturday 25 January*

As expected, Pallister's hamstring is tightish, so I don't risk

him. That means we are without a complete back four –
Pallister, Johnsen, May and Phil Neville. Also as I expected, it's
a hard game. With no score a quarter of an hour from the end,
I go gung-ho and bring on our two strikers, Andy Cole and Ole
Solskjaer, and push Roy Keane back into midfield.

It's a gamble, but it comes within an inch of paying off when
Scholes heads in a cross from Cantona with just a minute of
normal time remaining. I think we're home and dry but
Wimbledon are one of those teams who never say die. They
grab an injury-time equaliser through Robbie Earle.

If a couple of our players had got back to reorganise themselves instead of wasting time arguing with the referee about
the free kick which led to the goal, perhaps we'd have made it.
I thought we might have had a penalty when Karel Poborsky
was brought down by the goalkeeper but I can't begrudge
Wimbledon their replay, because they played their part in a very
entertaining match. They came to play an open game and
matched us strike for strike.

*FA Cup R4 / Old Trafford / Att: 53,342*

**Manchester United 1**
Schmeichel, G Neville, Irwin, Clegg, Poborsky (Solskjaer), Casper, Cantona,
McClair (Cole), Keane, Scholes, Giggs
*Scorer: Scholes*

**Wimbledon 1**
Sullivan, Cunningham, Kimble, Jones, Blackwell, Perry, Leonhardsen, Earle,
Ekoku (Holdsworth), Ardley (Jupp), Gayle
*Scorer: Earle*

*Sunday 26 January*

For the third time this season, we play the same side in the
League that we faced in the Cup in our last game. I couldn't
begin to calculate the odds of that happening. It worked that
way with Leicester in the Coca-Cola Cup, then Spurs after the
FA Cup third round, and here we are facing Wimbledon at Old
Trafford again this coming Wednesday. We will also face the
Dons at Selhurst Park in a Cup replay. I can live with that

because Wimbledon are men, and I don't mind playing against men, however much of a threat they may pose.

Incidentally, I'm told that there wasn't so much persistent standing up by supporters at Old Trafford yesterday. Perhaps they read my programme notes after all.

# 7
# Wright v Schmeichel

We must start making it clear that we're not a one-man team. Eric Cantona was booked against Wimbledon at the weekend, triggering an automatic two-match ban. Some people are saying his absence is a big blow to our Championship hopes. Certainly, Eric is an important player for us, but we aren't quite as dependent on him as we once were.

There's no doubt that he was the catalyst for the club's first Championship success for 26 years, and that he's been a key figure since. The statistics show that we've lost very few games when he's been playing; in fact, he's become a kind of talisman. But we are capable of winning without him.

It was the same when Bryan Robson was playing. Robbo was such a key player that people said we were a one-man team, and that when he wasn't playing, we had no chance. When we had to learn to live without Captain Marvel, we did. Now that Eric's turned 30 I guess we must accept that he can't play for ever, either.

I'm not too worried about his current suspension since the rest will do him good. He and David Beckham have been our only regulars this season and we gave David a rest recently. Overall, Eric misses very few matches, and he plays more often than most top strikers.

The break will charge him up, although of course I'll be glad to see him back. He still makes an impressive figurehead and gives us a presence which is often worth a head start. Other teams are never quite sure how to handle us tactically when he's playing. Eric's not changed much. He can still lose his temper, but he hasn't made a bad tackle all season. Perhaps the influx of other foreign players has helped him, in that he's not constantly under a glaring spotlight.

None of the foreign players who have followed Eric into our game have made the same impact. Zola and Vialli have done well, Di Matteo comes good in spells, but Ginola is terribly mercurial. OK, so Juninho's had a wonderful season for Boro, but Eric's been much more consistent over a long period.

We have to start looking for other players who will give us the kind of authority Eric normally supplies. Roy Keane and David Beckham, for instance, have emerged as not just Premiership players, but as European class, capable of playing against anyone. That's a measure of the progress we have made.

You have to keep a careful eye on strikers once they reach the wrong side of 30, but Eric's fitness and strength should give him another couple of years at the top. In the meantime, he'll be back to help us drive for the Championship and the Champions' Cup. He's the type who thrives on winning. Some players are afraid of the really big occasion, but not Eric; it inspires him, especially now he's our captain.

But at the same time, it's no longer such a major set-back when we have to be without him.


*Monday 27 January*

I fly out to watch Roberto Rios play for Real Betis in a Cup tie against Vallodolid. It's the second time I've seen him; I also watched him play for Spain against Yugoslavia. He can play in midfield, but I'm interested in him as a centre back in view of Gary Pallister's back problems. I could do without being away, because we need to prepare to meet Wimbledon in the League at Old Trafford on Wednesday. But if I'm going to move for Rios then I want to see him in action at first hand.

My conclusion is that he's an impressive player but unfortu-nately, from my point of view, the game against Valladolid doesn't stretch him and he just gives a comfortable performance. I'll need to see him again.

I flew first to Madrid, then had a car for the two-hour journey to Vallodolid, so there was plenty of time to mull things over. I had a chuckle to myself as I reflected on yesterday's game between Chelsea and Liverpool. I pictured the scene in the Liverpool dressing room at half time, with Liverpool two goals up and Roy Evans saying to his players, "Great, you're doing all the right things, just don't do anything stupid and this match is won." I could picture Ronnie Moran in the background, barking at them to keep it going.

Then Chelsea bring on Mark Hughes for the second half and give a marvellous display to win the game 4–2. Sparky's performance was superb. He forced Liverpool to play deep, and Chelsea were a stride ahead all over the pitch. Afterwards, Ruud Gullit suggested that the transformation came about when they put Roberto Di Matteo on to John Barnes, but we must have been watching different games. Hughes made the difference for me.

I really felt for Roy Evans... no wonder managers go grey! It was a great game which made for compulsive viewing. I'm not surprised that television is making a fortune selling English football round the world. It was wonderful stuff.

On the way back to Madrid, the driver points out the spot where Laurie Cunningham, who played for Manchester United in Ron Atkinson's day, lost his life in a car crash. It must have been a similar scene: late at night on a deserted road.

*Wednesday 29 January*
I only caught the tail end of training yesterday on my arrival back from Madrid, but Brian Kidd must have prepared the troops well. They give a brilliant performance to win 2–1 against Wimbledon at Old Trafford tonight, which means we are top of the Premiership for the first time since early in the

season. It's the kind of game which will have the fans in the pubs afterwards saying we should have scored ten. Well, so we probably should, but we only secured the victory after a typical home game drama of the kind our players seem to love.

So often at home, when the opposition is digging in and soaking up all our attacks, we go behind and have everyone biting their nails. Remember the game against Sheffield United in 1992/93, the season we won the first of our three Championships this decade? Against Southampton, when we were behind until Ryan Giggs scored twice late on? Against Sheffield Wednesday, when we equalised so late in protracted injury time that Trevor Francis said we had scored in the second leg? Or Liverpool, when we were two goals down before Mark Hughes banged in a couple?

You must never give up hope, and sure enough Giggs scored with a back header before Andy Cole came on as a substitute to hit the winner. So ended another thrilling match in this season's serial with Wimbledon.

*Premiership / Old Trafford / Att: 55,314*

**Manchester United 2**
Schmeichel, G Neville, Irwin, Clegg, Pallister, Keane, Cantona, Beckham, Scholes (Cole), Solskjaer, Giggs
*Scorers: Giggs, Cole*

**Wimbledon 1**
Sullivan, Cunningham, Kimble, Blackwell, Leonhardsen, Earle, Ekoku (Holdsworth), Gayle (Goodman), Perry, Jupp, Fear
*Scorer: Perry*

## Thursday 30 January

The most satisfying part of last night's match was seeing Andy Cole score, so soon after he returned to action after his pneumonia and broken leg. People frequently talk about the chances Cole misses rather than the goals he actually gets. He does miss – last night, he stabbed a gilt-edged opportunity wide soon after he came on. But you have to remember the superb positions he takes up to create all those openings.

It's all a matter of percentages. I'm still convinced Andy can become a leading scorer again and one of the best strikers in the game. He and the fans just have to focus on the positive side of his game, and accept that he's going to miss as well as hit. His goal last night was pure Cole. He's a predator: if a goal-keeper drops the ball or can only parry, he'll be first on the scene. You have to also acknowledge the original shot from Ole Solskjaer, who hit the bar twice and could easily have had a first-half hat-trick. I thought he and Gary Neville were probably our best players.

It was another super game, played at a great tempo which was maintained throughout; the kind of match which drains managers as well as players and supporters. I found it frustrating, as I am sure our crowd did, waiting for us to score.

The outcome is that we are top of the table, but there's certainly no daylight up there. Usually by New Year the main contenders have begun to pull away, but that hasn't happened yet. There are a number of teams threatening. Don't forget that Wimbledon themselves still have to play most of the other leading clubs at Selhurst Park. It seems to be one of those seasons where you have to hold your breath, keep playing well – and wait.

The players are in to loosen off, and they have smiles on their faces. A victory like that means plenty of banter, laughter and mickey-taking among the players. Me, I'm not so cheerful, because tonight is one evening of the year I always dread. It's the moment the schoolboys and their parents come to learn who will be given contracts to join the club as YTS trainees, and who will be released. There are 16 of them and I have to let three go. Another three will be given a little longer to prove themselves because they've been injured or had some other difficulty.

It's a tense evening, even for the lads who have made it. Their parents are naturally apprehensive when they come into the office, and though I've been through it many times before

I'm not comfortable either, so everyone is nervous. I know I'll be destroying the dreams of three youngsters and that they will be terribly upset. I just don't like doing it. But I assure the parents of the boys we're releasing that we will find them other clubs and that the coaching and experience they've had with us will stand them in good stead. On the positive side, we have some promising youngsters joining us, but I'm still glad when it's all over.

*Saturday 1 February*

Here we go again ... a goal down to Southampton after 10 minutes, just like our games against Everton, Blackburn, Derby, Forest, Sheffield Wednesday, Southampton and Wimbledon. Perhaps the players are as surprised as me when they see the Southampton line-up, because despite their embarrassing Coca-Cola Cup defeat in midweek against Stockport, they come out all gung-ho with a team of forwards.

Talking to Graeme Souness in my office before the game, I spot Steve Basham on his teamsheet, a name that's new to me. "I suppose he's a midfield player," I say, and Graeme nods in agreement. It just goes to show you should never trust a Scotsman ... Steve Basham is a centre forward.

The Saints' attack is loaded with strikers. They have a right go at us, play some great stuff and take the lead after 10 minutes through Egil Ostenstad. Fortunately we equalise quickly through Gary Pallister, and in the second half we go at them like a battering ram until they submit. Eric Cantona gets the winner, his first goal from open play for some time. With luck, that's the cue for him to take over and start running the show, as he normally does at this time of the season.

I like games like this. Southampton play with a bit of style and I am impressed by their attitude; it is much more positive than their League position suggests, perhaps because Graeme seems to have got a good staff together. He's got

# Wright v Schmeichel

Terry Cooper, Alan Murray, who used to be at Hartlepool, and Phil Boersma, who is a real character. I hope they pick up and do well.

*Premiership / Old Trafford / Att: 55,260*

**Manchester United 2**
Schmeichel, G Neville, Irwin, Clegg (Johnsen), Pallister, Keane, Cantona, Beckham, Poborsky (Cole), Solskjaer, Giggs
*Scorers: Pallister, Cantona*

**Southampton 1**
Taylor, Neilson, Monkou, Dryden, Le Tissier, Maddison, Magilton, Berkovic (Hughes), Ostenstad, Basham, Charlton (Robinson)
*Scorer: Ostenstad*

## *Sunday 2 February*

Another trip to Spain to watch Roberto Rios, this time in Bilbao. There's a direct flight from London so it's an easier trip. I reminisce with the driver on the way to Bilbao's ground; I played them three times, with Dunfermline and Rangers. I ask him if he can find Cortez Street, which I remember as the hub of Bilbao's night life. In a bar there, I once lost a watch Cathy had given me, but the driver's not optimistic about my chances of finding it since Cortez Street has apparently all closed down. So I ask him if he remembers the Bilbao centre half Echevario. "Ah, the Butcher," he says, and I tell him I still have the scars to justify the nickname.

As for the game, Real Betis slaughter Bilbao. Once again it is too easy for Rios and I can't make a definitive judgment. I fly back to London and stay overnight to wait for the team, who are travelling down for our Cup replay at Wimbledon on Tuesday.

## *Tuesday 4 February*

A really good Cup tie at Selhurst Park, which we are desperately unlucky not to win. I don't hide my displeasure at the way we concede the goal which costs us the match, and I would criticise of some of our play, but once the initial disappointment subsides I'm not too upset. Deep down, I know it would be impossible to win the League, the Champions' Cup and the FA Cup. Maybe it's for the good that one is now out of the way; it would have been asking too much of the players.

I'm happy with the commitment of our lads, which is the main thing. They don't shirk it – and we go out gloriously. It's probably Wimbledon's turn to win after three stirring battles, and I can't begrudge them their success. Indeed, I go into their dressing room at the end of the game and shake the hand of every player – not just to congratulate them on reaching the sixth round, but to thank them for their attitude and the football they played in all three games. Neither team ever wilted, and I like that.

I am especially pleased to have a word with Neil Sullivan, recently called up by Scotland, so I can tell him that the master race has produced another great goalkeeper. They all laugh at that, but the boy has done marvellously after coming back from a broken leg. I really rate him.

*FA Cup R5 / Selhurst Park / Att: 25,601*

**Wimbledon 1**
Sullivan, Cunningham, Kimble, Jones, Blackwell, Perry, Leonhardsen (McAllister), Earle, Ekoku, Holdsworth (Harford), Gayle (Goodman)
*Scorer: Gayle*

**Manchester United 0**
Schmeichel, G Neville, Irwin (McClair), Pallister, Johnsen, Keane, Cantona, Beckham, Poborsky (Solskjaer), Cole, Giggs

*Wednesday 5 February*

There's no game on Saturday because of the international fixtures next week. Because of Cup commitments involving our opponents the following Saturday, we haven't got a fixture until we go to Arsenal on 19 February. It's a good opportunity for a break. Unlike some clubs, I won't be fixing up a friendly match in the gap. We already have enough on our plate. I really can't understand managers who complain about playing too much football, then promptly fly off for a game abroad when they get a break. Maybe it's something to do with money.

I want all the players to have a rest while I head off with Cathy for the sunshine of Cyprus to attend the 10th anniversary of the United Supporters' Club there. There will be a big group of players, wives and girlfriends, including Brian Kidd, Barry Moorhouse (our membership secretary), Ronny Johnsen, Ole Solskjaer, Phil Neville (who's recovering from glandular fever), and our young Scottish midfielder Grant Brebner. We will be among friends, so the only problem for me will be the hospitality ... all that good food, not to mention the wine!

*Monday 10 February*

After a relaxing time in Cyprus, it's more of the same in Barcelona. Cathy and I flew here yesterday, and I know she'll love the city. However, I can never get away from football completely ... I can't resist watching the match between Espanol and Barcelona on television.

I felt quite sorry for Bobby Robson, who's having a relatively rough ride with Barcelona this season. When he was interviewed after the match he got quite animated and upset, and started waving his arms about. I wondered why, at the age of 63, he's still putting up with that kind of treatment. The answer, of course, is that football is in his blood, like a drug he clearly can't give it up. I wonder if I'll ever reach that point?

*Wednesday 12 February*

We fly home and I quickly get up-to-date on events at Old Trafford. Paul Scholes has had a cartilage operation which also involved the removal of a cyst; it's bad luck for him, because I'd just started to involve him again after he'd waited patiently for his chance.

In the afternoon, I hear the line-up announced on the radio for this evening's England v Italy World Cup qualifier at Wembley. I also catch an interview with Matt Le Tissier's brother who, with hardly any prompting, proudly tells the whole world that Matt is in the team and reveals the tactics Glenn Hoddle is planning against Italy. I'd love to be a fly on the wall next time the brothers meet up. Matt is sure to get a blasting from the England manager. Cesare Maldini, the Italian manager, must be laughing his socks off. Personally, if I was Glenn and heard the broadcast, I'd be tempted to change my selection. If he had any doubts about picking the controversial Le Tissier, this is his chance to leave him out.

Hoddle sticks by Le Tissier, but in my view substituting him is a mistake. I would certainly bring on Ferdinand, but I would keep Le Tissier on to look for something to drop off the two strikers on the edge of the box. That's his forte.

Italy showed why they win things. In England, when we clear the ball in a hurry, it can land in row six. The Italians put it in row 20.


*Thursday 13 February*

The criticism of Glenn Hoddle today after the 1–0 defeat by Italy has been hysterical. It was a very narrow defeat; in fact, England could easily have won. Italy only had one shot at goal and they showed nothing new. Indeed they confirmed that, despite their reputation for smooth, sophisticated defence, at times they belt the ball as if they intend to burst it, and anywhere will do.

That hasn't stopped the critics, who only last week were lauding Glenn Hoddle's tactical awareness. Now they're savaging him, calling his judgment poor and comparing him unfavourably with Terry Venables. Yet if England are to do well, the media must show some trust and confidence in the manager. If they don't, then they take all the joy out of the job, and there's nothing more destructive and draining on a manager's confidence than that. Even more significant, a manager under pressure is damaging for the players. Of course there has to be criticism, but these days it's always so overstated. There's no happy medium: winning is heaven and losing is hell. That can't be right.

In the evening I'm a guest of the University of Manchester's Institute of Science and Technology for the Queen's Award ceremony at the London Guildhall. I enjoy hearing about their latest scientific advances, and I'm pleased to establish contact with the University because they've got some great facilities for measuring and monitoring the fitness levels of athletes. The Duke of Kent was there, as was Lord Woolfson – who turned out to be quite a character, not to mention a chatterbox. He talked all night, even through some of the speeches. He told me his father came from Glasgow. I replied that I was well aware Isaac Woolfson had actually been born not far from me, in the Gorbals.

*Friday 14 February*

The players reported back for training yesterday. On the evidence of today's session, the break has really done them good. Their work was out of this world: so slick and sharp. As I remarked to Kiddo, it's a great bonus to have them looking so good at this stage of the season. I took David Beckham and Gary Neville out of it quite early because they'd played at Wembley in midweek, and we talked about the England match. I think it's good for a manager to get into the minds of the young players – especially a manager who's getting older!

*Saturday 15 February*

A day off for the players this Saturday. We don't play until next Wednesday, against Arsenal, who I go and watch at

Tottenham. I have lunch at White Hart Lane and thoroughly enjoy it. We're clearly not the only club doing a good line in catering, which is never easy on a big scale. On a match day, United serve over 2,500 lunches in the various dining rooms.

The match itself is a typical derby. Spurs should have won but don't, thanks mainly to three fantastic stops by John Lukic in the Arsenal goal. I watch Arsenal in particular, and note some aspects of their play which we'll have to address before we play them.

Over the years, Arsenal's defensive record has spoken for itself, but the downside has always been their notoriously stuffy and uncompromising style, which made them unattractive to watch. These days there's no doubt that their defenders look to join in the play more, and that makes them much more fluid. Now they drop balls into space a lot, which we'll also discuss before our visit.

Spurs, meanwhile, are struggling to find consistency. Gerry Francis will be pleased by this performance, even if they only get one point.

I leave ten minutes from the end so I'm back in the house by 7.45 pm. Before long I get a call from John Boyer, who does a fantastic job as the club's chaplain. John tells me that he has to see me tomorrow to discuss the future of one of our young players, Chris Calderone, who's apparently far from happy.

Chris is an outstanding young goalkeeper. He's suffered badly from colitis, a debilitating illness which drains you and results in weight loss and lethargy. Not only that, John tells me, but the lad also has another problem to deal with: there's been a lot of mickey-taking in the dressing room. This concerns me greatly. You can never be sure where teasing stops and bullying starts, and bullying is something that, as I've always stressed to my youth team coaches, I simply won't tolerate.

The upshot is that the boy wants to quit football, but doesn't know how to break the news to his father. I shall see both John and Chris in the morning.

# Wright v Schmeichel

*Sunday 16 February*

When it comes to football, parents can be terribly obsessive, perhaps because they want to see their boy achieve their own unfulfilled dreams. Sometimes they believe the road will be paved with gold, but there are a lot of hurdles to clear and only a few actually manage it.

It soon emerges when I talk to Chris that he wants to quit, but he knows his dad will be tremendously disappointed.

First of all I establish that there has been mickey-taking, but no bullying. Chris says he can live with the teasing but that he simply isn't enjoying playing football any more. So I suggest that rather than give up – because he does have great promise – we should look for a club nearer Nottingham, where his home is, and where the expectations might not be so high. He's clearly uncomfortable at Manchester United and this compromise might be easier for his dad to accept.

I don't want any boy at Old Trafford to feel neglected; the most important thing is that they're all happy. We'll start looking straight away for another club where Chris can make a fresh start.

With that sorted out, I can watch our first team squad train – and they're even better than they were on Friday. It's obvious that everyone is looking forward to getting back into action and tackling next week's big games at Arsenal and Chelsea. They're all looking fresh, and the precision of Cantona's passing is particularly brilliant.

At times like this, there's very little you can say to the players. It's pointless urging them on because they're already doing that for themselves. They have their own standards and ambitions, so I simply let them get on with it and take pleasure in watching them at work. I know that what they do in training will manifest itself in games, so I'm more than happy with what I'm seeing. If I could just get Butt and Scholes back to fitness then we'd have a full squad. But you never get everything you want in football.

*Monday 17 February*

In the wake of my talk with Chris Calderone, my priority for this Monday is a staff meeting to assess the amount of leg-pulling in the junior dressing room and find out if it's got out of hand. Eric Harrison and Neil Bailey confirm that, while there is a degree of mickey-taking, there's no bullying. Just to make sure, I call in three of the more experienced second-year boys to stress that I don't want any nasty goings-on in their dressing room. Some players can take it, others can't, and I tell them that I will hold them responsible if any occurs. Chris, meanwhile, wants to go home today. I arrange a car for Dave Bushell, our youth development officer, to take the boy to Nottingham. Dave will help explain the situation to Chris's parents and express the hope that they'll allow him to settle down while we find him a club in the area.

I'm supposed to be going to Buckingham Palace tonight for a presentation of sporting awards, but it's too late to travel and I still have to see the chaplain again. I'd love to have gone, but the kids come first. The Calderone situation – and the issues that his unhappiness have raised – have to be dealt with properly. I'm satisfied we've done what is best for the boy, and we've also found him a club: I'm delighted to say that Sheffield United have agreed to take him.


*Tuesday 18 February*

With Eric Cantona suspended for this week's two games, there's been a great deal of speculation about who will replace him. Scholes is not available. I could play with just one striker, but my plan is to play Cole and Solskjaer up front together. We've been practising this way for the last few days and I'm confident. Arsenal are always a hard side to beat, but their pitch is good and will suit our passing game.

Arsene Wenger has done marvellously since his arrival. Arsenal's abundance of older players, like Wright, Adams and

Bould, probably needed a fresh approach and new ideas, and he's provided them. The players clearly like him, which is important, and he's already something of a messiah at Highbury. But his real test will come in two or three years' time.

We practise our set pieces in training before setting off for London.

*Wednesday 19 February*

I couldn't ask for a better performance. To produce so much style and penetration as the end of February approaches is really quite astonishing. We are well worth our 2–1 win at Highbury, with goals from Solskjaer and Cole.

Everything is going along fine until 20 minutes from the end, when Ian Wright loses it. I'm sorry, but I can't find any other word for his behaviour. The best that can be said for his temperament is that he's got a short fuse, and I always instruct our players not to get involved with him. In fact, so volatile is Wright that I tell them not even to tackle him but just to protect the space. Today, our players say at half time that he's been going bananas during the first half, so I emphasise again that they should keep away from him.

Midway through the second half, Wright has a dig at Denis Irwin. It was the kind of thing which would probably have got him sent off if he'd been playing away from home. Despite the warnings, my players inevitably react. Ironically, in view of what is to come, it's Peter Schmeichel who acts as peacemaker.

The game settles down again ... until Wright jumps in at Schmeichel. The crowd react furiously to the tackle. If Eric Cantona had done the same, he'd have been locked up on Devil's Island. I don't know what prompts it; perhaps Wright is angry that Dennis Bergkamp's goal was ruled offside. It might also be on Wright's mind that he's never scored against Peter, except in the Charity Shield.

There's no question the man is a top quality striker. Indeed, I've often wondered whether I should try to get him to Old Trafford. But his temperament is another matter. He seems to attract controversy.

Unfortunately, the tackle is not the end of the matter. At the end of the game, I go straight to our dressing room to wait for the players when I hear a hullabaloo outside. I go back just in time to hear Wright's voice down the tunnel. He's shouting "Don't you dare make racist remarks to me." By this time, Peter is inside our dressing room so I ask him what it's all about. He says he had no idea, and that all he had said to Wright as they came off the field was, "You tried to do me."

The problem is that when the race issue crops up everyone panics and immediately jumps to conclusions. The press want to go big on it, with the assumption that Peter said what Wright alleges. However, I believe that Peter did not make a racist remark.

I can tell you, however, that there was one racist remark in the tunnel – and that came from an Arsenal player who called Roy Keane an Irish bastard. I heard it and said, "For goodness sake behave yourself." Actually, a couple of Arsenal players did apologise to me. Nigel Winterburn, last into the Arsenal dressing room, came up, shook hands and congratulated us on our performance. That was a nice touch of class, which is something you associate with the Arsenal of 20 years ago but regrettably, not so much these days.

I must say I wonder about Highbury now. A couple of years ago, Wright punched Steve Bruce in the tunnel and the police wanted to prosecute. We chose not to lay a complaint and Arsenal assured us that they would deal with Wright. And what do we get as thanks? A complaint by Arsenal to the Football Association that we had been trying to poach Matthew Wicks, one of their junior players. Why couldn't they have been up front and approached us first with their allegations?

Arsene Wenger: "The media in London are trying to turn him into some sort of guru ... he just can't know what it's like to play four games in eight days"

12 January 1997: Smiling through the abuse at the Sky TV awards

15 April 1997 v Celtic (h), Brian McClair's testimonial: "His loyalty and dedication to Manchester United has been unswerving"

19 April 1997 v Liverpool (a): "Even after such a fantastic victory, I still felt sorry for David James"

Whipping up support at Anfield: "Fergie, Fergie, give us a wave"

5 May 1997 v Middlesbrough (h): A bit of the old "Fergie fury" when a penalty decision goes against us

7 May 1997: Celebrations at the Cliff

Dressing room congratulations to our Reserves for winning the Pontin's League

8 May 1997 v Newcastle (h): The title is ours

Newcastle's guard of honour: A classy gesture by Kenny Dalglish and his players

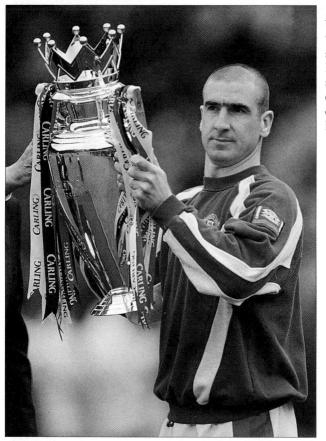

11 May 1997 v West Ham (h): "My eyes keep straying back to Eric Cantona. He seems deep in contemplation, especially when he lifts the trophy"

18 May 1997: "*Au revoir* and thanks for so many wonderful memories"

June 1997: Markus
Babbel (above) and
Brian Laudrup (left)
Two that got away…

A grateful fan!

"Although winning feels different now, it's still exhilarating"

# Wright v Schmeichel

*Premiership / Highbury / Att: 38,172*
**Arsenal 1**
Lukic, Dixon, Winterburn, Vieira, Bould, Adams (Hughes), Wright, Merson,
Bergkamp, Keown, Parlour
*Scorer: Bergkamp*

**Manchester United 2**
Schmeichel, G Neville, Irwin, Pallister, Johnsen, Keane, Beckham,
Poborsky (Butt, McClair), Cole, Solskjaer, Giggs
*Scorers: Solskjaer, Cole*

## Thursday 20 February

After last night's match, we travelled to the hotel England
use. We're here to prepare for our match at Stamford Bridge
on Saturday.

There are a few journalists hanging around, and we've
spotted photographers in the bushes. They're obviously looking
for reaction following Ian Wright's allegations. But the boys are
calm, and the players in the squad who weren't involved in the
match are training.

We organise a shooting session, much to the misery of
Raimond van der Gouw, who finds himself on the receiving end
of some ferocious, wind-assisted shooting by David May. David
is not recognised as a marksman – as a defender he doesn't see
much of the opposition goal – but he does pack one hell of a
shot. Today he's 99 per cent accurate, with shots that rocket
into the top corners. Raimond gets some stick, but he's a great
guy and takes it in good heart.

It's good to take the team away from time to time, especially
when it means I get away from the telephone. The players go to
the cinema in the evening while I excuse myself to have dinner
with Sir Richard Greenbury and his wife Sian.

I have no qualms about letting the players go off on their
own. I don't think I'd have been quite so relaxed about seeing
the squad I inherited ten years ago setting off together for an
evening out! Today's players are more ready to accept their
responsibilities. They know Chelsea is a big game for them.

*Friday 21 February*

I cannot believe an article in today's Daily Express. I'd heard that they were preparing something to do with Schmeichel and Wright, and I actually got up at 3.45 am to read the paper. The story claims that another Arsenal player heard Peter calling Wright a "black bastard", but significantly the player isn't named. Paul McCarthy, the reporter concerned, names the race issue as the reason Wright lost his temper.

Peter is raging and denies it wholeheartedly. We telephone Maurice Watkins, the club director and solicitor, and ask him to look at the legal implications.

Next, the News of the World phone to say that they could arrange to bring Ian Wright to the hotel for a photograph of the two players shaking hands and apologising. I refuse, because Wright still has some explaining to do. A meeting like that would imply that Peter has something to apologise for.

I spend the rest of the day talking to Maurice Watkins. We set up a meeting for Monday of next week, by which time we'll be back in Manchester.

In the evening we get a visit from Sir Roland Smith, chairman of the plc board. Thank goodness for his arrival; he helps us get things into perspective. I really appreciate his vast experience of business and the media in these kind of situations. Talking to him, you can see a pattern emerging; it's interesting that so far, Arsenal as a club have said nothing. I know silence is golden, but Highbury must be paved with gold at the moment! Ian Wright seems to stand alone on this issue. Arsene Wenger has made it clear that no one complained to him about racist remarks.

*Saturday 22 February*

We had a pre-match light training session this morning, which Ray Wilkins brought his son to watch. Peter was in great form and he's keen to play. With a second game in London so soon after the Arsenal row, I wonder about the wisdom of him playing, but anger seems to have made him even more determined. The only concession I've made to the controversy is to go on Sky television and the BBC's Grandstand programme and state categorically that there had been no racist talk from Peter Schmeichel at Arsenal.

As for the game, Chelsea started like a whirlwind and Zola had the ball in our net after a couple of minutes. Mark Hughes might well have added to their lead but for a Schmeichel save. I always worry in the early stages after a hard midweek match, and my worst fears were being realised. We were poor, with no flow to our play. Though I rate Gerald Ashby as a referee, I thought he had a stinker, which didn't help. He pulled Roy Keane up for a couple of tackles and booked him for the second one, and I thought both were perfectly OK. I know Roy doesn't help himself at times, and he does make the kind of constant protests which are bound to anger any official. But I do feel there's a degree of victimisation where he is concerned. This game was played in good spirit and I thought the referee should have been more prepared to let the players get on with it.

We were all over the place until I changed our formation and played Ryan Giggs through the middle. He was a constant threat and we started to do really well. David Beckham secured a 1–1 draw with another of his spectacular shots – this one was measured at 97.8 miles per hour. The draw was still good enough to keep us one point in front at the top of the table; after all that had happened, I was just glad to get out of London with four points out of a possible six.

Overall, I thought our players behaved with a lot of dignity when they could have been tempted to say things to introduce a little more truth into the situation. Peter may well need to take legal action; for the time being, it's best if we keep quiet while we wait to see what action the FA are going to take. They're talking about bringing a disrepute charge against him. I'm afraid we've not yet heard the last of this.

# A Will to Win

*Premiership / Stamford Brook / Att: 28,336*

**Chelsea 1**
Hitchcock (Grodas), Petrescu (Gullit), Leboeuf, Clarke, Hughes, Wise, Di Matteo, Minto (Johnsen), Sinclair, Newton, Zola
*Scorer: Zola*

**Manchester United 1**
Schmeichel, G Neville, Irwin, Pallister, Johnsen (May), Keane, Beckham, McClair, Cole, Solskjaer, Giggs (Cruyff)
*Scorer: Beckham*

## *Monday 24 February*

These kind of situations are a perfect example of what the assistant manager does. The Schmeichel-Wright issue has reached boiling point, and I'm relying on Brian Kidd to keep working with the players while I attend to outside matters.

The FA is getting more involved, but we know from our experience over the Cantona episode at Selhurst Park that you can't always take what one man might say at face value. For instance, a major figure at Lancaster Gate might promise something which he may or may not be able to deliver; a committee, such as a disciplinary commission, may decide its own course of action contrary to an official's assurance ... You have to proceed with caution.

Recent history also suggests that the FA doesn't necessarily have the all-encompassing power it once did. Tottenham showed that when they took the FA to court over their 12-point deduction and FA Cup ban.

Everyone has a legal avenue these days. Right now several avenues are open to Peter who has been cast as the villain of the piece.

## *Tuesday 25 February*

The FA has chosen to make public a letter it sent to us. The letter suggested Peter and Ian Wright meet at Lancaster Gate to shake hands and make some kind of apology.

Graham Kelly is a good man, who one can't help but like.

Some people reckon he comes over as a bit of a cold fish on television, but in fact he's a very amusing character who talks well. However, I cannot understand why the head of a big organisation wants to go running to the media with this. Perhaps he's more concerned with sending out a message to the fans, along the lines of "I'm doing my best but the others won't help me."

Our position remains unchanged. Peter's done nothing wrong and there's nothing for him to address. The chairman, incidentally, is away on holiday. His timing is impeccable!

*Wednesday 26 February*

Tonight's rearranged fixture, at home to Middlesbrough, is off. Bryan Robson's team have to replay against Stockport in the Coca-Cola Cup. This may give us problems later on, but at least it clears the decks for our match against Coventry on Saturday and the big one against Porto next week. Kiddo has been preparing the troops, and I want to make the most of this week's training time. If we're successful, we'll end up facing a glut of matches with very little time in between to prepare.

I tell the players that this morning might be their last gruelling session of the season. Someone – it might have been Gary Pallister – cynically replies, "Oh yes, that'll be right!"

In the evening I go over to the Baseball Ground to watch the FA Cup tie between Coventry and Derby. Some things, like Derby's pitch, never change: it is dreadful. Coventry go 2–0 up, but Derby draw level thanks to two corner kicks. "Derby will win it now," I say to my son Jason, who is watching with me. When you lose a lead like that in a Cup tie it's terribly dispiriting, and you could see the Coventry heads go down.

On the way back Jason phones Darren, who'd been playing for Wolves reserves. Apparently he had quite a good game, but he's generally a bit low at the moment because he's not getting a regular game in the first team. It surprises me, because he's the one really good passer of the ball Wolves have got. All I can do is try and make sure he doesn't get so downhearted that he stops enjoying his football.

I hurry home to catch the televised highlights of the Leicester v Chelsea Cup tie. I heard on the radio about the controversial penalty in extra time which had given the Londoners a 1–0 victory. Referee Mike Reed ruled that full back Spencer Prior had body checked Erland Johnsen – and when I see it on television for myself, I don't blame the ref one little bit. Johnsen's dive deserved top marks for technical merit and made it very difficult for the official; only a televised play-back would have shown the incident in its true light. I wonder if referees will ever be given technical assistance? The thing is, you can't stop progress, but you can't have long breaks in the play to study television evidence, either.

However, the real problem in this case was Johnsen. He didn't conduct himself at all well. Martin O'Neill did, although you could see the anger in his face after the match. Despite being helpless, he said all the right things in what was a terrific interview.

As for Ruud Gullit, he said he hadn't seen the incident and that the penalty kick wasn't important anyway. Who's he kidding? It only decided the whole match, and could make Chelsea's year. It was a surprisingly crass comment from a man who talks well on television. Mind you, when you've been a great player and have three European Cup winners' medals on your mantelpiece, you can get away with murder. A cv like that can cover up a lot, and I thought Ruud definitely fudged this one.

At the same time, he has done extremely well in his first year as a manager. Management must be an adventure for him. He's shown great imagination, both in the way he gets his team to play and in his dealings in the transfer market. As with Arsene Wenger, the time to judge him will come in two or three years' time. British football is very demanding, both on and off the field, and it'll be interesting to see how he stands up to the test.

Being Dutch, at least Gullit will always have an opinion. All Dutch players do, which is one reason why Holland seldom go all the way in major tournaments. When it comes to the nitty-gritty towards the end of a tournament, the stories start circulating about rows in the Dutch camp over team selection and tactics. So many times at international level you hear about Dutch players not being happy with the manager, or even refusing to play for him. They have more difficulties between players and managers than any other country in the world.

*Thursday 27 February*

The Professional Footballers' Association entered the Schmeichel-Wright debate today. It's hardly surprising, since they've worked hard on racial issues in football and are duty bound to play a role. Like the FA, they seem to be after a joint statement of conciliation from the two players. The whole thing hinges on Wright's terrible tackle, and until he's prepared to apologise for that, I can't see a solution.

In the evening I'm a guest at an Institute of Bankers' dinner. I am scheduled to make a speech after Sir Brian Pitman, a guru of the banking world. How do you follow that? Luckily I seem to get a reasonable reaction to my words describing what we're trying to achieve at Old Trafford.

*Friday 28 February*

Tomorrow we're at Coventry. I wonder whether their manager, Gordon Strachan, is finding management a little harder than he expected. He's certainly walked into a critical situation; in his case, time is the manager's greatest enemy so he's having to learn quickly. I can't remember another season with so many teams locked into such a tight battle in the bottom half of the table.

I hope Coventry stay up. You never get their fans chanting

"Stand up if you hate Manchester United"; their concern is for Coventry, and that's admirable. It would be sad for a club which has had shown such a great pioneering spirit over the years to go down. Coventry were the first to commit themselves to an all-seater stadium, and they had the idea of providing proper restaurants even before we developed that kind catering at United. It would be sad if all that enterprise were to go out of the Premiership.

There'll be a special welcome tomorrow for David Busst, who'll be our guest at the match. None of us will forget the Coventry player's horrendous injury at Old Trafford last season, and we're looking forward to playing in a testimonial for him. We are trying to arrange something towards the end of the season at Highfield Road. Courage comes in many forms, and David has particularly brave in facing up to the 15 operations he's undergone since breaking his leg. We wish him luck.

Five pals and their wives from Scotland are staying with Cathy and I and coming to watch tomorrow's game. I've known them for 50 years: I went to nursery school with three of them, and we all played football for the Boys' Brigade, at Secondary School and for a Boys' Club in Glasgow.

So, with a party in mind, I send David Beckham to buy me a CD system. He knows about these things. My plans are going fine until I drop it while trying to set it up in the lounge. I chip the fireplace and smash my favourite piece of porcelain sculpture, which I've had for 20 years. Cathy doesn't say a word because she knows I am ready to explode. The silence is deafening.

But it doesn't spoil the evening, and my visitors – Duncan Petersen, Tommy Hendry, Jimmy MacMillan, Angus Shaw and Harry Campbell – are all in great singing form. When it's my turn to sing, I launch into "Moon River", whereupon they all get up and walk out. They eat my food, drink my drink and then insult me ... and they call themselves my friends!

# Wright v Schmeichel

*Saturday 1 March*

I couldn't have chosen a better game as preparation for Europe. Coventry presented us with two own-goals in the first five minutes and that was really game, set and match; the rest of the afternoon became a stroll. I'm not degrading Coventry at all, it was just one of those unfortunate moments and it left them shell-shocked. We scored again early in the second half through Karel Poborsky, which afforded me the luxury of being able to take off Denis Irwin, David Beckham and Ryan Giggs in readiness for Wednesday's tie against Porto. As an added bonus, I could give Phil Neville, Brian McClair and Ronny Johnsen a run out in their places.

David Busst received a great ovation from both sets of fans when he went out. I was touched that all the Coventry players lined up at the start to applaud his entrance into the directors' box. You can expect that kind of gesture from Dion Dublin's team. Dion's one of the finest lads you could meet, a really good pro. It was interesting to see him playing as a centre back. I thought he did well.

*Premiership / Old Trafford / Att: 55,230*

**Manchester United 3**
Schmeichel, G Neville, Irwin (P Neville), May, Pallister, Cantona, Cole, Beckham (McClair), Giggs (Johnsen), Cruyff, Poborsky
*Scorers: Breen og, Jess og, Poborsky*

**Coventry City 1**
Ogrizovic, Shaw, Williams, Jess, Whelan, Dublin, McAllister, Hall (Telfer), Evtushok (Ndlovu), Breen, Huckerby
*Scorer: Huckerby*

*Sunday 2 March*

Porto is on my mind constantly now. My big concern is Roy Keane, who is jogging but nothing more; I know he's struggling to make it. But the rest of the players have a nice spring in their step as we go into match countdown. It's the first time since I came here that United have been in the quarter finals of this competition, and I have a great sense of anticipation. As I consider my approach, I try to think back to my Aberdeen days when we were involved in Europe. But my mind is racing ahead to picking the team and whether rehearsing tactics would just put more pressure on the players.

I know they are desperate to get on with it. At the moment it's as if they're in the dentist's waiting room, worrying about the pain and agony that could lie ahead but also relishing the thought of how it will feel if everything works out right.

I've been in these kind of pressure situations before, and I'm counting on that experience to help see us through.

*Monday 3 March*

Decide to leave the training session open. We're an accessible club and I don't see any point in retreating behind closed doors, even if it means the Portuguese press and cameras will be watching us work. The journalists have a job to do too, and they seem pleased.

*Tuesday 4 March*

Roy is getting closer to fitness but today is decision day. As I go to talk to the players, armed with my pens and magnetic men to draw tactics on the board, I send Roy out with Kiddo for a test. I've just told the players that if he is fit, he will play, when the pair of them come up to say it's no use. Roy is still feeling the injury. But now I know for certain he's not available, at least I can work out my plans.

I want a system in which we can press the ball in midfield and make it busy in that area. I'm looking to Giggs, Beckham and Johnsen to condense the midfield; that way we can get our full backs on to their wide players. Porto's defensive record suggests the makings of a 0–0 draw, but I don't want that. I don't want them going back home psychologically satisfied that they've been to Old Trafford, hatched their plot and got a no-score draw. That would get them thinking that a penalty, or something like it, would be enough to win the second leg 1–0 on their own ground. That's happened so often. I'm determined we must get a goal, so I'll play as many goalscorers in my team as I reasonably can. I'm aiming for a 1–0 win.

It could be cat and mouse, but I want to set the pace in attack with Eric Cantona as the catalyst playing behind our two strikers, Cole and Solskjaer. I want Beckham to play in central midfield, and I'm giving Giggs the freedom to go wide or attack the space in front of him through the middle. Porto normally play 4–3–3 and they may find us difficult to handle if we play like this. We've been studying videos of them for the past two weeks, and Les Kershaw and Jimmy Ryan have seen them play four or five times. A lot of people have been involved in the planning for this tie.

After talking to the players, I have the doors of the training ground closed while we stage a practice match. However, just as we are finishing I see the Daily Mirror reporter walking across the car park. I instantly think there's no way my team selection is going to stay secret now. He explains he's come to get a shirt signed, but I don't trust anyone at this stage of our preparations. I'm furious. He takes the full blast of my anger, but there is a lot at stake.

When I give my press conference at Old Trafford to the English and Portuguese press, the man from the Daily Express asks if pursuit of the European Cup has become an obsession. I tell him I'm refusing to allow the European quest to become a personal albatross. I've achieved too much in my career for everything to depend on one competition, however important.

Someone asks whether we will be playing for England, but I'm not having that either. We shouldn't worry about carrying a torch for anyone but ourselves. Of course it's good for English football if English clubs do well, and I genuinely hope Liverpool and Newcastle also win their European ties this week, but my thoughts are mostly with our players and supporters.

*Wednesday 5 March*

Match day gets off to a disappointing start. I pick up the papers to find that some of the journalists seem to be trying to blow up a row between me and Glenn Hoddle. At yesterday's press conference I was asked for my views on England's plans to play in a summer tournament. I couldn't see what it had to do with our match against Porto, but I said I considered it folly to arrange that kind of tour. The players would be better off resting. The papers have twisted that into a declaration that I will pull my players out. That's an entirely different matter.

At times like this, I miss having the likes of Steve Curry and Richard Bott as number one writers for their papers. They were newspaper men who showed a sense of balance and fairness that allowed you to build up a degree of trust. It's sad that the media is a cut-throat business these days. I don't know how young managers coming into the game will ever establish a decent working relationship without trust.

All that, however, was soon forgotten. The way the match works out was beyond my wildest dreams. I've seen a lot of good performances at Old Trafford in my time, but this was the most emphatic in Europe I have known as a manager.

I don't think anyone anticipated that we could win 4–0 – even I was prepared to settle for 1–0. Our positive approach really worked, and so many of the players excelled. Gary Pallister played for most of the second half with a groin injury but never gave in. You can normally expect to win a match when around eight of your players deliver performances you can rate at nine out of ten. Well, tonight all 11 performed at that standard, with one or two really distinguishing themselves.

It was a searching examination for Ryan Giggs. Just to be critical of the boy, what has he won at world, international or European level? This was a test for him, playing against one of the tournament favourites, and he was absolutely magnificent. The deeper midfield role suited him, and he has an electricity and balance that opponents just can't handle. He showed a maturity and passing awareness that bodes well for the future; in two years he will be a truly wonderful player.

But I was delighted with them all. Eric Cantona carried his responsibilities as captain brilliantly. With a four-goal advantage, we're well placed to reach the semi finals.

*European Champions' League / Old Trafford / Att: 55,415*
**Manchester United 4**
Schmeichel, G Neville, Irwin, May, Johnsen, Pallister, Cantona, Cole, Beckham, Giggs, Solskjaer
*Scorers: May, Cantona, Giggs, Cole*
**Porto FC 0**
Hilario, Aloisio, Conceicao, Drulovic, Artur (Barros), Barroso, Paulinho Santos, Edmilson, Jorge Costa, Costa (Jardel), Zahovic

*Thursday 6 March*

Not to put too fine a point on it, I'm knackered. It's all right for the players; they're young. I'm 55 and I still ran every yard, made every pass, headed every ball and made every tackle against Porto. Needless to say I played a blinder, but I still finished with a deep pain in my chest.

I had lots of friends down for the match who stayed over, including my son Mark, whose early morning taxi to catch a train back to London didn't turn up. I didn't get to my bed until 3 am and Cathy woke me three hours later to tell me I'd have to run him to the station.

My son Jason, who works for Sky television, was also there. When he was directing one of our games, he was heard to say down the line, "Get the camera on Fergie, he's looking angry." Even my family are playing up the "Fergie Fury"angle.

Just as I get into my car with Mark, the taxi turns up. I go back to bed, but there's no way I'm going to get back to sleep, so I go into training. I'm glad I do; the players are pleased as punch and there's a warmth about the place. It's the same for all of us, even the likes of Teresa in the canteen kitchen, who's cooked for all Manchester United's great players over the years;

you get a glow from her as well. These are the moments that make your life and give you the will to continue when times aren't so good.

At some stage, I'll have to bring the players back down to earth, but not now. It will do them good to reflect on their glory. Belief is the key; it was the main theme of my talks with the players leading up to the game. I had no worries about our form. We've been playing with great confidence in the Premiership, during a run which has taken us to the top of the table. But European football is a different ball game.

We know what a lack of belief does to us – it happened in the first half against Juventus in Turin, when we lost faith in our ability. Porto are up there with the Italian champions: they squeezed AC Milan out of the competition and finished top of their group with the same record as Juventus. Our players were all well aware they would face a top-class team in the quarter final, but I didn't want them to be apprehensive. In reality, they need fear no one these days, but I knew I had to convince them that Porto weren't the only side who could boast four or five brilliant players. I told them Porto's Brazilian stars were sure to have talked to Emerson and Juninho at Middlesbrough, and would have heard exactly how Manchester United had got to the top of the Premiership, and exactly what we'd achieved in recent seasons.

I emphasised to the players that they wouldn't be the only ones out there thinking they were up against a good team. Porto would definitely treat us with respect. They might even be a little fearful that they'd get a far more severe test than they're used to in their domestic league, which they dominate: once again, they're running away with the Portuguese Championship.

I explained that people are talking about Manchester United these days because they are the best. If the players don't believe they were the best, then they're at the wrong club. I urged them not to go out there thinking that all they could do was their best; I wanted them to take the field believing they *were* the best, and to play to their true abilities. I warned they'd had their lesson in Turin, and that that was the last time I ever expected to see them playing without faith in the their own – and their team-mates's – abilities. I wrapped up by telling them to enjoy themselves, because that's when we see them at their best.

A visit to St Ann's School in nearby Stretford, accompanied by Eric Cantona, makes a pleasant end to the day. At the request of Father Keegan (who has been as persistent getting us to his parish as he is fanatical as a United fan), we plant a rowan tree to mark a landscape project for the nursery which I opened 18 months ago. The kids are brilliant. So is Eric, who has even brought photgraphs of himself to give out. After the ceremony, I tell the boys and girls that Robert Burns wrote a poem about a rowan tree ... except that for the life of me I remember it.

# 8
# Cantona bombshell

Football has a nasty habit of bringing you down to earth with an almighty bump. After floating around on the euphoria of our great result against Porto, we hit the deck with a resounding smack in our next match.

We were at Sunderland, which on paper shouldn't have presented us with too many problems. But we were awful and we lost 2–1. I was particularly down. Quite a few of the fans weren't happy with the team I picked, and a manager should ask himself questions when he makes decisions which don't bear fruit. I felt quite guilty as I listened to the familiar criticisms surrounding my unnecessary "tinkering" with the team.

To my mind, the changes I made were all for a purpose. Andy Cole and Ole Gunnar Solksjaer had run their socks off against Porto, so I left them on the bench, along with Ryan Giggs, who I also thought needed a rest. We had good players to replace them – that's the whole point of having a quality squad. I felt sure we could get something out of the game with the side I selected. Sunderland are struggling to score goals and Peter Reid knows it. That's why he's so desperate to get Niall Quinn and Paul Stewart, both of whom have some physical presence, to Roker Park. I thought if we defended properly we'd be sure to get a goal and take the points.

Forget team selection: on the day, we didn't have one player who hit 60 per cent efficiency. At that low level you can't expect to do well. It was a hot day too. But no excuses – we simply gave a bad performance. Sunderland weren't much better, but they deserved their victory.

Was it me who made a mess of it, or did other factors contribute to what was a total team collapse? I asked the players afterwards if they'd had a late night on Wednesday to celebrate the win against Porto. Most of them were honest enough to admit they hadn't prepared as well as they might have done for Sunderland. It's a responsibility that the players must take on board.

*Saturday 8 March*

The trip to Sunderland had started well enough, when Bob Cass visited our hotel. Bob is one of the most likeable football writers on the circuit; he's very loyal to the North East, and it's always a pleasure to trade insults with him. I had half an hour with him before dinner, as usual. After he'd wheedled a story out of me, I told him I was under the impression he always came to see me as a friend. "Don't kid yourself ... business is business," he replied.

Sunderland grabbed their goals through Michael Gray, a former United junior, and John Mullin, a one-time Stretford Ender. We only got on the scoresheet thanks to an own-goal.

*Premiership / Roker Park / Att: 22,225*

**Sunderland 2**
Perez, Hall, Kubicki, Ball, Bracewell (Williams), Ord, Melville, Kelly, Gray, Mullin, Bridges (Russell)
*Scorers: Gray, Mullin*

**Manchester United 1**
Schmeichel, Irwin, P Neville, May, G Neville, Johnsen, Cantona, Beckham, McClair, Poborsky (Solskjaer), Cruyff (Cole)
*Scorer: Melville (own goal)*

*Monday 10 March*

It's the dinner season again. Along with a few other players and representatives from Old Trafford, I attended the annual function of the North Wales and Chester branch of our membership club. A lot of the people there were glued to their earpieces, listening to radio commentary of the match between Liverpool and Newcastle at Anfield.

I don't normally tune into games which have a bearing on our own fortunes. If I'm watching at the ground itself, I'm OK; the professional side of me prevails and I become detached. If I'm at home, I get so uptight that it just isn't worth the stress. However, I couldn't avoid being told the score as Liverpool took a three-goal lead. Newcastle's fight-back coincided with a speech made by Eddie Mansell, the chairman of the club, and people kept interrupting him as the score became 3–3. Finally, Eric Cantona got to his feet and started waving his arms around in disgust – Liverpool had grabbed a winner. Poor Eddie was trying to finish his speech throughout all this. He can rest assured that the both the gift Eric received as the branch's Player of the Year, and the gift I got to mark my ten years at Old Trafford, were much appreciated.

*Tuesday 11 March*

Encouraging news today from the Crown Prosecution Service. They won't be proceeding with charges against Peter Schmeichel for racist remarks allegedly made to Ian Wright. That's really put the cat among the pigeons: what are the FA going to do now? Perhaps, after treating Peter miserably by prolonging this affair, they will finally get round to examining Wright's tackle. After all, that's what started this whole furore.

*Wednesday 12 March*

There can't be many university lecturers who switch from teaching chemistry to assessing players and matches, but that's what Les Kershaw did. He joined us as chief scout, and he's really good at it. Les is a fantastic man, a brilliant worker and a shrewd judge. He travels all over the world looking at possible transfer targets and checking out our European opponents. He also came to my rescue today when I was stuck at the station waiting for my sister-in-law's delayed train from Scotland. I'd planned to drive to Hillsborough for Sheffield Wednesday's match against Sunderland, since Wednesday are our opponents at Old Trafford on Saturday. But as I was stranded I put in a call to Les, who immediately volunteered to go. I do hope he's not getting like Bill Shankly, whose idea of a birthday treat for his wife was to take her to a football match.

Speaking of which, it's my wedding anniversary today. We're going to celebrate our 31 years of marriage tomorrow, when I'm taking Cathy to the races at Cheltenham (well, at least it's not football) and then on to London for a night out on the town.

*Thursday 13 March*

I didn't win a penny at the races, but I did have a smashing lunch with Mike Dillon of Ladbrokes, John Mulherin the Irish trainer, Dessie Scahill the RTE commentator and the journalist Hugh McIlvanney. There's always good conversation when Irish people are around, and this was no exception.

At the London Hilton, we're greeted with a big anniversary cake courtesy of the hotel, which is a lovely gesture.

*Friday 14 March*

The break was welcome, but all good things have to end. We got up early catch the 7 am train, to be back in Manchester in time for training for tomorrow's game with Sheffield Wednesday.

Hillsborough's change of fortune has been remarkable since David Pleat's arrival. He's got Wednesday playing with a confidence which has taken them from last year's relegation dog-fight to, currently, sixth place in the Premiership. They've also enjoyed a good FA Cup run, which only ended this week. They lost two players through injury in their quarter final against Wimbledon and understandably went down 2–0. It was only their second defeat in 23 games, and David Pleat must be pleased with their consistency.

We're also going into the match on the back of a defeat, but I'm not worrying too much. I expected a backlash after the Porto game. You often pay a price for the big games.

*Saturday 15 March*

I had a feeling on Wednesday that we might suffer from three big games in six days, and I was right. We made an edgy start and presented David Hirst with a great chance to score. When I realised who it was that we had left unmarked in front of our goal with the ball at his feet, I groaned. Usually Hirst only has to burp and the ball's in our net. Happily, on this occasion he missed a gilt-edged chance. We recovered to show a sharpness that produced a brilliant goal after 20 minutes. Giggs set Eric Cantona away, and Cantona threaded an exquisite ball through the visitors' defence for Andy Cole to smack home.

Andy pulled up with a thigh strain after scoring. I replaced him with Karel Poborsky, who scored a fine goal in the second half. I was pleased for Karel, who is a fabulous lad and trains very hard. He's improved a lot lately. I'm sure if he's patient, he'll end with plenty of United appearances under his belt.

*Premiership / Old Trafford / Att: 55,267*

**Manchester United 2**
Schmeichel, G Neville, Irwin, May, Pallister, Cantona, Butt, Cole (Poborsky), Beckham, Giggs, Solskjaer (Scholes)
*Scorers: Cole, Poborsky*

**Sheffield Wednesday 2**
Pressman, Atherton, Nolan, Walker, Whittingham, Carbone, Hirst, Blinker (Briscoe), Nicol (Booth), Stefanovic, Humphreys

*Sunday 16 March*

It's Sunday, but the players are in for training because we go to Portugal on Tuesday. I was thinking of flying out tomorrow to take advantage of the sunny weather our opponents seem to be enjoying, but too many arrangements have been made by the directors and the rest of the party sharing the charter team plane. At his stage of the season, with so many important fixtures looming, I have to make sure the players get enough time to rest and relax.

*Tuesday 18 March*

The flight to Oporto is relaxed, thanks to our four-goal advantage from the first leg. It's a nice cushion. Of course we could simply aim to avoid losing, but in fact that's the last thing I want. It's important we get into the habit of performing correctly and winning in Europe.

*Wednesday 19 March*

We have a nervy 10 minutes but then play so well, and with so much discipline, that I can't see Porto scoring against us. We are solid. It's a reflection of our improvement in Europe as the season has progressed. David May makes one very important tackle for us to deny Porto's Brazilian striker Jardel. We are possibly a bit frightened to tackle because of the threat of yellow cards, but once the players realise the refereeing is good, our tackling improves and we take a grip on the game. Perhaps if we'd have been more careful on the counter-attack, the game might not have finished goalless, but a clean sheet away from home in Europe is nevertheless a good result.

In fact, our biggest scare came on the journey from our hotel to the stadium. Thanks to the police escort, the drive was more like a high-speed car chase from an American movie. I was telling the directors and staff sitting next to me about the time when, during a trip to Portugal with Aberdeen, our police escort forced an ambulance into a ditch, when blow me if there isn't an ambulance coming towards us. Nothing has changed over here; the police simply waved it off the road to let us speed by.

*European Champions League / Estadio das Antas / Att: 40,000*
**FC Porto 0**
Wozniak, Joao Pinto (Zahovic), Rui Jorge, Mendes (Mielcarski), Drulovic, Jardel, Barroso (Wetl), Joao Manuel Pinto, Paulinho Santos, Edmilson, Jorge Costa
**Manchester United 0**
Schmeichel, G Neville, Irwin (P Neville), May, Johnsen, Pallister, Cantona, Butt, Beckham (Poborsky), Keane, Solskjaer (Scholes)

## *Thursday 20 March*

The full extent of the rough treatment meted out to our supporters in Portugal emerged today. As part of the official party, we didn't have any problems, but Cathy and her sister had a terrible experience at the game. It appears that the police just couldn't handle the crowd on the other side of the stadium. They'd installed barriers to funnel people through so they could be searched, but it was a totally inadequate system. To make matters worse, one of the turnstiles couldn't recognise the barcoding on the visiting fans' tickets, so people with perfectly valid tickets were refused entry. The result was chaos; there was so much delay that the pressure on the barriers built up. The police reaction was simply to lash out with their batons on the people nearest them. Cathy told me the police were very menacing.

There was a similar crush after the game. The police opened fire with rubber bullets which caused some nasty wounds, as photographs in today's newspapers clearly show.

We'd seen a lot of our supporters at the airport when we arrived out in Portugal, and the impression I got was that they were in a good-natured mood. Some of them had obviously had a few drinks, but it was clear they were there to enjoy themselves. This has to go down as an over-reaction by the Portuguese police to a situation which was too big for them to handle properly.

I arrived home to find there was worrying news on the domestic front, too: one of my twin granddaughters has pneumonia. Cathy's going to take the first train to London tomorrow and stay for a week to help Tania with the twins and Jake.

*Saturday 22 March*

Our recent record coming off the back of European matches gives me good cause for worry, especially today. We can expect a real battle in our fixture at Everton. They load a lot on big Duncan Ferguson's shoulders.

That's the way the match turns out. In the first half, we do little more than simply hang on, and I wonder how losing Gary Pallister's height – he limps off with a groin strain seven minutes before the interval – will affect us. In fact, David May is superb against Ferguson. That might explain why the striker catches May in the face with his elbow later on in the game. I know players often throw their arms about when they are grappling and trying to free themselves; I also know that Ferguson can lose his temper. Nevertheless, I don't associate Duncan with this kind of crude challenge. It's an offence which is creeping back into the game and must be stopped. It could have caused a bad injury.

Just before losing Pallister, we'd taken the lead on a breakaway which saw Ole Gunnar Solksjaer conjure a goal out of nothing. I didn't see how he was going to get in a shot; that he scored was typical of the lad's opportunism. Eric Cantona put the game beyond doubt on another counter attack in the second half.

The fact that we have beaten the post-European match blues (after five unsuccessful attempts at winning a match immediately after a Champions' League game) is almost as valuable as the points. This time, the game was won in the plane on the way back from Oporto. Not one player took a drink. Normally,

# Cantona bombshell

they have three or four on a flight home to relax. I hadn't said anything; perhaps they'd just learnt their lesson from the repercussions of the late night after the home game against Porto. The value of preparation is seeping through, and it's good that the players can take responsibility for their own discipline.

It was a good win for us. The same cannot be said for Joe Royle. I get on well with Joe. I picked up a bad undercurrent in the Goodison boardroom and a sense of dissatisfaction about the whole place. I could see that Joe himself was pretty down, so when we had our usual pre-match cup of tea we talked about things in general rather than about the club. He feels under pressure – which is hardly surprising. His chairman told him before their game against Forest a few weeks ago that the situation was out of his hands if he didn't get the right results.

The departure of Andrei Kanchelskis in November must have been a blow. I think it hurt; it always does when you spend a lot of money on a player who lets you down. Joe's position couldn't possibly have been helped by Cliff Finch, an Everton director, holding a phone-in on local radio to field questions from fans. To me, that's undermining the manager's position. I'm surprised that Peter Johnson, who seems a decent chairman, allowed it. If he considers Everton to be a big club, then they should behave like one. I can't imagine Philip Carter countenancing that kind of event when he was Everton chairman and I doubt it would have happened when Jim Greenwood was chief executive, either.

When the news broke that Joe was was leaving Everton, I can't say I was surprised. He did the honourable thing, and I just hope the club look after him.

*Premiership / Venue: ??? / Att: 40,079*
**Everton 0**
Gerrard, Barrett, Thomsen (Rideout), Unsworth, Watson, Phelan, Stuart, Parkinson, Ferguson, Speed, Barmby
**Manchester United 2**
Schmeichel, P Neville, Irwin, May, Keane, Pallister (Johnsen), Cantona, Butt, Solskjaer, Beckham (McClair), Giggs
*Scorers: Solskjaer, Cantona*

*Sunday 23 March*

I wake up to newspaper headlines declaring war between Glenn Hoddle and myself. I've pulled Gary Pallister, Gary Neville and David Beckham out of the England squad for the match against Mexico on Saturday.

It's true that I believe friendly internationals at this stage of a season is crazy, but I'm not in the business of deliberately trying to wreck Hoddle's selections. The plain fact is that all three of the withdrawn players were injured. Neville hadn't even been able to start at Everton, while the other two were both substituted during the game because of injury.

Anyway, I don't really know why I should have to put a case across for the withdrawals. The onus should be on the FA to justify their decision to arrange a friendly match at the busiest time of the season. I can tell them that if our chairman Martin Edwards had his way, none of our players would be selected during the season for a friendly match.

While the FA are at it, they might like to argue the case for the players taking part in a friendly international summer tournament instead of enjoying a well-earned rest. Again, I can't see the sense in piling on even more commitments. What we really need is an extension to the season to give us a decent run-in. At the moment it looks like we'll have to play four fixtures in the final week,

Happily, Glenn was at Goodison. He saw the substitutions for himself and I think he understands, despite the efforts of the press to stir up trouble between us. Nicky Butt is the only survivor out of Glenn's original four United selections ... until he tells me he wants David May and Philip Neville as replacements. I have no problem with that. In fact I'm delighted, especially for David, because like Steve Bruce – who was never capped – David's an unsung hero. Neither of them is a flamboyant player, but they exert great influence in defence. I'm glad that unlike Steve, David is being recognised internationally as an important defender.

# Cantona bombshell

Cathy is still down in London with Jason and Tania, but nevertheless I feel obliged to go to Manchester cabaret artiste Frank Lamar's birthday party in the Rover's Return at Granada Studios. Frank does such a lot for charity, and I can't believe he's 60. He receives messages from people like Danny La Rue and Bernard Manning, while I meet up with two of my old warriors, Bryan Robson and Steve Bruce. It's a good night.

*Monday 24 March*
We have a fortnight clear of club fixtures because of the international weekend, but social fixtures soon fill up the gaps. Today I have lunch with Martin Buchan, the former Manchester United captain, and Hymie Wernick, a car dealer who is chairman of Martin's testimonial committee, to celebrate the 25 years they have known each other. Under Hymie's guidance we have a Jewish lunch in Prestwich. I can hardly move afterwards – which is unfortunate, because in the evening I am due to dine out again, this time at a fund-raising dinner for local football club Radcliffe Borough. I'm pleased to support them because they're a club who get off their backsides to do things. However, it does mean I have to confront Bernard Manning again, and that means more stick. As he points out, he's a Manchester City fan. His most insulting barb is reserved for the 82-year-old former president of Radcliffe, who is quietly minding his own business down at the other end of the table. Bernard grabs the mike and announces to the assembled guests, "Eat up your soup, because if you don't, you'll end up looking like that old beggar."
I don't know how he gets away with it.

*Tuesday 25 March*
The Schmeichel/Wright issue came up again at today's board meeting. Peter is still adamant that he won't cooperate

with the FA because he feels he has no case to answer. I'm glad to say that the directors are backing him. Indeed, they admire the stand he has taken and don't see why he should be subjected to what amounts to harassment.

*Thursday 27 March*

I fly to Hamburg to watch Borussia Dortmund, our European semi-final opponents, in action against St Pauli. I'm told around 7,000 Scots work in Hamburg, mostly in the insurance and fishing industries. Amazing how the master race gets everywhere!

The game doesn't tell us a lot. What it does underline, however, is the importance to Dortmund of Andreas Moller. They wouldn't have won the game without him.

It's deadline day for transfers in the Premiership, and some of the media have been chasing me. I've got nothing to tell them, though. For one reason or another there's nothing on. I'll wait until the summer to finalise my plans on that front.

*Saturday 29 March*

So many players are away that training has just ticked over this week. In the morning I watch our A team beat Burnley 3–1; they look likely to win their League again, for which Eric Harrison deserves credit. In the afternoon, I watch England play Mexico on television and I'm pleased to see Nicky Butt get on for the last 15 minutes. I don't expect the pundits will be ecstatic with the result, but I thought England do quite well and look comfortable. They do what they need to do. As you would expect, the South Americans are gifted enough to test England, so no-one was short-changed watching the game.

As I sit twiddling my thumbs watching the telly, I feel more disturbed than ever about another blank weekend in the Premiership. I can understand why Glenn wants a fixture. He's a young man with lots of energy to burn, and he must be finding the switch from club to international management very difficult. You go from the daily involvement of training, buying and selling players, and arranging contracts, to a great void, with no players to handle from day to day and weeks between fixtures. No wonder he wants to grab some action.

I've always felt that the job of national manager is better suited to an older man. The appointment of Jock Stein in Scotland, for instance, was perfect timing. Here was an older man with 20 years' experience and considerable success behind him at club level, who was more likely to show patience. Glenn is a young man in a hurry. Having lost to Italy, I'm sure he thought it was important to establish some team unity and get a grip again. But why at Easter, when the fixtures are piling up for the successful clubs? And why on the Bank Holiday, which invariably pulls in big crowds and is the point of the season when the League traditionally takes its final shape?

Perhaps Glenn wants to try out new players. But from my experience, that never works out because you get so many withdrawals. I make no apology for my attitude. I've got a key European quarter final coming up, and at this time of the year the players suffer from strains, pulls, aches and general fatigue.

David Beckham is a case in point. His fitness at the moment concerns me. How far can he run now? How much more does he have in his tank to give the team? Because he is young, people say – himself included – that he can run for ever, but there is running and there is running. I'm talking about the explosive runs, and the accuracy of his work. The boy doesn't see it; he can't see it. I keep telling him I'll phone his house to make sure he's resting. I probably won't, of course; it's only a threat. But he knows better than to doubt me.

Glenn knows my feelings about friendly games. He also knows, I'm sure, that I won't let him down when it comes to the real thing.

*Tuesday 1 April*

One of the compensations of having no matches over Easter was being able to watch Hugh McIlvanney's three-part BBC documentary examining that trio of great football managers, Sir Matt Busby, Bill Shankly and Jock Stein. If any journalist could capture the poetry and romance of those men, it's undoubtedly Hugh. The only disappointment for me was that the series was not long enough. I wanted to get right inside their heads. Nevertheless, it was an absorbing programme.

I first met Shanks when I was chairman of the Professional Footballers' Association in Scotland. Jock Stein kindly arranged for me to watch Liverpool play at Derby in a League title decider. I was with Jock's son in the boardroom when Bill came in, hands in pockets Cagney fashion, and proceeded to show us all the photographs of Anfield's famous players displayed on the walls. He had a comment to make about each of them: Raich Carter, Dally Duncan, Billy Steele, Steve Bloomer ... and he described Peter Doherty as the greatest player of all time, blessed with power, pace, dribbling and control. I was aching to tell him that my father had played with Peter Doherty for Glentoran, but I was so in awe of Bill that I couldn't get the words out.

But when it got to just ten minutes to kick off and we were still touring the boardroom, I did manage to say, "Excuse me Mr Shankly, do you realise it's 7.20 pm?"

"Son," he said, "if I've got to be with my team tonight in a League decider, there's something wrong with them." I've never forgotten that. To this day, once I've said my piece I leave the players alone just before the start of a game.

Years later, I met Shanks at Liverpool when I was manager of Aberdeen. He told me he'd heard about the great things I was doing at Pittodrie. I was still a bit tongue-tied, because it was like meeting the Pope. He said to me, "Are you here to see my team, son?" I replied that I was, to which he said: "Aye, they've all tried that."

*Thursday 3 April*

It's a free week, apart from World Cup qualifiers. We're just fiddling about in training and practising things like free kicks and set pieces. There's no need to demand anything physical from the players at this stage of the season.

The Republic of Ireland played in far-flung Macedonia last night, so we arranged for a private jet to pick up Denis Irwin and Roy Keane after the match to get them back early. I think we'll save 24 hours that way, and that day is valuable if they've been injured.

We're at home to Derby on Saturday, but my mind is already racing forward to next Wednesday's Champions' League semi-final first leg against Borussia Dortmund in Germany. We must take care of every angle.

*Friday 4 April*

Most people would be flattered to have a plane specially arranged to fly them half way across Europe. All dead-pan Denis Irwin could do was complain that there were no beers on board to go with the sandwiches. That's footballers for you!

Meanwhile, the Premier League chairmen have referred our request for an extension to the season to the League's board of directors, its chairman Sir John Quinton and chief executive Peter Leaver. Middlesbrough face a hectic run-in as well and would welcome some leeway, but Leeds were the only other club to support us at the meeting of the chairmen. What you see is what you get from Bill Fotherby, the Leeds chairman, who spoke with typical Yorkshire bluntness.

The most vocal opposition came from Peter Robinson of Liverpool, which I find surprising. Liverpool know what fixture pile-up is all about. As Alan Hansen recently wrote of the season when Liverpool played three FA Cup semi-finals against Arsenal, "You got up in the morning and didn't know if any part of your body was all right." The game is even tougher now.

Everything, from cars to athletes, goes faster these days – and footballers are no exception.

Roy Evans has also spoken out against our request. At least the manager of Liverpool has experience of playing football and if that is what he genuinely believes, then so be it. But among all the opposition from Anfield, one man was strangely quiet. When we lost the Championship in 1992, we collapsed through fatigue after too many matches in too short a time. At that time Rick Parry was chief executive of the Premier League, and he said that that kind of fixture congestion would never happen again. Now he's chief executive at Liverpool and there's not been a word from him.

Arsene Wenger has also had a pop at me, and not for the first time. The media in London are trying to turn him into some sort of guru. Just because he's French, and different, the press seem to love getting him to comment on this and that. Perhaps they wind him up and lead him into controversy. But when it comes to our request for an extension to the season, he's not got the experience to entitle him to pass comment. He just can't know what it's like to play four games in eight days.

We went into that final week five years ago with a four-point lead over Leeds. We then drew at Luton, lost at home to Nottingham Forest and lost at West Ham and Liverpool. Nothing in our form that season suggested we would start losing like that; it was because we were tired from having to play four games in eight days. That's exactly what we are being asked to do now.

The Premiership should not be decided by a test of endurance over the last lap. It should be about going to places like Anfield, Highbury, Elland Road and Goodison Park and proving yourself by playing football.

It was a disappointing day on the home front, too. The twins are getting better now so Cathy's back home, but she's poorly with a virus. We had to pull out of going to the wedding of her hairdresser, Rachel.

# Cantona bombshell

*Saturday 5 April*

An unexpected home defeat against Derby to the tune of 3–2, and I'm suspicious. Did someone from television give Derby advance knowledge of our team? They hadn't played with a flat back four all year, and today they suddenly sprang it on us and caught us on the hop.

But it was a fantastic game, and Derby played better than any other visiting team at Old Trafford this season. We did help them by shooting ourselves three times in the foot with careless concentration at the back. The second goal saw Paulo Wanchope, their new Costa Rican player, run 40 yards through the middle to score. I bet he was thinking to himself, "I like it in this country, nobody tackles you."

At half time I had to ask our players if they thought tackling had suddenly been outlawed. I was angry: we had been slip-shod. Perhaps they were already preoccupied by the thought of our big game in Dortmund next week.

For the second half I took off Nicky Butt, who was still feeling his way after injury, and put on Ole Gunnar Solksjaer. He partnered Andy Cole upfront in a bid to peg back Derby's two-goal lead. Eric scored immediately after the interval from Solskjaer's great pass. The Frenchman's control and balance were superb; it was one of his best performances of the season. He was the driving force. But the rest of the team were off the pace and Derby went 3–1 up before Ole Gunnar scored our second.

In the post-match television interview I was in just the right mood to give my views on an extension to the season and on Arsene Wenger's comments criticising me. I didn't mince my words, though I admit I'm no longer hopeful of getting an extension. Manchester United, of all clubs, won't get any help; there's too much self-interest around in the rest of the League. We must look after ourselves, and remember this episode when an issue such as pay-per-view television is on the table and everyone wants United on their side as the one club they need to secure the best deal. Losing today is a kick in the teeth, but it serves as a reminder that no one else is going to help us.

The match wasn't the only disaster of the day. I discovered I was double-booked for the evening as a result of my electronic organiser breaking down. I had to give back-word to Harold Riley, the Royal portrait painter, who had invited me to a dinner in aid of Sir Matt Busby's charities. I felt awful, but Cathy and I had Jimmy Steele and his good friend Margaret down from Scotland for the weekend. Jimmy, the old Celtic masseur who has also worked with our players on special occasions over the years, is in his eighties. I knew they were really looking forward to their visit. He's a great character as well as a lovely man; he's always full of stories about his days in football and as a second for the boxer, Freddie Mills.

I deserved to enjoy myself with Jimmy, after spending the rest of the weekend feeling angry with Arsene Wenger, guilty at letting Harold down and full of despair after losing at home to Derby.

*Premiership / Old Trafford / Att: 55,243*

**Manchester United 2**
Schmeichel, G Neville (Irwin), P Neville, Pallister (Scholes), Cantona, Butt (Solskjaer), Cole, Beckham, Giggs, Keane, Johnsen
*Scorers: Cantona, Solskjaer*

**Derby County 3**
Poom, C Powell, D Powell, Van der Laan, Sturridge, Ward, Trollope, Laursen, Dailly, Wanchope (Simpson), McGrath
*Scorers: Ward, Wanchope, Sturridge*

*Sunday 6 April*

The house is even fuller today. Jason is visiting and my brother Martin has arrived in readiness for tomorrow's trip to Dortmund. We all settle down to watch Middlesbrough play Leicester in the final of the Coca-Cola Cup. I'm enjoying it, when Cathy bursts in to tell me that Liverpool are a goal up against Coventry. I roar at her and ask if she's trying to ruin my day. She slams the door on her way out.

Later on, she comes in again and asks if I still don't want to hear the Liverpool score. I'm just about to shout at her again when she says, "So don't you want to know Coventry have equalised?" This time I send her on her way with a "I love you, darling."

Later that evening, Gary Pallister tells me he's been saying the same kind of thing. Apparently, he'd been watching his old club Middlesbrough when his phone rang. It was Dion Dublin from the visitors' dressing room at Anfield.

"Who's your favourite player then? Who's just scored the winner for Coventry?" asked big Dion.

"I love you," shouted Pally, who now wants to vote for Dublin as Manchester United's Player of the Year. And why not? Our former striker scored against Arsenal, and now he's done it against Liverpool. He deserves to be our top man. What a break for us – though at the end of the day, our fate will lie in our own hands. We can't depend on others.

*Monday 7 April*

We're setting off for the tie against Dortmund a day earlier than usual. It's a big, big game, and now the weather is getting better there may be a chance of the players getting some fresh air and sun on them to help them relax.

People keep coming up to tell us we're representing England, the fans are pleading with us not to let them down and the directors are joking about the share prices. Football cuts across so many people's lives. Me, I'm just concentrating on trying to attend to every little detail. If I can improve our preparation by just five per cent, it could make all the difference. We are taking 21 players to Germany, and for the first time in ages the whole squad is fit.

We trained in the morning before we set off. After a flight of just over an hour, we spend the rest of the day settling into a very pleasant hotel perfectly situated out of town.

*Tuesday 8 April*

A long lie-in for the players, followed by massages. Then a trip to the stadium, where we'll be playing tomorrow night, for our permitted one hour of training. The actual pitch is disappointing, but I put it out of my mind. It will be just as bad for Dortmund. We practise with a Derby ball, which they use in Germany. Everything is going fine, until Peter Schmeichel and David May pull muscles: May has a thigh strain and Schmeichel a ricked back. A complete squad was too good to be true.

Now I have to rethink the team. I had intended to leave out Nicky Butt in order to put Ronny Johnsen on to the dangerous Moller, but now Butt is back in. Schmeichel wants to wait for a fitness test tomorrow, but I have to prepare Raimond Van Der Gouw to take over just in case. He knows he is in the firing line. If I wait until the last moment for a decision on Peter's fitness, it's hardly a vote of confidence in his number two. We consider giving Peter a painkilling injection but Mike Stone, the club doctor, says the damaged area is too big to make that practical. I'll sleep on it, and see how Peter is tomorrow.

*Wednesday 9 April*

In the afternoon I tell Peter that he can do his warm-up before the match as usual and that I'll include his name on the team-sheet we hand in at 6.30 pm. According to UEFA, we can change the goalkeeper up to half an hour before kick-off if necessary. Then I tell Raimond that I don't think Peter has any chance of making it, and that he'll definitely be playing. It's only fair that he should be able to prepare himself. I'm quite happy to have Rai in goal; he is a fantastically good keeper. It's a real bonus for us that he's such a patient number two.

As expected, Peter can't get through his warm-up, and UEFA issue a second team-sheet with a goalkeeping alteration. That, however, is not the end of the crisis. The game has only been going for 20 minutes when Raimond is involved in an almighty collision with Gary Pallister. They both go down and lie motionless, and I'm thinking we don't even have a reserve goalkeeper on the bench now. Eventually they both carry on, though it takes Gary half an hour to get back into top gear.

The half wears on, and with Keane on Moller and Butt marshalling Sousa we're doing OK. We even begin to make inroads ourselves, and after half an hour Eric has a great chance. I think he might at least hit the target.

I can see there are certain things Dortmund can't handle, though at half time I tell the players it seems as if they are waiting for me to reinforce their belief in themselves. We do well in the second half. But you also need that little bit of luck and it's missing when Nicky Butt hits the post after a great run. David Beckham beats the goalkeeper, only to see defender Kree make a last-gasp interception. As if that wasn't bad enough, Tretschok gets in a shot 15 minutes from the end which takes a deflection off Pallister and goes in.

We didn't deserve that. There is great disappointment in the dressing room afterwards. I'm still optimistic: five or six of our players didn't perform as well as they can, yet we still managed to create three very good chances. A one-goal deficit is not insurmountable.

*European Champions League / Westfalenstadion / Att: 48,500*
**Borussia Dortmund 1**
Klos, Reuter, Moller, Herrlich (Zorc), Lambert, Kree, Heinrich, Ricken (Freund), Sousa, Feiersinger, Tretschok (Reinhardt)
*Scorer: Tretschok*

**Manchester United 0**
Van Der Gouw, G Neville, Irwin, Johnsen, Pallister, Cantona, Butt, Beckham, Giggs (Scholes), Keane, Solskjaer (Cole)

*Thursday 10 April*
In an effort to prepare better for our next League game, we stayed over in Dortmund last night instead of flying home straight after the match. We trained this morning before an

afternoon flight, and I hope we will return to winning ways. After two defeats, the media are beginning to ask questions. Inevitably, Saturday's visit to Blackburn is being built up as a clash of the great rivals. Certainly, Blackburn beat us to the Championship two years ago, but a bee only stings once. It would cost Jack Walker the remainder of his fortune to put Blackburn on a par with the likes of Liverpool and ourselves. Don't get me wrong; Blackburn Rovers is a warm club and I love going there. They have the best boardroom spread of half-time eats in Britain, bar none.

I think it's time to rest David Beckham. A lot of people said how disappointing he was in Dortmund, but it's no use blaming the boy. This was always going to happen. I've tried to help as much as possible by resting him, and even pulled him out of the England game. The big question is: is he taking enough rest when he's not playing football?

*Saturday 12 April*

We were without Schmeichel and May again against Blackburn. I left David Beckham out, as planned, and went with both strikers, Cole and Solskjaer – partly because Colin Hendry, the Blackburn centre half who's such a key player for them, has been playing with a hernia problem for weeks. I've read that he keeps delaying an operation and he's obviously not in the best physical condition. We planned to try to turn him as much as possible; the passing ability of Paul Scholes would help exploit any gaps behind him. It might not sound very sporting, but you've always got to try and take advantage of the opposition's weaknesses.

There was a tasty start to the game when Tim Sherwood rattled Gary Neville within the first couple of minutes. It wasn't long before we got a penalty for Jeff Kenna bringing down Butt, although I've got to admit that Nicky made a meal of it – his dive was worth nine out of ten for technical merit. Then, lo and behold, the great man missed it. Eric Cantona was not a happy bunny, but when I ask him later what happened, all I got was a "Je ne sais quoi." However, I still felt confident of victory because our rhythm was so good, as the first goal showed. It was a superb piece of football, ending with a shot into the net by Andy Cole from Cantona's pass.

Cole was razor sharp through the whole game, and went on to make goals for Scholes and Cantona. The 3–2 win was important, and my main thought now is that we must keep on winning, regardless of how our leading rivals do.

*Premiership / Ewood Park / Att: 30,476*
**Blackburn Rovers 2**
Flowers, Kenna, Berg, Hendry (Pearce), Le Saux, Gallacher (Pedersen), Flitcroft (Donis), Sherwood, McKinlay, Wilcox, Warhurst
*Scorers: McKinlay, Warhurst*
**Manchester United 3**
Van der Gouw, G Neville, P Neville, Pallister, Johnsen, Scholes (Beckham), Butt, Keane, Cantona, Solskjaer, Cole
*Scorers: Cole, Scholes, Cantona*

*Sunday 13 April*
I fly to London to watch the FA Cup semi final at Highbury between Wimbledon and Chelsea. I'm struck by the movement of Gianfranco Zola, who makes the difference between the two teams. Mark Hughes scores two smashing goals. On the day it proves all too much for Wimbledon, brave as they are.

It's the Professional Footballers' Association dinner tonight, so after the game I book in at the Grosvenor Hotel and watch the other semi final, between Chesterfield and Middlesbrough, on television. What a fantastic game. It has everything: drama, romance, controversy, excitement, skill, blood and thunder. Full marks to John Duncan for preparing his team to play so far above themselves. Their last-gasp equaliser was extraordinary. I did feel for Bryan Robson and the other ex-pats from Old Trafford who are with Boro now: Viv Anderson, Clayton Blackmore and Gordon McQueen. But deep down, I feel it's more important for Robbo to keep his club in the Premiership.

What a disappointing evening the PFA dinner turned out to be. It wasn't the actual awards, or Sky's presentation – both were fine. But the audience has become a rabble. There were just too many drunken people. I'm sure Gordon Taylor was cringeing with embarrassment, especially when one of the speakers was forced to sit down because everyone was talking. I spoke for about seven minutes, which was long enough, though I frightened them all when I said I'd applied for an extension to the evening. That got a laugh from everyone but David Dein, Arsenal's vice chairman, who was sitting right in front of me with a face like a grave robber's dog.

He might have smiled if he'd seen me earlier when I was in the gents. A guy in the next stall recognised me, swung round to say hello – and left me absolutely soaking. It summed up the night!

*Tuesday 15 April*

Today I went to the unveiling of a controversial new painting at Manchester City Art Gallery by local artist Michael Browne. The picture includes Eric Cantona, several of the players and me in historical garb in a resurrection scene, based on two Renaissance paintings, Piero della Francesca's "Resurrection" and Mantegna's "Julius Caesar". Eric is portrayed as Christ, which some regard as blasphemous. However, according to Michael, he is simply trying to convey the importance of football in people's lives (including his own). It's not putting it too strongly to say that there are fans out there who worship Cantona, and certainly look upon him as a hero.

I can understand the criticism, but I think Michael – who spent a year on what is a massive project – never intended to offend the ecclesiastics. I try to fend off any criticism because it's a marvellous piece of work.

# Cantona bombshell

We have a wonderful night at Old Trafford. United play against Celtic in a testimonial for their former player, Brian McClair. The crowd is stunning, around 40,000, and if ever a player deserved this kind of appreciation it's Brian; his loyalty and dedication to Manchester United has been unswerving. We lose the game 2–1, which shouldn't surprise me. We've played five testimonials against Celtic in my time here and lost the lot.

There's a good atmosphere. The evening gives me the opportunity to introduce a few young players later on in the match, namely Chris Casper, Graeme Tomlinson, John Curtis, Ronnie Wallwork, Philip Mulryne and goalkeeper Paul Gibson. We have several young players I expect come through, but they may have to be patient. They certainly won't be given their chance as early as, say, Ryan Giggs, because the standard of the first team is higher now and it's harder to force a way in.

There's no question that the standard of our young players is the best it's been in my time. It's unfair to name too many names at this stage, but we certainly have high hopes for John Curtis, a former England schoolboy captain from Nuneaton; Wes Brown, a local boy, and Alex Notman, a great little Scottish striker.

Unfortunately, Celtic have problems behind the scenes. There seems to be uncertainty surrounding the future of their manager, Tommy Burns. I think he's having a hard time with his chairman Fergus McCann, who's putting him through the mill, and I fear for his job. Tommy's the type who cares deeply about his club and his job, but he's an emotional man who speaks his mind. All I can advise is that he should hold fire and see how things transpire. Celtic would be very foolish to think they could easily get someone as committed and passionate as Tommy to replace him.

I do wonder about the decisions of directors at times. The behaviour of supporters is often criticised, and we managers come under fire when we lose our tempers with referees. By contrast, by and large directors escape scrutiny because they are the people in control. You'd think that the examples of Manchester United and Liverpool would show how it pays to persevere with your original appointment as manager. All too often, directors chop and change their managers when there's no guarantee that change will bring success. Martin Edwards stood by me when things weren't going too well. He supported my youth policy, and today we're reaping the benefits. In fact, all the directors at Old Trafford have been great, and people like Sir Bobby Charlton have been solidly behind me. Directors, who after all are generally older men, should show more patience, but not many of them do.

*Wednesday 16 April*

Today, in preparation for our game against Roy Evans' team on Saturday, I went to Goodison Park to watch Everton play Liverpool.

I didn't realise how much passion there is among the fans on Merseyside. On one side were the Liverpool fans, shouting at me that I was here to see the champions. On the other side, the Evertonian cries of "Don't let that Liverpool mob win the title" were just as vehement.

I got a lot of pleasure from watching the fans and I admire their passion. All players should watch games and support a team so that they know what it means to care. It would make them more aware of their responsibilities to the supporters.

Liverpool scored a smashing goal. David James, who is getting a lot of criticism, made three good saves and kept Liverpool in the game. Nonetheless, Everton deserved their equaliser from Duncan Ferguson. It was a replica of the one he got at Old Trafford: control, turn and hit. The lad has certainly got ability, it's just a matter of someone harnessing it.

His goal did us a favour since the draw was a good result for us. We're now two points clear of Liverpool with a game in hand, which can't be bad.

# Cantona bombshell

*Thursday 17 April*

I'm picking my team for the clash with Liverpool. Ryan Giggs is not 100 per cent and is complaining of pain in the stomach area, so we're sending him for an abdominal scan. David Fevre is convinced there's nothing seriously wrong but it looks as if I must forget him for Saturday. We'll aim to have him right for Dortmund next week. In the meantime, my strategy for Anfield is geared to making sure that we don't allow Liverpool to settle into a flow, as that will lift their supporters. This match could prove to be the League decider.

*Saturday 19 April*

What a fantastic result! We did it without Giggs and with a slightly different system, which worked very well in the first half when we showed great ability to keep the ball. Our performance was first-class and we were well worth our 3–1 victory. Gary Pallister doesn't score many goals, but he powered home two headers from corner kicks and Andy Cole got one late on.

After the game, I was asked if we'd been practising set-pieces. I denied it because I wanted to hide the fact from Borussia Dortmund. Unbeknown to me, Pallister had already been interviewed and had revealed that we'd been rehearsing corners and free kicks all week. I blasted him on the coach, "Thanks Pally, why don't you tell the whole of Germany?" I guess we'll have to start singing from the same hymn sheet!

Even after such a fantastic victory, I still felt sorry for David James when I saw him standing on his own afterwards. I don't like to see players under pressure from criticism, and goalkeepers in particular can become very isolated. I couldn't help going over to tell him, "Keep your chin up, your form will come back." And I'm sure it will.

It had been an early morning kick-off and the victory made it an easy afternoon, especially when Blackburn scored a controversial last-minute equaliser to hold Arsenal to a 1–1 draw. Arsenal put the ball out of play so that an injured player could be treated. Chris Sutton, following the sporting custom, threw the ball back to Arsenal's Winterburn, but then put him under pressure to force a corner which led to the goal.

Arsene Wenger said later that England had created a fair play tradition which had now gone to pot. I can't agree. It would be a shame to let that one incident signal the end of a sporting habit which the fans love. Sutton was out of order, but maybe he was feeling the pressure of relegation.

Nevertheless, it was another great result for us; we're now five points in front of Liverpool and Arsenal with a game in hand on both. Newcastle, after the same number of matches as us, are nine points behind.

*Premiership / Anfield / Att: 40,892*

**Liverpool 1**
James, Kvarme, Wright, Harkness, McAteer (Collymore), Thomas, Barnes (Berger), Bjornebye, Redknapp, McManaman, Fowler
*Scorer: Barnes*

**Manchester United 3**
Schmeichel, G Neville, Johnsen, Pallister, P Neville, Keane, Butt, Beckham, Cantona, Scholes (McClair), Cole
*Scorers: Pallister 2, Cole*

*Sunday 20 April*

I'm feeling good. We're in a smashing League position. If we focus our minds and carry on working hard, the title will be ours.

Les Kershaw is back from watching Dortmund play Bayern and reports that all their big guns are back after injury. It doesn't worry me. It just means they'll revert to their normal two-up system, which I'm confident we can handle.

*Monday 21 April*

I tell Ryan Giggs the scan on his stomach problem is clear and try to assure him that there's nothing to worry about. I hope it will buck him up a bit, but he's not had a problem like this before. Despite my best efforts, will probably continue to worry. My big concern is that, even when he declares himself ready to play again, he'll have had no real training.

We have a light session and practise set pieces again. They could be important. We try out a free kick I once used with some success against the Germans many years ago at Aberdeen. Two players shape up to take a free kick, but pretend to get in each other's way and collide. Hopefully, the opposition loses concentration for a econd, whereupon you quickly take the kick and catch their defence off guard. I remember Aberdeen were 2–1 down against Bayern Munich in 1983 with 12 minutes to go when we pulled this stunt. The diversion not only got us an equaliser, but the Germans were so unnerved that they allowed us to score again a minute later and we won 3–2. Perhaps we'll try it tomorrow if the opportunity crops up – and the players manage to remember it in all the excitement.

Our line-up will rely on the same system we used so successfully against Porto at Old Trafford, except this time we won't have Ryan Giggs. Our priority is to avoid giving a goal away, and it's crucial that the defence concentrates. Ronny Johnsen's role is to sit in front of the defence and take care of Andreas Moller, who'll try to break from midfield into the hole behind the strikers. If we can get that right, we should have enough firepower with three up – Cantona, Cole and Solskjaer – to get us a goal.

I have to break the news to Denis Irwin that he won't be playing. He's terribly disappointed and asks what he's done wrong. I tell him absolutely nothing, that he's only out because of the niggling groin strain he's had and the great form of young Philip Neville. His youth is not a valid reason to ignore Neville, who's been playing out of his skin, showing real maturity and looking very strong. Over the last five years Denis has probably been our most consistent player, but I still feel that Philip is playing too well to be left out of this one.

In my pre-match press conference I do what I can to get across the confidence that I feel. I really think we're ready for this game.

*Wednesday 23 April*

Beaten 1–0. What can I say? If I'd thought beforehand that we were going to play as well as we did on the night, I'd have felt even more confident. People will remember the chances we missed rather than the performance, and those missed opportunities cost us a place in the final. But even the most cynical observer must agree that we played some great football and had Dortmund under constant pressure.

After this performance, I won't let anyone tell me that we're not good enough to win in Europe. If we had taken our chances, we could have gone on to get a really emphatic victory. Where the Germans had the luck was in scoring so early on in the first of the two ties – and with the help of a deflected shot. It gave them a sense of purpose and something to hang on to under all our pressure. It came across clearly in the performance of Jurgen Kohler, who'd been ill prior to the game, but flew out late to become the star of the night. His defending was inspirational and he made some remarkable clearances and interceptions.

A lot of things go through your mind after a shock defeat like this – such as the appointment of the Swiss referee as a late replacement. He'd never been in charge of a Champions' League game before, and to be given a debut at a semi final seemed strange. He chalked off two goals we thought were legitimate, and I had serious doubts about his capability.

But the referee apart, we have no excuses. We had the chances to secure our place in the final against Juventus in Munich. Dortmund were very fortunate to overcome us. The number of chances we had in both legs was unbelievable, and quite out of keeping for a team going out of Europe.

# Cantona bombshell

It's a devastating blow, and I just don't know how long it'll take me to get over it; I suspect it's going to hurt like hell for some time. Fortunately, we're still in an excellent position to win the League ... That challenge will help us all to get our act back together.

*European Champions' League / Old Trafford / Att: 53,606*
**Manchester United 0**
Schmeichel, G Neville, P Neville, May (Scholes), Pallister, Johnsen, Cantona, Butt, Cole, Beckham, Solskjaer
**Borussia Dortmund 1**
Klos, Reuter (Tretschok), Chapuisat, Moller, Riedle (Herrlich), Lambert, Kohler, Kree, Heinrich, Ricken (Zorc), Feiersinger
*Scorer: Ricken*

## *Thursday 24 April*

There's an air of depression about the place. Eric Cantona in particular is in a broody mood. I suspect success in Europe has become very important to him, a personal Holy Grail, and I think he has reached a crossroads in his career. It looks as if the chances he missed – not to mention his relatively quiet performance – have prompted him to question his future. But my immediate concern is that we still have a Championship to win, and I'm worried that Eric's depression will affect his form over the remaining four fixtures.

I purposely keep away from the players. They are in low spirits, too, and I reckon they're best left alone to sort themselves out. Anyway, I'd probably find it hard to lift their spirits because I'm down myself. The fact that most of them are going away now on international duty is a bonus; it will give them a break from the pressures at Old Trafford. Me, I've got plenty of thinking to do.

At lunchtime I go to Oldham for the opening of a new synthetic pitch at Breeze Hill School. One of the aims of the project is to encourage Asian girls to play outdoor sports, which can prove difficult because of their culture. I admire them for trying, and make sure there's a smile on my face. After the opening ceremony I'm cornered by Bob Cass and Joe Melling from the Mail on Sunday, who have been trying to track me down all day. They interview me sitting in a car outside the school, and in a funny way it helps take my mind away from my disappointment and focus on the trip to Leicester. It has become a vital game for us.

*Friday 25 April*

I travel up to Scotland today to speak at a Newspaper Press Fund lunch in memory of Jim Rodger. I know his widow Cathy will be there, and I'm worried that talking about Jim will upset her. However, she tells me to do what I have to do, so I recount some of my favourite stories about him. I only get to Scotland a couple of times a year these days and it was refreshing, despite the sad occasion.

As if to rub it in that it just isn't my week, I fall down a two-foot hole full of water as we are being manoeuvred around for a group picture by the photographers. I scrape a big gash in my shin and end up with soaking wet trousers. It's an unhappy reminder of the episode in the gents at the PFA dinner. Naturally I let fly at the photographers with a few choice words, and Paul Sturrock, the former Dundee United player who's now manager of St Johnstone, laughs and says, "I thought you were supposed to have mellowed!" Steve Paterson, who played for United as a youngster and is now manager of Inverness Caledonian Thistle, was also there.

*Wednesday 26 April*

I watch the B team win at Bury to clinch the Lancashire League Division Two title. Actually, it isn't one of their best displays, but they've scored 109 goals this season so they deserve it. It's good to see young boys progressing, even at this early stage. Two local boys in particular catch my eye: Michael Ryan from Stockport and Richard Wellens from Manchester though I really don't know why, at eight stone wet through, Wellens wants to fight everyone. Big Norman Davies, our recently retired kit man, is there, and I enjoy bacon butties afterwards at his new house in Bury.

*Sunday 27 April*

Cathy and I attend a reception for Pendlebury Children's Hospital today. There may not be much football being played at the moment, but there are plenty of social occasions to take its place.

*Monday 28 April*

More social engagements. This time it's a dinner to welcome new members, of which I'm one, at the Caledonian Club in London. As you might imagine from the name, the club is for those members of the master race who've had to leave Scotland for one reason or another. It's a lovely place with a real sense of history.

*Wednesday 30 April*

It's international day. I've got everything crossed, because the last thing we want is an injury blitz as we prepare for four games in eight days. I arrange for a charter jet to bring Roy Keane and Denis Irwin home quickly from Romania. It's a four-seater, so Aston Villa share it with us to pick up Steve Staunton and Andy Townsend.

I watch Italy play Poland on satellite TV, but catch snatches of England against Georgia. Gary Neville and David Beckham seem to play well and England win 2–0. Nevertheless, I expect Glenn Hoddle will still get slaughtered in print tomorrow.

And to think that could have been me on the receiving end! Not many people know this, but I was offered the England job after Terry Venables left. I turned it down in favour of staying with Manchester United. However, all that is water under the bridge now; not even the European defeat has made me regret my decision.

*Thursday 1 May*

It's a late night tonight. I watch television until the wee small hours as Labour sweep to success in the General Election. So, the first leg of my Double is up ... sorry chairman!

*Saturday 3 May*

It is a terribly hot day at Leicester – already 85 degrees by 11 am – but we are on fire as well. Andy Cole could easily have had a hat-trick before we go to sleep and concede two early goals. I think we are in real trouble, but we manage to salvage a 2–2 draw.

Andy Cole sets up Ole Gunnar Solskjaer twice for the Norwegian to take his tally for the season to 17. The lad has a good attitude, and to reach this kind of total in his first Premiership season is tremendous. We think he'll be even better next season.

I am delighted to get a point, and pleased with the players for their determination to get something out of what had become a very difficult situation. We've got three home games now in which to secure three points, and if we perform up to our usual standard, we're surely there.

After the game we are straight on to the coach – no visit to the players' lounge at Filbert Street, no beer. I explain to the players that I need their patience. We are going to Mottram Hall Hotel for the weekend to rest up for Monday's game against Middlesbrough at Old Trafford.

# Cantona bombshell

*Premiership / Venue: Filbert Street / Att: 21,068*
**Leicester City 2**
Keller, Grayson, Elliott, Walsh, Kaamark, Izzet, Lennon, Parker (Campbell),
Heskey, Marshall, Claridge (Whitlow)
*Scorers: Walsh, Marshall*

**Manchester United 2**
Schmeichel, G Neville, P Neville, May, Pallister, Keane, Butt (Beckham),
Cantona, Scholes, Cole, Solskjaer
*Scorer: Solskjaer 2*

## Monday 5 May

In my pre-match talk, I stress the need to close Juninho
down quickly. I wonder if the players were listening: the little
Brazilian destroys us. He scores the first goal of the day and
triggers Middlesbrough's terrific performance. Roy Keane brings
us level, but we were all at sea and 3–1 down after 40 minutes.

I suppose I mustn't grumble; we do claw our way back to
3–3. But I'm far from happy at conceding eight goals against
three sides in the bottom half of the table over the last three
weeks. In fact, we have lost 23 goals against the bottom seven
sides this season. It's a point I make at the press conference.
Sometimes it's a mistake to be over-protective of the team, and
this is the worst we have defended in the last six years. I won't
criticise individuals in public, but as a team they cannot escape.

*Premiership / Venue: Old Trafford / Att: 54,589*
**Manchester United 3**
Schmeichel, G Neville, Irwin, May, Pallister, Cantona, Cole, Beckham, Keane,
Johnsen (Scholes), Solskjaer
*Scorers: Keane, G Neville, Solskjaer*

**Middlesbrough 3**
Roberts, Pearson, Emerson (Kinder), Mustoe, Juninho, Ravanelli (Freestone),
Fleming, Blackmore, Festa, Stamp, Hignett (Vickers)
*Scorers: Juninho, Emerson, Hignett*

## Tuesday 6 May

Eric's still not looking right as we loosen off in training. We
don't do any work, not even with the ball, because I remember
only too well a similarly hectic finish to the season five years

ago, when we just went to pieces. Drawing the last two games suggests we're not at our best, even though we staged tremendous fight-backs in both of them. But what was I worrying about? By the end of the night we're Champions again, thanks to West Ham, who draw with Newcastle, and Wimbledon, who oblige with a 2–1 win over Liverpool.

I deliberately went to the gym for an hour in the evening, then had a sauna and a meal. I wasn't going to put myself through the torture of watching Teletext, and really, I'm more concerned with planning Thursday's game against Newcastle. I got into my car at 9.45 pm and switched on my mobile, which promptly rang. The call was from Amer Midani, the United director, to congratulate me.

So that's how I learned we were Champions again. I was near Amer's house, so I dropped in and had a glass of champagne. I had just got home when chairman Martin Edwards came round, so I had another drink, but it was all very civilised. I was in bed before midnight.

How do I feel about winning the title without kicking a ball? Well, some people would no doubt prefer to see us win it live in the games against Newcastle or West Ham, but to be honest I'm quite relieved. At least this way the Championship has been decided by football, not by a test of endurance. I've made no secret of my dislike of being asked to play four games in eight days. Who knows how the players would have reacted to playing too many games too quickly? Now the issue has been settled for us. I think we've answered all the questions asked of us over the course of the season.

*Wednesday 7 May*

I was up before 5 am walking round the house, and thought I might as well get down early to the training ground. Father Keegan, a long-time United fan, is another early bird. He insists we celebrate with an Irish breakfast: black pudding, sausages, the whole works. Teresa cooks it for us, singing away, and as the players begin to arrive I shake hands with each one and congratulate them.

*Thursday 8 May*

The phone hasn't stopped ringing with congratulatory calls from friends and colleagues. We still have a game tonight, and it's a very important one for Newcastle, who are chasing second place and entry into the Champions' League.

Ryan Giggs and Nicky Butt, who are both injured, are going to London to represent the club and receive an award from the Variety Club of Great Britain for our support of children's charities. Karel Poborsky will definitely play because he has only made 13 starts in the League so far and we don't want any trouble with his work permit.

Before the game, Kenny Dalglish is very complimentary about our success. I see a change in him. He's more relaxed; I think the break from football has done him good. He tells me he really appreciates the passion of the supporters at Newcastle.

As for the game, it would have been nice to celebrate with a few goals, but it was still a reasonably entertaining match. Our opponents worked very hard. At least we defended quite well and didn't give any goals away, which is something.

*Premiership / Old Trafford / Att: 55,236*
**Manchester United 0**
Schmeichel, G Neville, P Neville, May, Johnsen, Keane (McClair), Scholes, Beckham, Cantona, Poborsky, Cole (Solskjaer)
**Newcastle United 0**
Srnicek, Watson, Elliott, Batty, Peacock, Albert, Barton, Beresford, Shearer, Ferdinand (Asprilla), Gillespie

*Friday 9 May*

I make an early start to drive to London and pick up my grandchildren – and then a receive a bombshell on my arrival back in Manchester. Eric Cantona comes to see me to say that he wants to retire from football this week. I thought he'd been very preoccupied; now I know why.

Of course I'm enormously taken aback by Eric's decision. But I try not to get too heavy on him, and by the end he's laughing a bit. I tell him I want to get our final League game out of the way, and that we mustn't make any snap decisions before talking about it more next week.

Afterwards, talking to Brian Kidd, I wonder if this is just Eric's excuse to get away from Manchester United. But I don't think so. I believe Eric is seriously wondering whether he's now run his course at Old Trafford. Maybe he's influenced by this last season; by his own high standards, he's been disappointing. I don't think he's ready to throw himself off a bridge just yet, but he knows he hasn't had the same influence of late. He is still a charismatic figure with great vision, but at 31, perhaps he's lost his cutting edge. It happens. I know my best years as a striker were between 25 and 29. By the time I turned 30 I didn't have quite the same drive as a young buck.

In the evening I attend the show at the Opera House in aid of the Prince Charles Trust. I find the Prince very clued up about football and we chat at the interval about the game against Dortmund. He says he was disappointed we hadn't won, and certainly knows all about the chances we had missed. Maybe the young princes had briefed him to meet our players!

*Saturday 10 May*

I have a meeting with the chairman and Johann Cruyff at Mottram Hall to discuss Jordi's future. Johann is a forthright character but it is all quite harmonious. I have an open mind about the situation. You can't simply dismiss Jordi's ability, even though he's failed to establish himself as a regular in the team. I say that if he wants to try again next season he is quite welcome, only he will have to work a lot harder. I explain that

I am trying to buy another player who could affect his position, so we agree to wait and see what develops.

Along with Sir Bobby Charlton, I am invited to open Hulme Bridge. It's a spectacular arch to represent the crescents which were knocked down, which now links the regenerated Hulme area with central Manchester. The bonus is that I get to ride in the most expensive motor car in the country: a silver-plated Rolls Royce, made in the original Rolls Royce factory which is near the bridge. The car is over 100 years old and said to be worth millions of pounds.


*Sunday 11 May*

The last game of the season. There's a carnival atmosphere at Old Trafford as all four of our Championship-winning teams receive their trophies. Eric Harrison's A side and Neil Bailey's B side top Lancashire League Divisions One and Two respectively. Jimmy Ryan's Pontin's League winners are on parade too and, of course, we're up for the Premiership.

The feeling of winning the League for the first time in 26 years, back in 1993, will never be bettered. It was a precious moment for everyone connected with Manchester United. But although winning feels different now, it's still exhilarating. The demands on us are greater each season and we can bask in the satisfaction of having met those demands.

I've always wanted to create attacking teams. The fact that we've increased our goal tally each season is a measure of our progress. As if to emphasise the point, today we score twice against West Ham, with goals from Paul Scholes and Jordi Cruyff. It is a pleasing result after we fired blanks against Newcastle. Towards the end of the game Peter Schmeichel starts waving frantically at our bench and tapping an imaginary watch on his wrist as the fans urge him to go upfield and play centre forward. The switchboard has been jammed all week with calls asking if I'm going to play him up front.

# A Will to Win

Perhaps word has got out that Albert, our kit man, has had a red shirt printed with number one and Schmeichel's name on it. But even if the match is a celebration for us, it would be wrong to turn it into a circus. All I have in mind is to let him go up for a corner kick. Unhappily for Peter, we just don't get one!

Everyone is deliriously happy, and I'm busy waving to my grandson Jake in the directors' box. But my eyes keep straying back to Eric Cantona. He seems deep in contemplation, especially when he lifts the Premiership trophy at the end. Perhaps it is just my fevered imagination ... I guess I'll find out soon enough when we talk.

*Premiership / Old Trafford / Att: 55,249*

**Manchester United 2**
Schmeichel, Irwin (Clegg), P Neville, May, Johnsen, Cantona, Butt, Beckham, Poborsky (McClair), Scholes (Cruyff), Solskjaer
*Scorers: Scholes, Cruyff*

**West Ham United 0**
Miklosko, Potts, Hall, Bilic, Ferdinand (Hughes), Moncur, Lomas, Porfirio, Lazaridis, Dowie, Kitson

# 9

# Life after Eric

It's the end of the Premiership season. We certainly couldn't have done any better than win it, but in many ways I feel the hardest challenges are just beginning. For starters, I've got to sort out the problem with Eric Cantona. At the same time, I've got to try and bring in new players. They will have to be top class if they are to improve the quality of our squad.

I'll probably be busier during the close season than I was from August to May.


*Monday 12 May*

I was delighted to accept my Manager of the Year award at a marvellous dinner held by the League Managers' Association at Burnham Beeches just outside London.

All is not well among us managers. Our Association is concerned at the depths to which radio phone-ins have sunk. The BBC used to stand for decency and reason, but broadcasters like Danny Baker, Dominik Diamond and David Mellor now go in for personal abuse. It is a disgrace. The BBC commentator Alan Green even described Roy Keane as a lout the other day. That is way out of order.

David Pleat, an experienced and long-serving manager, spoke of his anger at David Mellor's mocking criticism of Roy Evans. With so-called pundits like the former Tory MP leading campaigns for managers to be sacked, cynicism seems to have overtaken radio journalism. We have to find an answer.

*Wednesday 14 May*

I'm now holding peace talks with Eric.

It doesn't seem as if much has changed. I think he is depressed about the European defeat. But I tell him that this is not the time to decide his future. I ask him to go away on holiday and come back refreshed enough to take a proper look at his position.

We end up having a good conversation and agree that we will talk some more later in the summer. He has an appointment with Martin Edwards tomorrow. Perhaps after that I'll have a better idea of his feelings.

*Thursday 15 May*

Eric saw the chairman today. It's clear that he's made up his mind and is intent on leaving football. Martin tells me that he did his best to get him to change his mind, but that Eric was adamant. As I well know, once Eric makes up his mind he's not usually one for turning. All we can do now is work out how we are going to break the news.

There's already a lot of speculation around about a new contract, and various clubs are supposed to be ready with bids. We don't want the news just to trickle out; Eric deserves a proper, formal tribute. Can we persuade him to come and say his farewells to the media himself? The answer is no. Eric plans to go straight off on holiday with his family. So we decide to hold a press conference on Sunday to announce his retirement properly. At the conference, we'll read out a message from Eric.

I arrange all this on the phone with the chairman, because in the afternoon I travel down to London for the Football Writers' Association dinner and presentation of their Footballer of the Year award. It's a pleasant occasion.

Sir Stanley Matthews, the first recipient of the award 50 years ago, makes the presentation to Gianfranco Zola, whose acceptance speech is charming. There's no disputing he's played brilliantly for Chelsea, and for Italy against England, but he only arrived halfway through the season. If I'd had a vote, it would have gone to Juninho of Middlesbrough. The Brazilian is another pint-sized player with an incredibly big heart and fantastic talent, but he's also done the business throughout the winter – and a North East winter, come to that!

*Saturday 17 May*

I spoke to Bryan Robson yesterday. He told me that one of his tactics for the FA Cup final was to have Robbie Mustoe manmark Roberto Di Matteo. I remember his plan as I watch the game at Wembley on television this afternoon. Di Matteo scored for Chelsea after 43 seconds – probably before Mustoe even had time to locate him.

I fear for Middlesbrough after such an early goal because it means they have to chase the game, which isn't easy after all their recent exertions and a fixture logjam. I feel sorry for Robbo. It seems to me that he was more preoccupied by the consequences of relegation – like how on earth he is going to hang on to his foreign players and stabilise his team for next season's promotion campaign. The only advice I can give him is to trust his own instincts and ability, and to remember that he's done it once before – without the Italian and Brazilian stars.

*Sunday 18 May*

We didn't circulate the afternoon media call until this morning, so as not to alert the papers that there was a big story brewing. There is still a big turn-out to hear the chairman announce that Eric's four and a half years with us are over. We both pay tribute to him, and I describe it as a sad day. I've had a terrific relationship with Eric, and we arrived at a good level of understanding. Perhaps that was why I was able to pick up the vibes over recent weeks that all was not well with him. Now everything is out in the open, it's simply a matter of *au revoir* and thanks for so many wonderful memories.

I've got to be honest: while Eric Cantona has been good for Manchester United, Manchester United has been good for Eric as well. We gave him what I believe is the best stage in Europe to play on, as well as a blend of talented stars and richly promising youngsters to play alongside. We supported him when he was at his lowest ebb after the kung-fu incident. And both the club and its fans appreciated him, which I believe was very important to Eric.

Now he has gone it won't be easy to replace him – but we will. My plans to sign a world-class player, perhaps even two or three, have become even more urgent.

*Friday 23 May*

I attend a meeting of the plc board in London. The main subjects on the agenda are transfers, and the money available to me. The outcome is not exactly what I want to hear. I've always had the board's backing for transfers, but it's obvious that there are going to be constraints on the amount of cash we can spend.

My job is to improve Manchester United enough to win the European Cup. It's also important to keep faith with our present players, and make it clear to them that the club is ambitious and wants only the very best. But it could take a lot of money to bring in players who would improve the side, and I can see a potential area for conflict. There's nothing I can do about the board's decision, so I must just bite the bullet and get on with it.

*Saturday 24 May*

England are at Old Trafford tonight for their friendly against South Africa. We get an incredible crowd of nearly 53,000.

Following the call-up for Andy Cole and Paul Scholes, Manchester United now have five players in the England squad, which must have created more interest for our supporters. I'm really pleased for Andy; it's a fair reward for the way he's battled back from injury and illness.

England selection couldn't have come at a better time for young Scholes, too. Don't think that because he hasn't made as many first-team appearances as some of the youngsters from the class of 1992 that he's not as good a player.

Earlier this season he had a cartilage operation, which kept him out for 10 weeks, and then of course Eric Cantona stood in his way. Now the Frenchman has departed, Scholes will come into his own. I've always earmarked him as Eric's understudy: he passes as brilliantly, has superb vision and a comparable eye for goal. He'll be a first-team player next season all right. The responsibility won't faze him; he has a great temperament.

*Monday 26 May*

Ryan Giggs is making good progress following his double hernia operation. The injury puzzled us at first, but we eventually managed to get to the bottom of it and Ryan will be as relieved as anyone that everything is now sorted out. He's got ample time to recover and regain his fitness for the start of next season.

*Tuesday 27 May*

I have lunch with Peter Schmeichel and his wife. Peter is concerned about his son's education. The boy is growing up in England and the Schmeichels feel that it may be time for him to go to school in Denmark. Peter's agent is there as well, and it's all very amicable. We agree to talk again later in the summer.

*Wednesday 28 May*

I'm in Munich for the final of the European Champions' League. It's a bitter-sweet experience: I can't help looking round the stadium and feeling that Manchester United should be here. Just to rub it in, my seat is in the front row of the directors' box and the European Cup itself is displayed almost exactly in front of me. I can't take my eyes off it!

Though we aren't involved on the pitch, it's still a fantastic occasion. It started with a splendid dinner last night, and UEFA invited the Manchester United survivors from the Munich air crash. Sir Bobby Charlton was there anyway as a United director, but it was good to see players like Dennis Viollet (who had come from America), Harry Gregg, Bill Foulkes, Jackie Blanchflower, Kenny Morgans, Ray Wood and Albert Scanlon.

Flying into Munich Airport, scene of the disaster 39 years ago, proved an ordeal for Albert, so UEFA arranged for him to return home by train and ferry. It made me wonder whether, if we'd got to the final, the emotion of the occasion might have proved a bit much for us all.

As for the game, I do an interview for ITV beforehand and say that I can't see any other result than Juventus winning. Cathy, of course, was tipping Borussia Dortmund. When the Germans pulled it off she called me a smart Alec, and there wasn't a lot I could say. It just made me even more frustrated that we hadn't got to the final.

*Saturday 31 May*

England are riding high after pulling off a great win in Poland. I see no reason why they shouldn't be in France next summer for the World Cup. I know I make a fuss about our players being called up for international friendly games when the club is heavily committed during the season, but in principle I'll always do my best for the international managers.

Players like David Beckham are getting invaluable experience. Playing in the wing-back role means another string to his bow.
*Monday 2 June*

We have agreed transfers which will take Pat McGibbon to Wigan and Colin Murdock to Preston. The moves will give them both a good chance of regular first-team football.

*Tuesday 3 June*

Getting players into the club is proving not quite as straight forward as transferring them out, but at least I've finalised the arrival of 19-year-old Erik Nevland from Viking Stavanger. He's a Norwegian Under-21 international who impressed on trial with us in October. He is one for the future, rather than a player who will have an immediate impact.

Money, as I suspected, is proving a stumbling block in my quest to recruit experience. I've had discussions now with the agents of a number of world-class players: Gabriel Batistuta, the Fiorentina striker; and Marcel Desailly, AC Milan's French defender. They are all talking mega-million pound deals which certainly don't fall within my guidelines.

Even if we were prepared to pay the extortionate transfer fees being asked for the players in contract, we would have difficulty agreeing personal terms. You create problems right down the line if you blow your salary structure apart for one player. In fact, you'd probably end up losing team unity and spirit, and they are more valuable than individual players. Some of the salaries sought are staggering. Even the agents are demanding commission running into six figures.

So the search goes on, with even more urgency since Eric Cantona isn't coming back to Old Trafford. I don't think he'll even return to say goodbye, much as the fans might want him to. Naturally, we'd prefer to say a proper farewell face-to-face as well, but I don't think Eric would be able to handle that emotionally. He's not the type. I always predicted that one day he would simply up sticks and go, and that's exactly what has happened. But I've come to terms with it now. In fact, I respect his decision to quit while he's still at the top. After analysing the whole situation I've concluded that he's made the right decision. My feeling is that he will surface in America. He's got a big contract with Nike and I'm sure they could use him over there to promote football in the States.

*Wednesday 4 June*

This week I'm holding a series of meetings to discuss our plans for coaching schools across Europe, with my coaching and scouting staff, representatives from the board of directors and chairman Martin Edwards.

At Old Trafford, we have kept pace with the changing face of football. The result has been four Championships in five years and a magnificent stadium with regular crowds of 55,000. Sponsorship, commercial interests and hospitality packages have given us a sound financial base, but we cannot afford to sit back. Other clubs are on the march, too, and of course we still have Europe to conquer.

Now I have a vision of another giant step forward. This doesn't just involve achieving our immediate ambition of winning the Champions' League, but putting down roots in Europe for the long term. I want to establish a scouting and coaching structure which includes our own centres of excellence for schoolboys in places like Ireland Norway and perhaps France and other countries. It could take time to establish, but we can start by appointing scouts based in certain Continental countries with a brief to look for outstanding young players. Perhaps we can catch 'em young and produce our own overseas stars!

It's really an extension of the "Busby Babes" philosophy, only on a global scale. Given our achievements, it's time to widen our horizons in preparation for the new millenium.

# Life after Eric

*Thursday 5 June*

The papers are full of Paul Scholes today, and rightly so. He put in a storming performance for England against Italy in France last night. It was his first senior international start and he was tremendous, making a goal for Ian Wright with a 60-yard pass and then marking his debut with a goal himself. Give Scholes his chance, and he takes it. Last night he simply confirmed everything I said about him when he was called up for the South African game. I had enquiries about him from other clubs when he wasn't in our starting line-up, but there was never any chance of him leaving. His future with us has always been guaranteed. What we saw of him against Italy will become a familiar sight.

It seems a long time ago that I was sunning myself in the South of France and writing the opening entries in this diary before the start of the season. My batteries need recharging again. So I'm off on holiday. I'll leave Old Trafford in the very capable hands of the chairman and our experienced and supportive secretary, Ken Merrett. His assistant, Ken Ramsden, is also our press officer; he's got the unenviable task of fending off the media during my absence.

I expect I'll stay in close touch with the chairman as we continue our search for new players. Who decided to call summer the close season, anyway?


*Monday 9 June*

I'm leaving for France today, but that didn't stop the phone ringing red hot over the weekend. We are trying to tie up deals for two players: Bayern Munich's German international defender Markus Babbel, and Brian Laudrup, Rangers' Danish star. The fees for the players are in the £5 million range and quite within our guidelines. Whether the players' personal contract demands are acceptable remains to be seen.

Maurice Watkins, the club solicitor, is off to Munich this

week to try and complete the Babbel signing. The boy is tall, strong and young – he's still only 24. He has shown with Bayern that he's organised and disciplined. Laudrup, meanwhile, is a quality player. He's marvellous at beating opponents and achieving penetration. Rangers are prepared to let him go as he only has one year left on his contract; if he stays another season at Ibrox, under the Bosman ruling they won't get a fee.

### Wednesday 11 June

The wage Babbel is demanding at the moment is unreal – around £1.5m a year. We won't be held to ransom. While it's frustrating from my point of view, I can understand the chairman digging his heels in.

Ajax, meanwhile, appear to be our main rivals for Laudrup.

### Thursday 12 June

Transfer negotiations continue. In the meantime, as I relax here in France, my mind keeps swinging back to Eric Cantona.

Eric's time with us has been one of the most dramatic in the club's history. I foresaw the impact he was going to have on us all as early as his first training session. When he had finished his normal routine, he requested two players to help him with what amounted to his own personal training performance. His 30-minute practice taught me two things. Firstly, it identified a problem in the British game, and perhaps explained why our players are technically inferior to the top European and world players. Up to that point, I'd always had a fixed approach to training – not helped by our winter weather (especially in Scotland), which doesn't encourage long skills sessions out on the pitch. Eric's routine opened my eyes to wider horizons.

Secondly, he showed me the value of practice. It's not playing games of football which makes the player; it's practice. Thanks to Eric's example, I'm now certain that's the only way to improve your game. Other factors come into it, such as temperament, speed, tactical ability and determination, but practice sharpens your skills so you can outplay your opponents.

Watching Eric's first training session, I immediately realised that he was a special player. I also realised he would require man management of the highest order, that communication and understanding were essential, and that there had to be trust. I'm truly sorry that Old Trafford won't ring with the strains of the Marsellaise quite so often now. But we'll have our memories: the strut, the upturned collar and, of course, the moments of breathtaking skill.

My own abiding memory of Eric will be a pass he produced in a game against Nottingham Forest in January 1993, the season of our first Premiership win. He received the ball with his back to goal, swivelled, and on the half-turn played a ball into the path of Mark Hughes, who scored our second goal. Oh, the vision of that pass ... Usually, watching from the touchline, I see a pass before the player spots it, but I couldn't see that one.

When I think about it now, the manner of his departure doesn't surprise me. It was so swift and precise, just like his football. Though Old Trafford was his second home for four and a half years, I always knew that one day he would suddenly up and go. But if ever a player was born to play for Manchester United, it was Eric Cantona.


*Tuesday 17 June*

We have come to no agreement about Babbel and it doesn't look like we will get Laudrup either. Our bid for Stephane Henchoz, the Swiss defender at Hamburg, has also been unsuccessful. He preferred to link up again with Roy Hodgson, his former manager, who is now in charge at Blackburn.

We will never stop trying to strengthen our squad, and if we start the new season without any major new signings, it will not be for the want of trying. As the Chairman points out, we have offered a total of £50 million to various clubs for at least six players in recent weeks.

Happily, we have reached a stage where we cannot be held to ransom. Nor do we have to buy in panic: we already have the best players in England. We're quite capable of mounting another winning challenge with or without reinforcements.

# Other titles available from Manchester United Books

☐ 0 233 99135 2   Manchester United Official Review 96/97       £9.99
☐ 0 233 99045 3   Cantona on Cantona                          £14.99
☐ 0 233 99047 X   Alex Ferguson: Ten Glorious Years             £9.99
☐ 0 233 99046 1   Ryan Giggs: Genius at Work                    £9.99

*For children:*
☐ 0 233 99041 0   Manchester United Little Devils               £4.99
☐ 0 233 99034 8   Manchester United Ultimate Football File      £5.99

## Forthcoming titles Autumn 1997:

☐ 0 233 99115 8   Odd Man Out: A Player's Diary
                  *by Brian McClair*                           £14.99
☐ 0 233 99148 4   Living the Dream
                  *by David Beckham*                            £9.99
☐ 0 233 99220 0   Manchester United Diary 1998                  £4.99

*For children:*
☐ 0 233 99164 6   Manchester United Annual 1998                 £5.50

All these books are available at your local bookshop or can be ordered direct from the publisher. Prices and availability are subject to change without notice.

*Send order to:*
Manchester United Cash Sales, 106 Great Russell Street, London WC1B 3LJ
Please send a cheque or postal order made payable to André Deutsch Ltd for the value of the book(s) and add the following for postage and packaging (remembering to give your name and address):
*UK:* £1.00 for the first book, 50p for the second and 30p for each additional book up to a maximum of £3.00.
*OVERSEAS including EIRE:* £2.00 for the first book and £1.00 for the second and 50p for each additional book up to a maximum of £5.00